I0650434

Henry Thomas Loomis

Spelling and Letter Writing

A Textbook for Use in Commercial Schools, Normal Schools, Colleges....

Henry Thomas Loomis

Spelling and Letter Writing
A Textbook for Use in Commercial Schools, Normal Schools, Colleges....

ISBN/EAN: 9783337158613

Printed in Europe, USA, Canada, Australia, Japan

Cover: Foto ©Paul-Georg Meister /pixelio.de

More available books at **www.hansebooks.com**

Spelling

AND

Letter Writing,

A TEXT BOOK FOR USE IN

COMMERCIAL SCHOOLS, NORMAL SCHOOLS,

COLLEGES,

ACADEMIES AND HIGH SCHOOLS.

TWENTY-FOURTH THOUSAND.

PREFACE.

No subject can be of more importance to a young man or young woman who seeks employment in business, or would have a practical education of every-day use in life, than Spelling and Letter-writing.

Any person desiring a business position should be able to write a good letter. Such ability, together with good penmanship, often secures valuable positions for clerks, book-keepers, amanuenses, teachers and others. Few branches taught in our schools are of more consequence, and few more neglected.

It is equally important that a person be a good speller. While one may not always receive the credit he is entitled to for spelling correctly, if he does not acquire the qualification he is sure to be humiliated in consequence of bad spelling.

Much time and labor have been devoted to the preparation of this work, and it is the earnest hope of the authors that the time shall not prove to have been spent in vain.

We acknowledge our indebtedness to Messrs. Ivison, Blakeman & Co., publishers of the Spencerian system of penmanship, 755 Broadway, New York, for the privilege of using most of the engraved script illustrations to be found in this book.

Copyrighted, 1886, by Spencer, Felton & Loomis.

Printed by The Cleveland Ptg. & Pub. Co., Cleveland, O.

INDEX.

SPELLING AND DEFINING.

Agriculture	29	Fruit	28
Animals	101	Furniture	57
Annoyance	68	Geography	53
Architecture	30–31	Government	42
Arithmetic	49–50	Groceries	25
Authority	43–44	Hardware	21–22
Birds	102	Hatred	83
Book-keeping	18	Homophonous Words . . . 17, 21, 25,
Business	10–15	30, 34, 41, 47, 52, 56, 62, 67, 73, 79,
City	111	85, 90, 95, 101, 104, 106.
Cities of U. S.	112–113	Human Body	36
Cities, Foreign	115–117	Humor	96
Clothing	20	Injury	68
Color	100	Insects	103
Confusion	66	Intemperance	84
Conversation	86–87	Joy	95
Crimes and Criminals	41	Kindness	84
Death	93	Law	37–40
Dictation Exercises . . . 10, 15, 16, 19,		Laziness and Fatigue	55
20, 24, 27, 29, 31, 35, 40, 42, 46, 48,		Lineage	81
52, 54, 55, 56, 61, 64, 67, 69, 70, 72,		Lines and Forms	51
74, 76, 78, 82, 84, 85, 87, 89, 91, 93,		Literature	62–63
97, 99, 103, 106, 111, 118.		Manners	79–81
Disaster	69	Men	76
Disease	34–35	Mind	59–61
Drugs	32	Miscellaneous . . 15, 19, 23, 27, 31, 37,
Dry Goods	19	45, 49, 54, 59, 64, 69, 75, 82, 87, 92,
Expenditure	18	98, 110.
Festivity	97	Months and Days	118
Finished	94	Motion	54
Fire and Fuel	57	Music	55
Fish and Fowl	26	Mystery	92
Flowers	98–99	Nations	78
Food	26	Navigation	71

Oratory   46
Orthography   9
Persons   77
Physics   33
Pictures   58
Politics   44
Praise   88–89
Precious Stones   105
Quantity   106
Religion   90–91
Requiring Careful Discrimina-
    tion 107–110
Schools   45–46
Sciences   47–48
Size   104
Skill   17

Society   75
Sorrow   94
States and Territories 113–115
Stationers' Goods   23
Temper and Disposition . . .   83
Theatre   96
Time   73–74
Traveling   70
Trees 100
Vegetables   28
Vehicles   71
Vocations   16
War or Military Service . . .   65–66
Wind and Weather   72
Women   76
Writing   24

LETTER-WRITING.

Acceptances and Regrets . . . 167–168
Advertising 163–164
Body of the Letter 130–131
Capitals 143–145
Cards 168–170
Classification of Titles 179–184
Classified List of Abbreviations 188–190
Conclusion 131–135
Correct and Incorrect Positions 196
Correcting Letters 195
Diction and Construction . . . 143
Dinners 166–167
Folding 135–137
Forms of Address and Salutation 184–187
General Postal Information . . 174–175
Heading 123–125
Introduction 119–120
Introduction of Letters 126–130
Letters 120
Letters acknowledging Receipt
    of Money 156
Letters of Application 153–154

Letters of Condolence 162–163
Letters of Congratulation . . . 161–162
Letters of Credit 154
Letters enclosing a Remittance 157–160
Letters enclosing Invoice . . . 160–161
Letters of Introduction 152–153
Letters Ordering Goods 157
Letters of Recommendation . . 155
Materials 122
Miscellaneous Exercises 190–194
Miscellaneous Hints 149–152
Notes and Cards 164–165
Parties 167
Public Letters 161
Punctuation 145–149
Skeleton Letter 121
Stamp 142–143
Telegrams 163
The Superscription 138–142
Titles 170–174
Type-writing 175–178
Wedding Invitations 165–166

Spelling and Defining.

INTRODUCTION.

Had we believed, with a celebrated Congressman—not noted for skill in orthography—that "spelling is very small business," this book would not have been published. Considering the subject *important*, we have earnestly endeavored to prepare a work that should present it in the most attractive, interesting and useful manner.

The words have been selected with great care, our aim being to take only words in common use, and such as are liable to be misspelled. They are arranged alphabetically, classified to make the study of the lessons more interesting and at the same time give a knowledge of the proper use of the words. The part of speech of each has been given. Only one, two, or at most three words have been selected from a series of words derived from the same root, varying slightly in spelling or definition.

The Dictation Exercises are on the same subject as the respective lessons, and are the best thoughts of the best writers. They will add interest to the spelling lesson, afford excellent practice in penmanship and spelling of short and common words, and may be used or not, at the discretion of the teacher.

The definitions are short and comprehensive, and of the words in their most common use. It is as important to know what a word means as how to spell it.

Webster's Unabridged Dictionary has been the authority in spelling, pronunciation and defining.

The Key to Pronunciation, carefully studied, will enable the student to know, from a glance at its diacritical marks, the correct pronunciation of a word.

The geographical names include some of the largest cities in the world, and those most difficult to spell.   In a work of this kind it is impossible to give a very extensive list, as the number of geographical words is almost limitless.

Capital letters have been used to begin words only when required, and the lessons should be written in this respect as printed.

The use of the book may be varied to suit the taste of the teacher and needs or qualifications of the pupils.   We might suggest that spelling " by ear " is a poor method where the orthography is as arbitrary and inconsistent as in the English language.   We only need to spell when we *write*, and not when we pronounce words.   The dictation exercises should be read through first by the teacher, and again slowly, while the pupils write.   The short quotations may be written at the beginning of each lesson, and the long dictation exercises, as lessons, in the order they are given.   The teacher should read the definitions of each of the classified words, after he pronounces the word.   If the school is small, the teacher, or some one selected by him, may correct the lessons.   In large classes, the students could exchange blanks and correct each other's work.   A check mark should be placed opposite each misspelled word, and under each error in spelling, capitalization or punctuation of the dictation exercis :s.   100 per cent. may be taken as the standard of perfection, and five per cent. deducted for each mistake.   It is well to keep a record of each pupil's work, for which purpose the books should be collected after each lesson, and returned just before the beginning of the next.

To the student we would suggest that in studying the lessons you note carefully the definitions, and endeavor to learn the meaning of the words as well as how to spell them. *Use great care* in writing your lessons, with a view to neatness, legibility and good penmanship.   You will thus make the spelling lesson a valuable one in writing as well.

A correct position of the hand and pen, and of sitting at the desk, is of first importance in doing good writing.   We refer the student to the illustrations on page 196, instead of giving any instructions on this subject.

Rules for Spelling.

[Most rules for spelling have so many exceptions that they are not of much aid to the learner. The following may prove of some assistance.]

1.   Monosyllables and words accented on the last syllable, when these words end in a single consonant (except *h* and *x*) preceded by a single vowel, that consonant is doubled: as, *clan, clannish; plan, planned; hat, hat'ter; prefer', preferred'*. When the accent of the primitive is thrown back upon another syllable, the final letter is not doubled: as, *prefer', pref'erence; refer', ref'erence; defer', def'erence*. The following are exceptions: *infer'able, transfer'able, chagrin'ed*.

2.   A consonant standing at the end of a word immediately after a diphthong or double vowel is never doubled: as, *ail, haul, door, maim;* the word *guess* is the only apparent exception, as the *u* does not strictly form a diphthong with the *e*, but serves only to render the *g* hard.

3.   The plural of nouns ending in *y* when *y* is preceded by a consonant, is formed by changing *y* into *i* and adding *es:* as, *lily, lilies; lady, ladies*. When *y* is preceded by a vowel, the plural is formed by adding *s:* as, *valley, valleys*.

4.   The word *full*, used as an affix, always drops one *l;* and its compounds form their plurals by adding *s* to the singular: as, *handful, handfuls*.

5.   Words formed by prefixing one or more syllables to words ending in a double consonant, retain both consonants: as, *befall, rebuff*. The exceptions are, *withal, annul, until;* also *fulfill* and *instill*, which may be written *fulfil, instil*.

6.   In derivatives formed from words ending with silent *e*, the *e* is generally retained when the termination begins with a consonant: as *pale, paleness; hate, hateful; move, movement;* when the *e* is immediately preceded by another vowel (except *e*), it is often dropped from the derivative: as, *due, duly; true, truly; awe, awful*. The words *wholly, nursling, wisdom, abridgment, acknowledgment, lodgment*, and *judgment* are exceptions. When the affix begins with a vowel the *e* is generally omitted: as, *bride, bridal; use, usage;* the *e* is retained in the words *hoeing, shoeing, toeing, dyeing, singeing, tingeing*.

KEY TO PRONUNCIATION,
AND ABBREVIATIONS.

VOWELS.

	SHORT SOUNDS.
ā, long, as in . . . . . . grūy, ūle.	ă, short, as in . . . . făt, hăve.
ē, long, as in . . . . . . pēace, ēve.	ĕ, short, as in . . . . . . ĕnd, chĕck.
ī, long, as in . . . . . . fīne, īce.	ĭ, short, as in . . . . ĭll, fĭn.
ō, long, as in . . . . . . nōte, ōld.	ŏ, short, as in . . . . ŏt, tŏrrid.
ū, long, as in . . . . . . tūbe, ūse.	ŭ, short, as in . . . . ŭs, stŭdy, tŭb.
ȳ, long, as in . . . . . . stȳle, flȳ.	y̆, short, as in . . . çy̆st, trȳst, abȳss.

OCCASIONAL SOUNDS.

â, as in . . . . âir, fâre, pâir.	ô, like short u, as in . . . dône, sôu.
ä, Italian, as in . . ärm, fäther, fär.	ọ, like long ōō, as in . . . dọ, mọve.
à, as in . . . . . . àsk, pàss, dàuce.	ọ, like short ōō, as in . wọlf, wọmau.
ạ, broad, as in . . ạll, tạlk, swạrm.	ô, like broad ạ, as in . . . ôrder, stôrk.
ạ, like short o, as in . whạt, wạuder.	ōō, as in . . . . mōōn, fōōd.
ê, like â, as in . . . êre, hêir, whêre.	o̔o̔, as in . . . . . bo̔o̔k, wo̔o̔l, fo̔o̔t.
ẹ, like ā, as in . . . . . ẹight, prẹy.	u, preceded by r, as in . rude, rural.
ê, as in . . . . vêrge, êrmine.	u, like short o̔o̔, as in . fụll, pụt, pụsh.
ï, like long ē, as in . . . pïque, polïce.	û, as in . . . . . . ûrge, bûru, fûrl.
ï, like ê, as in . . . . thïrsty, ïrksome.	

REGULAR DIPHTHONGAL SOUNDS.

oi*, oy*, as in . . . . oil, toy.	ou*, ow*, as in . . . . . . out, owl.

CONSONANTS.

ç, soft, like s, sharp, as in . çēde, çïte.	th*, sharp, as in . . . thïng, breath.
e, hard, like k, as in . . eall, sueçess.	th, flat or vocal, as in thine, smooth.
çh, soft, like sh, as in çhaise, maçhine.	ng*, as in . . . . sing, single.
eh, hard, like k, as in ehorus, epoeh.	u, as in . . . . lip'', ụncle.
g̅, hard, as in . . . g̅et, tig̅er, beg̅in.	x, like gz, as in . . . exist, example.
g̣, soft, like j, as in g̣em, eng̣ine, eleg̣y.	ph*, like f, as in . phantom, sylph.
s*, sharp, as in . . . same, yes, rest.	qu*, like kw, as in . . queer, quail.
ş, like z, as in . . hạş, amuşe, reşide.	wh*, like hw, as in whạt, when, awhile.

ᵒUnmarked.

ABBREVIATIONS.

a. adjective; *adv.* adverb; *n.* noun; *p.* plural; *p. p.* participle past; *prep.* preposition; *v.* verb; *v. i.* verb intransitive; *v. t.* verb transitive.

WORDS, DEFINITIONS

AND

DICTATION EXERCISES,

FOR PRACTICE IN

Spelling, Defining and Writing.

LESSON I.

ORTHOGRAPHY.

" Now the old school house is banished, like so many of its race,
To the elements that wrought it—and a new one holds its place ;
And the spellers write their words down, with a chance their parents lacked,
For as Bacon hints, ' 'Tis writing that must make a man exact.' "

ăe'-çĕnt, *n.* Stress of voice on one syllable of a word more than another.

ăf'-fĭx, *n.* A syllable added to the end of a word.

ăl'-phà-bet, *n.* The letters of a language arranged in the customary order.

eŏn'-so-nant, *n.* An articulate sound usually combined and uttered with a vowel sound.

dē-rĭv'-a-tive, *n.* A word formed from another word.

di-a-erĭt'-ĭe-al märks, *n. pl.* Marks used to indicate the sounds of letters, and aid in pronunciation.

di'-grăph, *n.* A union of two vowels in one syllable and one sounded.

diph'-thong (dif'-thong), *n.* Union of two vowel sounds in one syllable.

dĭs-sŷl'-la-ble, *n.* A word of two syllables.

mŏn'-o-sŷl-la-ble, *n.* Word of one syllable.

ôr'-tho-e-py, *n.* Correct pronunciation of words.

ôr-thŏg'-ra-phy, *n.* Naming the letters of a word in their order.

pŏl'-y-sŷl-la-ble, *n.* A word of four or more syllables.

prē'-fĭx, *n.* A syllable placed before a word.

prim'-i-tive, *n.* Not derived from any other word.

tri'-grăph, *n.* A union of three vowels in a syllable representing a single sound.

tri-sŷl'-la-ble, *n.* A word of three syllables.

sŷl'-la-ble, *n.* A letter or letters uttered at a single impulse of the voice.

vow'-el, *n.* A letter uttered at a single impulse of the voice.

word, *n.* The sign of an idea, either written, printed or spoken.

LESSON 2.

DICTATION EXERCISE.

There they stood, like young globe batters, with no salary enriched,
Waiting for the words momentous that the dexterous teacher pitched.
And he hurled the first one at them, like a nicely twisted ball,
While the catcher just behind them was the horny-handed wall;
The first boy struck and missed it, and his face was deeply vexed
As the teacher scowled a cyclone, and vociferated "next."
Then a fair-haired maiden tried it with some sympathetic aid,
And avoiding certain blunders that her predecessor made;
But she happened, too, to wander from the orthographic text,
And the teacher smiled in pity, as he softly murmured "next."
Then a cross-eyed boy struck at it, who to this day spells by ear,
And a red-haired girl attacked it, with her pale eyes full of fear,
And the word flew on, till one boy, very ignorant but sharp-eyed,
Spelled it by the only method that had not as yet been tried.
Then the teacher smiled approval, and with satisfaction said,
"That is right, my studious scholar, you can go up to the head."—*Carleton.*

LESSON 3.

WORDS USED IN BUSINESS.

"No man is born into the world, whose work is not born with him; there is always work, and tools to work withal, for those who will."

ac-çĕpt'-ănçe, *n.* Bill of exchange, when accepted.

ac-crĕd'-ĭt, *v. t.* To give confidence or trust to.

ăc- crue', *v. i.* To increase; to augment.

ăc-cŭ'-mu-lāte, *v. t.* To collect or bring together.

ăd-vĕr'-tĭşe-ment, or **ăd-ver-tīşe'-ment,** *n.* A public notice.

ăd-vīş'-a-ble, *a.* Prudent.

a-mȧn-u-ĕn'-sĭs, *n.* One who writes what another dictates, or copies what another has written.

ȧ-măss', *v. t.* To accumulate.

ăs-sĭgn-ēe', *n.* One to whom an assignment is made.

băŋk'-rŭpt-çy, *n.* The state of being insolvent.

băr'-gain, *n.* A gainful or satisfactory transaction.

băr'-ter, *v. t.* To exchange.

bo-năn'-zȧ, *n.* Any successful venture.

bŏnd, *n.* The writing by which a person binds himself to pay a certain sum of money by a given date, under certain conditions.

bŭl'-le-tĭn, *n.* Official report.

bŭll'-ion, *n.* Uncoined silver or gold.

bŭş'-i-ness (bĭz'-nes), *n.* Employment; occupation.

bŭş'-tle, *v. i.* To be very active.

bŭş'-y, (bĭz-y), *a.* Not at leisure.

eăp'-i-tal-ĭst, *n.* A man who has capital or stock in trade; usually a man of large property.

LESSON 4.
Words used in Business.

"Our thoughts are ever forming our characters, and whatever they are most absorbed in will tinge our lives."

eär'-go, *n.* Load; freight.

eäsh-ĭĕr', *n.* One who has charge of money.

ehăr'-ăe-ter, *n.* The estimate which is put upon a person or thing.

ehärġe'-a-ble, *a.* Capable of being charged.

ehĕat, *v. t.* To defraud.

ehĕek, *n.* An order for money, on a bank, payable on sight.

elĕar-ĭng-house, *n.* The place where the business of clearing is carried on.

elĕr'-ĭe-al, *a.* Relating to a clerk or copyist.

eŏf'-fer, *n.* A chest or trunk for keeping money in.

eoin, *n.* A piece of metal on which certain characters are stamped, making it legally current as money.

eŏl-lăt'-er-al, *n.* Security given in addition to promise.

eŏm-bı-nä'-tion, *n.* Association; alliance.

eŏm'-mĕrçe, *n.* The exchange of merchandise on a large scale between different countries or places.

eŏm-mĕr'-cial, *a.* Relating to trade.

eŏm-mĭs'-sion, *n.* Allowance made to an agent for transacting business.

eŏm-mit'-tēe, *n.* Persons specially appointed to manage any business.

eŏm'-pa-nỹ, *n.* A corporation; a firm.

eŏm'-pĕn-sāte, *v. t.* To remunerate.

eŏm'-pe-tent, *a.* Answering all requirements.

eŏm-pe-tī'-tion, *n.* Common strife for the same object.

LESSON 5.
Words used in Business.

Fortune is ever seen accompanying industry, and is as often trundling in a wheelbarrow as lolling in a coach and six.—*Goldsmith.*

eŏm-pu-tä'-tion, *n.* Reckoning.

eŏn-sĭgn-ēe' (-sĭ-nee'), *n.* A person to whom goods are delivered in trust.

eŏn-sĭgn'-er, *n.* One who consigns.

eō-ŏp'-er-āte, *v. i.* To concur in action.

eō-pärt'-ner-ship, *n.* A joint interest in any matter.

eŏr-po-rä'-tion, *n.* A body politic, allowed by law to act as an individual.

eoun'-ter-feit, *n.* A likeness; an imposter.

eou'-pon (kōō'-pŏng), *n.* An interest certificate attached to a bond.

erē-dĕn'-tials, *n. pl.* That which gives credit.

erĕd'-ĭt-or, *n.* One who credits or trusts.

eŭr'-ren-çy, *n.* A continual passing from person to person.

eŭs'-tom-house, *n.* The house where duties are paid.

dăm'-age, *n.* Injury; loss of value.

dĕal'-er, *n.* One who deals or trades.

dĕbt'-or, *n.* One who owes another.

dĕf-al-ĕä-tor, *n.* One who embezzles money left in his care.

de-fault'-er, *n.* One who fails to account for public money left in his care.

de-fĭ'-cien-çy, *n.* Inadequacy; imperfection.

de-frăy', *v. t.* To pay or discharge.

de-prē'-çi-ate (-shĭ-āte), *v. i.* To fall in value.

LESSON 6.

Words used in Business.

In human life there is constant change of fortune, and it is unreasonable to expect an exemption from the common fate. Life itself decays, and all things are daily changing.—*Plutarch.*

dis-bûrse', *v. t.* To pay out.

dis-crĕp'-an-çy, *n.* Varience; inconsistent.

dis-hŏn'-est, *a.* Faithless; fraudulent.

drạw-êe', *n.* One on whom an order or bill of exchange is drawn.

drạw'-er, *n.* One who draws a bill of exchange.

ĕl'-e-vä-tor, *n.* A mechanical contrivance for lifting persons or freight to an upper floor.

ĕm-bĕz'-zle, *v. t.* To appropriate by breach of trust.

ĕm'-is-sa-ry, *n.* A person sent on a private mission.

ĕm-ploy-ḝ', *n.* One who is employed.

ĕm-pō'-ri-ŭm, *n.* Center of an extensive trade.

ĕn'-ter-prïṣe, *n.* An undertaking.

ĕs-tăb'-lĭsh, *v. t.* To found.

ĕx-äet'-ness, *n.* Accuracy; precision.

ĕx-chänġe', *v. t.* To give and take; to swap.

ĕx-pĕnse', *n.* Outlay; cost.

ĕx'-pŏrt, *n.* A commodity sent abroad.

fï-nănçe', *n.* Revenue; income.

fïn-ăn-çiêr', *n.* One who is skilled in money matters.

firm, *n.* Partnership.

flŭet'-ū-äte, *v. i.* To be wavering or unsteady.

LESSON 7.

Words used in Business.

Yet still there whispers the small voice within,
Heard through gain's silence and o'er glory's din:
Whatever creed be taught or land be trod,
Man's conscience is the oracle of God.—*Byron.*

fŏr'-eîgn, *a.* Not native; remote.

fŏr'-feit, *v. t.* To lose the right to, by some misdeed, fault or offense.

fŏr'-ġer-y, *n.* Producing an imitation, to deceive or defraud.

frạud'-ū-lent, *a.* Containing fraud.

freight, *n.* Cargo.

grän̈t-êe', *n.* One to whom a grant is made.

grän̈t'-or, *n.* One by whom a grant is made.

guär-an-têe', *v. t.* To make sure; to warrant.

hŏn'-est-y, *n.* Trustiness; integrity.

Im-pŏrt', *v. t.* To bring from abroad.

In-äe'-eu-ra-çy, *n.* Mistake; error.

In-eŏm'-pe-tĕnt, *a.* Insufficient; unfit.

In-eor-rĕet', *a.* Inaccurate; faulty.

Iu-erëaṣe', *v. t.* To extend; to spread.

In-dĕbt'-ed, *a.* Under obligation.

Iu-dĕm'-ni-fȳ, *v. t.* To make good.

Iu-dĕnt'-ūre, *n.* A mutual agreement in writing.

Iu-dôr-sêe', *n.* The person to whom a note or bill is indorsed or assigned by indorsement.

Iu-dôrs'-er, *n.* The person who indorses.

Iu-dŭs'-tri-oŭs, *a.* Diligent in business or study.

LESSON 8.
Words used in Business.

Next to knowing when to seize an opportunity, the most important thing in life is to know when to forego an advantage.—*D'Israeli.*

In-sŏlv'-en-çy, *n.* Without means to discharge debts.

In-tĕg'-ri-ty, *n.* Honesty.

In'-vĕn-to-ry, *n.* A list or account of goods and chattels.

In-vĕst'-ment, *n.* Laying out of money in property of a permanent nature.

In'-voiçe, *v. t.* To insert in a priced list.

jŏb'-ber, *n.* One who buys goods from importers and sells to retailers.

joint'-ly, *adv.* Together.

lĕs-sēe', *n.* One to whom a lease is given.

lū'-cre, *n.* Gain in money or goods.

măm'-mon, *n.* Riches; wealth.

măr'-gin, *n.* Difference between the cost and selling price of an article.

ma-tū'-ri-ty, *n.* Arrival of the time fixed for payment.

mĕr'-can-tĭle, *a.* Buying and selling of commodities.

mĕr'-çe-na-ry, *a.* Governed by greediness of gain.

mĕr'-chan-dise, *n.* The objects of commerce.

mĕth'-ŏd, *n.* A regular way of doing anything.

mĕt-ro-pŏl'-i-tan, *a.* Belonging to a metropolis.

mil'-li-nĕr-y, *n.* Articles sold by a milliner.

mill'-ion-âire, *n.* One whose wealth is counted by millions.

mis-çel-lā'-ne-oŭs, *a.* Consisting of several kinds.

LESSON 9.
Words used in Business.

"Be not amazed at life. 'Tis still
The mode of God with his elect,
Their hopes exactly to fulfil,
In times and ways they least expect."

mo-nŏp'-o-list, *n.* One who takes the whole of anything.

ne-gō'-ti-a-ble (-gō-shǐ-), *a.* Transferable by endorsement to another person.

nĭck'-el, *n.* A coin; a greyish white metal, very ductile and malleable.

ŏp-er-ā'-tion, *n.* Mode of action.

ŏp'-er-ā-tor, *n.* One who produces an effect.

ŏp'-u-lençe, *n.* Wealth, affluence.

pär'-çel, *n.* A small package.

pärt'-ner, *n.* One who acts, suffers or enjoys with another.

pā'-tent (pā- or păt-), *n.* To secure the exclusive right to a person.

pā'-tron, *n.* One who supports or protects.

păy'-a-ble, *a.* Justly due.

păy-ēe', *n.* The person to whom money is to be paid.

păy'-er, *n.* One who pays.

pe-cū'-ni-oŭs, *a.* Full of money.

pĕn'-sion, *n.* An annual allowance given from the public treasury.

pĕr-suāde' (-swād), *v. t.* To influence by argument.

pe-tī'-tion, *n.* A request; an entreaty.

plĕdge, *v. t.* To give as security.

pŏl'-i-çy, *n.* System of management; stratagem.

pŭs-sĕs'-sion, *n.* Ownership; having in one's power.

LESSON 10.
Words used in Business.

Be noble; and the nobleness that lies
In other men sleeping, but never dead,
Will rise in majesty to meet thine own.—*Lowell.*

prē'-mi-ŭm, *n.* A prize to be won by competition; something given for the loan of money.

prŏm'-ĭs-so-ry, *a.* Containing a promise of something to be done.

pro-pŏr'-tion, *n.* Symmetrical distribution.

prŏp-o-ṣi'-tion, *n.* Offer of terms.

pro-pri'-e-tor, *n.* An owner.

prŏs'-per-oŭs, *a.* Successful.

pŭnçt'-u-al, *a.* Adhering to the exact time of an appointment.

pûr'-chas-a-ble, *a.* Capable of being bought.

quạl'-i-fied, *a.* Fitted by accomplishments.

răs-eăl'-i-ty, *n.* Base fraud.

rēa'-ṣon-a-ble, *a.* Within due limits; just.

re-bāte', *v. t.* To deduct from.

rē-çēipt' (-sēet), *n.* Acknowledgment of payment.

re-çēiv'-er, *n.* One who receives or takes.

rĕe-om-mĕnd', *v. t.* To put in a favorable light before any one.

rĕe'-om-pĕnse, *n.* Reward; compensation.

rĕe'-ti-fy, *v. t.* To make right.

re-dēem'-a-ble, *a.* Purchasable or payable in gold and silver.

rĕf-er-ĕe', *n.* One to whom a thing is referred.

re-li'-a-ble, *a.* Trustworthy.

LESSON 11.
Words used in Business.

"Sum up at night what thou hast done by day,
And in the morning what thou hast to do.
Dress and undress thy soul."

re-mit'-tançe, *n.* The sum, or thing remitted.

re-mu-ner-ā'-tion, *n.* An equivalent given for service.

rē-sōurçe', *n.* Funds; dependence.

re-spĕet'-ive-ly, *adv.* Relating to each.

re-spŏn'-si-ble, *a.* Accountable.

rĕs-ti-tū'-tion, *n.* Making good a loss or injury.

sĕe'-re-ta-ry, *n.* One employed to write letters, etc.

sāl'-a-ble, *a.* In good demand.

săl'-a-ry, *n.* The amount agreed upon, to be paid for one's services.

sāleṣ'-man, *n.* One who sells anything.

sehĕd'-ūle (skĕd'-yṳl), *n.* A document, list or catalogue.

sehēme, *n.* A design; a project.

se-eū'-ri-ty, *n.* One who becomes surety for another.

sĕiz'-a-ble, *a.* Liable to be taken.

shil'-ling, *n.* An English coin equal to twelve pence.

ship'-ment, *n.* Goods that are shipped.

shrewd'-ly (shrṳd'-lỹ), *adv.* With good guess; sagaciously.

shriṇk'-age, *n.* Reduction in bulk or dimensions of anything.

sŏlv'-ent, *a.* Able to pay all just debts.

stew'-ard (stū-), *n.* An officer of a boat, church or college.

LESSON 12.

Words used in Business.

"We worldly men, when we see friends and kinsmen
Past hope sunk in their fortunes, lend no hand
To lift them up, but rather set our feet
Upon their heads to press them to the bottom."

sti'-pend, *n.* Settled pay for services.

stip'-ū-lāte, *v. i.* To settle terms.

stŏck, *n.* Money invested in business.

sŭe-çĕss'-ful, *a.* Prosperous; fortunate.

sŭre'-ty (shŭr-), *n.* A bondsman.

swĭn'-dler, *n.* A cheat.

tăx-ā'-tion, *n.* Assessing a bill of cost.

tĕs-ti-mō'-ni-al, *n.* A writing which testifies in favor of one's good conduct.

tŏn'-nage, *n.* The whole amount of shipping estimated by tons.

trăf'-fĭc, *n.* Commerce; trade.

trăns-ăe'-tion, *n.* Performing any business.

trĭb'-ūte, *n.* A personal contribution made in token of services rendered.

ŭn-fôrt'-ū-nāte, *a.* Unlucky.

ŭn-prŏf'-it-a-ble, *a.* Useless; not profitable.

vā'-căn-çy, *n.* A place or post to be filled.

văl'-ū-a-ble, *a.* Having value.

văl'-ūe, *n.* Rate or estimated worth.

wâre'-house, *n.* A store house for goods.

war'-rănt, *v. t.* To indemnify against loss.

wĕalth'-y, *a.* Rich.

LESSON 13.

DICTATION EXERCISE.

Literature, the ministry, medicine, the law, and other occupations, are cramped and hindered for want of men to do the work, not want of work to do. When people tell you the reverse they speak that which is not true. If you desire to test this you need only hunt up a first-class editor, reporter, business manager, foreman of a shop, mechanic, or artist in any branch of industry, and try to hire him. You will find that he is already hired. He is sober, industrious, capable and reliable, and is always in demand. He cannot get a day's holiday except by courtesy of his employer, or of his city, or of the great general public. But if you need idlers, shirkers, half-instructed, unambitious and comfort-seeking editors, reporters, lawyers, doctors and mechanics, apply anywhere.—*Mark Twain.*

LESSON 14.

MISCELLANEOUS.

Formerly, when great fortunes were only made in war, war was a business; but now, when great fortunes are only made by business, business is war.—*Bovee.*

a-băn'-don, *v. t.* To forsake wholly; to renounce.

ăb-brē'-vi-āte, *v. t.* To shorten.

ăb'-di-eāte, *v. t.* To cast off; to renounce.

a-bŏve'-bōard, *adv.* Without trick or deception.

a-brĭdge', *v. t.* To diminish.

ae-çĕpt', *v. t.* To receive with favor.

ae-çĕss' or ăe'-çĕss, *n.* Admittance.

ăe-çĕss'-i-ble, *a.* Approachable.

ăe-quire', *v. .* To gain; to procure.

ăet'-u-al, *a.* Truly and absolutely so.

ăd-ăp-tā'-tion, *n.* The act of fitting.

ăd-hē'-sive, *a.* Sticking to.

ăd-mĭt'-tançe, *n.* Permission to enter.

a-dŏpt', *v. t.* To receive as one's own.

a-dŭl'-ter-āte, *v. t.* To corrupt by mixture.

ăd-văn'-tage, *n.* Favorable circumstances.

ā-ē'-ri-al, *a.* Belonging to the air.

æ-rie (ē'-ry), *n.* A nest of a bird of prey.

æs-thĕt'-ies,}
ĕs-thĕt'-ies, } *n.* Theory of taste.

ăf-fĕe'-tion-ate, *a.* Fond; loving.

LESSON 15.

VOCATIONS.

"The highest excellence is seldom attained in more than one vocation. The roads leading to distinction in separate pursuits diverge, and the nearer we approach the one, the farther we recede from the other."

ā'-er-o-nąut, *n.* A balloonist.

ăp-prĕn'-tiçe, *n.* One bound to a person to learn his trade or art.

är'-ehi-tĕet, *n.* One skilled in the art of building.

är'-ti-san, *n.* A skilled mechanic.

aue-tion-ēer', *n.* One who sells goods at public sale.

au'-di-tor, *n.* An examiner of accounts.

brō'-ker, *n.* One who transacts business for another.

eär'-pĕn-ter, *n.* An artificer who works in timber.

eā'-tēr-er, *n.* A provider of provisions.

elōth'-ier (-yer), *n.* One who sells cloth or clothing.

eŏm-pŏṣ'-i-tor, *n.* One who sets type.

eŭs-tō'-di-an, *n.* A keeper or superintendent.

ĕd'-it-or, *n.* One who prepares or revises matter for publication.

ĕn-ġi-nēer', *n.* One who manages an engine.

glā'-zier (-zhur), *n.* One who sets glass.

hănd'-i-erăft, *n.* Manual occupation.

jän'-i-tor, *n.* A doorkeeper; a porter.

mä-chïn'-ïst, *n.* One versed in the principles of machines.

me-ehän'-ie, *n.* One who works with instruments.

tȳ-pŏg'-rä-pher (or tӯ-), *n.* A printer.

LESSON 16.

DICTATION EXERCISE.

He was one of those men who achieve
So little because of the much they conceive.
He knocked at each one
Of the door-ways of life, and abided in none.
His course by each star that would cross it was set,
And whatever he did he was sure to regret.
The man who seeks one thing in life, and but one,
May hope to achieve it before life be done;
But he who seeks all things, wherever he goes,
Only reaps from the hopes which around him he sows
A harvest of barren regrets.—*Owen Meredith.*

LESSON 17.

PERTAINING TO SKILL.

"There are two most valuable possessions which no search-warrant can get at, which no execution can take away, and which no reverse of fortune can destroy; they are what a man puts into his brain—KNOWLEDGE; and into his hands—SKILL."

a-bil'-i-ty, *n.* Power; skill.

a-dept', *n.* One skilled in any art.

a-droit', *a.* Ready in invention or execution.

eä'-pa-ble, *a.* Having ability.

eün'-ning, *n.* Skill; dexterity.

dex'-ter-oŭs, *a.* Expert; skillful in contrivance.

ef-fī'-cient, *a.* Energetic and useful activity.

ex-pert'-ness, *n.* Skill derived from practice.

ex-pē'-ri-ençe, *n.* To train by practice; to try personally.

fa-çil'-i-ty, *n.* Ease in performance.

in-a-bil'-i-ty, *n.* Lack of power, strength or resources.

in-eä'-pa-ble, *a.* Incompetent, unfit, disqualified.

knäek, *n.* Habitual easiness of performance.

män'-age-ment, *n.* Skillful treatment.

ma-nip'-ū-lāte, *v. t.* To operate with the hands in a skillful manner.

niç'-e-ty, *n.* Delicate management.

pös'-si-ble, *a.* Capable of being done.

pro-fī'-cient, *a.* Well skilled.

skill'-fŭl, *a.* Able in management; well versed.

tŏl'-er-a-bly, *adv.* Moderately well.

LESSON 18.

HOMOPHONOUS WORDS.

"Of all the good things in this good world around us,
The one most abundantly furnished and found us
And which, for that reason, we least care about,
And can best spare our friends, is good counsel, no doubt."

Ā'-bel, *n.* The name of a man.

ā'-ble, *a.* Having ability or competency of any and every kind.

āil, *v. i.* To be sick.

āle, *n.* A kind of liquor.

âir, *n.* The atmosphere.

hêir, *n.* One who inherits.

aisle (īl), *n.* A passage in a church.

isle, *n.* An island.

ănt, *n.* An insect.

äunt, *n.* A parent's sister.

al'-ter, *v. i.* To make some change in.

al'-tar, *n.* The communion table.

ăs-çent', *n.* Motion upward.

ăs-sent', *n.* Consent.

āte, *v. t.* Past of eat.

eight, *n.* A number.

au'-ğer, *n.* A carpenter's tool.

au'-gur, *v. t.* To predict or foretell.

awl, *n.* A shoemaker's tool.

all, *a.* The whole quantity.

LESSON 19.

WORDS USED IN BOOK-KEEPING.

"Success in business is seldom owing to uncommon talents or original power which is untractable and self-willed, but to the greatest degree of commonplace capacity."

ãe-eount'-ant, *n.* One employed or skilled in keeping accounts.

ãe'-eû-ra-çy, *n.* Exactness.

ãg'-gre-gãte, *n.* Whole amount.

ãn'-nu-al, *n.* Yearly.

bãl'-ançe, *n.* The excess on one side added to the other to make equality.

bãl'-ançe-shĕet, *n.* A paper giving a summary and balance of accounts.

blãnk, *a.* Unwritten; white.

bŏŏk'-kĕep-ĭng, *n.* The keeping of accounts.

eount'-ĭng-house, *n.* The room for keeping accounts.

dãi'-ly, *a.* Happening every day.

dãy'-bŏŏk, *n.* An account book of original entries, giving details of the transactions.

dĕb'-ĭt, *v. t.* To charge with debt.

doûb'-le-ĕn-try, *n.* A mode of book-keeping in which two entries are made.

joûr'-nal, *n.* An account book in which the transactions are arranged for posting.

lĕdg'-er, *n.* The final book of record in business transactions.

sŭm'-ma-ry, *n.* A general statement.

tō'-tal, *n.* The whole sum or amount.

sĕm-ĭ-ãn'-nu-al, *a.* Half yearly.

sĕt'-tle-ment, *n.* Payment of accounts.

tri-ĕn'-ni-al, *a.* Once in every three years.

LESSON 20.

PERTAINING TO EXPENDITURE.

Beware of little expenses; a small leak will sink a great ship.—*Franklin.*

ãl-low'-ançe, *n.* A sum or portion appointed.

ē-eo-nŏm'-ĭe-al, *n.* Managing with frugality.

ĕx-ôr'-bĭ-tant, *a.* Extravagant; excessive.

ĕx-pĕud'-i-tûre, *n.* Paying out, as of money.

ĕx-pĕn'-sĭve, *a.* Costly.

ĕx-tôr'-tĭon, *n.* Unlawful exaction.

ĕx-trãv'-a-gaut, *a.* Profuse in expense; wasteful.

fru-gãl'-ĭ-ty, *n.* Prudent economy.

ĭm-prŏv'-ĭ-dent, *a.* Not providing for what will happen in the future.

lãv'-ĭsh, *a.* Wasteful; profuse.

mĭ'-şĕr-ly, *a.* Stingy.

nĭg'-gard, *n.* A person meanly close and covetous; a miser.

out-rã'-ġeoŭs, *a.* Exceeding the limits of reason.

pãr-sĭ-mō'-nĭ-oŭs, *a.* Frugal to excess; close; saving.

pe-nū'-rĭ-oŭs, *a.* Very saving in the use of money.

pĭn'-mŏn-ey, *n.* A sum of money allowed a wife for her private expenses.

prŏd'-ĭ-ġal, *n.* One who spends money extravagantly.

prō-fūse', *n.* Liberal to excess; lavish.

spĕnd'-thrĭft, *n.* One who spends money profusely.

stĭn'-ġĭ-ness, *n.* Extreme avarice.

LESSON 21.

DICTATION EXERCISE.

"Foolish spending is the father of poverty. Do not be ashamed of hard work. Work for the best salary or wages you can get, but work for half price rather than be idle. Be your own master, and do not let society or fashion swallow up your individuality—hat, coat and boots. Do not eat up nor wear all you can earn. Compel your selfish body to spare something for profit saved. Be stingy to your own appetite, but merciful to others' necessities. Help others, and ask no help yourself. See that you are proud. Let your pride be of the right kind. Be too proud to be lazy; too proud to give up without conquering every difficulty; too proud to wear a coat you cannot afford to buy; too proud to be in such company that you cannot keep up with expenses; too proud to lie or steal, or cheat; too proud to be stingy."

LESSON 22.

MISCELLANEOUS.

Study yourselves, and most of all, note well
Wherein kind Nature invites you to excel.—*Longfellow.*

ä'-li-as, *n.* Otherwise called.

al-lāy', *v. t.* To abate; to subside.

al-lē'-vi-āte, *v. t.* To make light or easy to be borne.

al-loy', *n.* A baser metal mixed with a finer.

al'-ter-nāte, *v. t.* To perform by turns.

al-to-gēth'-er, *adv.* With united action.

am-bī'-tion, *n.* Desire for office or honor.

an'-i-māte, *v. t.* To give life to.

an-nex-ā'-tion, *n.* Addition; union.

an-nounçe'-ment, *n.* Giving public notice.

ap-par'-ent, *a.* Plain; easy to be seen.

ar-ti-fi'-cial (-fish'-al), *a.* Not genuine.

a-sy'-lum, *n.* A place of retreat and security.

at-tach', *v. t.* To bind, fasten or tie.

at-tempt', *v. i.* To make an effort or endeavor.

at'-tri-būte, *n.* An essential or necessary property or characteristic.

ben-e-fi'-cial (-fish'-al), *a.* Profitable.

bev'-er-age, *n.* A drink.

bom'-bast, *a.* Inflated; big without meaning.

brick'-kiln, *n.* A kiln for burning brick.

LESSON 23.

DRY GOODS.

And why take ye thought for raiment? Consider the lilies of the field, how they grow; they toil not, neither do they spin.—*Bible.*

al-pac'-a, *n.* A thin kind of cloth made of the wool of the alpaca.

ban-dan'-na, *n.* A kind of silk or cotton handkerchief.

cal'-i-co, *n.* Cotton cloth.

cam'-bric, *n.* A fine, thin, white fabric of flax or linen.

cash'-mere, *n.* A fine woolen dress goods.

cas'-si-mere, *n.* A thin, twilled woolen cloth for men's garments.

cor'-du-roy, *n.* A thick, cotton stuff, corded or ribbed on the surface.

flăn'-nel, *n.* A woolen cloth of loose texture.

ğĭnğ'-ham, *n.* A kind of cotton cloth, · the yarn of which is colored before it is woven.

hănd'-ker-chĭef, *n.* A cloth carried for wiping the face and hands.

mŭṣ'-lĭu, *n.* A thin, cotton cloth of any kind.

me-rī'-nŏ, *n.* A thin fabric of merino wool for ladies' wear.

păr'-a-ṣŏl, *n.* A small umbrella used by ladies to protect them from the rays of the sun.

rĭb'-bon, *n.* A narrow web of silk.

skĕịu, *n.* A quantity of yarn or silk taken from the reel.

tăp'-ĕs-try, *n.* A kind of woven hanging of wool or silk.

ŭm-brĕl'-là, *n.* A shade carried in the hand to shelter one from the sun, rain or snow.

va-lĕn-çĭ-ĕnneṣ', *n.* A rich kind of lace.

vĕl'-vet, *n.* A soft material woven from silk, or silk and cotton mixed, having short thread or pile on the surface.

wạd'-dĭng, *n.* Sheets of carded cotton for stuffing garments.

wạ'-ter-prŏŏf, *n.* A kind of cloth impervious to water.

LESSON 24.

DICTATION EXERCISE.

Stick to your legitimate business. Do not go into outside operations. Few men have brains enough for more than one business. To dabble in stocks, to put a few thousand dollars into a mine, and a few more into a manufactory, and a few more into an invention, is enough to ruin any man. Be content with fair returns. Do not become greedy. Do not think that men are happy in proportion as they are rich, and therefore do not aim too high. Be content with moderate wealth. Make friends. A time will come when all the money in the world will not be worth to you so much as one good staunch friend.—*Beecher.*

LESSON 25.

PERTAINING TO CLOTHING.

Costly thy habit as thy purse can buy, but not expressed in fancy; rich, not gaudy; for the apparel oft proclaims the man.—*Shakespeare.*

ăp-păr'-el, *n.* Garments; dress.

băl-mŏr'-al, *n.* A kind of figured petticoat.

bŏn'-nĕt, *n.* A covering for the head.

era-văt', *n.* A piece of fine cloth worn by men around the neck.

ĕm-broid'-er-y, *n.* Ornamental decoration.

făsh'-ion-a-ble, *a.* Dressing according to the prevailing fashion.

fī-çhụ', *n.* A light pointed cape worn by ladies, usually made of lace.

ma-tē'-ri-al, *n.* The substance of which anything is made.

ō'-ver-ạllṣ, *n. pl.* Loose trousers worn over others to protect them from being soiled.

pĭn'-a-fŏre, *n.* A child's apron.

rāi'-ment, *n.* Clothing.

shawl, *n.* A loose covering for the neck and shoulders.

slip'-per, *n.* A kind of light shoe which may be slipped on with ease.

sēr'-vīçe-a-ble, *a.* Prepared for giving good service.

sŭs-pĕnd'-erş, *n. pl.* Straps worn for holding up pantaloons.

toi'-let, *n.* Mode of dressing.

trous-seau' (trōō-sō'), *n.* The outfit of a lady when about to be married, including clothes, etc.

trou'-şerş, *n. pl.* A loose garment worn by males, covering the lower limbs.

vōgue, *n.* The fashion of people; temporary mode.

wāist'-eōat, *n.* A vest.

LESSON 26.

HOMOPHONOUS WORDS.

But you who seek to give and merit fame,
And justly bear a critic's noble name,
Be sure yourself and your own reach to know,
How far your genius, taste and learning go —*Pope.*

aught (aᵥt), *n.* Anything; any part.
ought, (aᵥt), *auxiliary.* Should.

bāil, *n.* Security.
bāle, *n.* A large bundle.

ball, *n.* A globe.
bawl, *v. i.* To cry noisily.

bāse, *n.* The foundation.
bāss or **bāse,** *n.* The lowest part in music.

bĕll, *n.* A resounding metallic vessel.
bĕlle, *n.* A beautiful young lady and much admired.

blew (blū), *v. t.* Past of blow.
blūe, *n.* A color; azure.

been (bĭn), *v. i.* Past of be.
bĭn, *n.* A kind of box or enclosed space.

bough (bou), *n.* A branch of a tree.
bow (bou), *n.* To bend.

beau (bō), *n.* A lady's attendant or suitor.
bow (bō), *n.* A weapon; doubling of a string in a knot.

brĕad, *n.* A kind of baked food.
brĕd, *v. t.* Trained; educated.

LESSON 27.

HARDWARE.

What stronger breast-plate than a heart untainted?
Thrice is he armed that hath his quarrel just;
And he but naked, though clothed in steel,
Whose conscience with injustice is corrupt.—*Shakespeare.*

ădz, *n.* A carpenter's tool for chipping.

ăn'-vĭl, *n.* An iron block upon which metals are hammered and shaped.

au'-ger-bĭt, *n.* A bit with a cutting edge or blade like that of an auger.

ăx'-le, *n.* A transverse bar connecting the hubs of the opposite wheels of a car or carriage.

bŭek'-le, *n.* An instrument, usually of metal, consisting of a rim with a movable tongue or catch, used for fastening things together.

ehĭş'-el, *n.* An iron or steel instrument, sharpened to a cutting edge at the end.

eŏl'-an-der, *n.* A vessel with a perforated bottom.

fau'-çet, *n.* A fixture for drawing liquid from a cask or vessel.

fer'-rule (fer'-ril), *n.* A ring of metal put around a cane, tool handle, etc., to prevent splitting.

ham'-mer, *n.* An instrument for driving nails, consisting of a metal head fixed crosswise to a handle.

ham'-mock, *n.* A kind of hanging bed.

hatch'-et, *n.* A small ax with a short handle, to be used with one hand.

i'-ron (i'-urn,) *n.* One of the metallic elements, hard, and very malleable when hot; it is the most useful of all metals.

knife, *n.* An instrument usually consisting of a thin blade of steel, with a sharp edge, fastened to a handle.

knob (nob), *n.* Part of a lock.

knock'-er, *n.* A kind of hammer fastened to a door, to be used in seeking admittance.

latch, *n.* A small piece of iron or wood used to fasten a door.

lē'-ver or lĕv'-er, *n.* A bar of metal, wood or other substance, used to exert a pressure or sustain a weight.

mat'-tock, *n.* A kind of a pick-ax, having the iron ends broad instead of pointed.

mouk'-ey-wrench, *n.* A wrench having a movable jaw.

LESSON 28.
Hardware.

Iron sharpeneth iron, so a man sharpeneth the countenance of his friend.—Proverbs

nip'-pers, *n. pl.* Small pincers for holding, breaking or cutting.

pinch'-ers, *n. pl.* An instrument for drawing nails or gripping things to be held fast.

pul'-ley, *n.* A wheel with a grooved rim, for transmitting power from or imparting power to the different parts of machinery.

ra'-zor, *n.* An instrument for removing the beard or hair.

re-volv'-er, *n.* A repeating firearm.

riv'-et, *n.* A pin of iron or other metal with a head.

scis'-sors, *n. pl.* An instrument for cutting, smaller than shears.

scut'-tle, *n.* A wide-mouthed vessel for holding coal.

scythe, *n.* An instrument for mowing.

shov'-el, *n.* An instrument used for throwing earth or loose substances.

sieve, *n.* A utensil for separating the fine part of any substance from the coarse.

sti-let'-to, *n.* A small dagger with a round, pointed blade.

tongs, *n. pl.* An instrument used for handling fire or heated metals.

trow'-el, *n.* A mason's tool used for spreading and dressing mortar.

twine, *n.* A strong thread composed of two or three smaller threads, or strands twisted together.

waf'-fle-i-ron, *n.* A utensil for baking waffles.

wash'-er, *n.* A ring of metal or other material used to relieve friction and to secure tightness of joints.

wire, *n.* A thread of metal.

wring'-er, *n.* An instrument for forcing water out of anything.

zinc, *n.* A metal of a brilliant white color.

LESSON 29.

MISCELLANEOUS.

Honor and shame from no condition rise,
Act well your part, there all the honor lies.—*Pope.*

ca-jōle', *v. t.* To deceive or delude by flattery.

cal'-loùs, *a.* Hardened.

can'-çel, *v. t.* To efface.

çel'-lu-loid, *n.* A compound manufactured from several ingredients, and resembling coral, ivory, amber, etc.

çen'-sus, *n.* An official registration of inhabitants.

çiv-il-i-zā'-tion, *n.* Refinement; culture.

cŏg-nō'-men, *n.* A surname.

cō-in'-çi-dençe, *n.* Occurrence of events at the same time.

cŏm'-ma, *n.* A mark used to denote a short pause.

cŏm-mū'-ni-ty, *n.* A society of people having common rights.

cŏn-çeal', *v. t.* To hide.

cŏn-çen'-trate, *v. t.* To bring to a common center.

cŏn-çil'-i-āte, *v. t.* To win over.

cŏn-crēte', *v. t.* To form into a mass.

cŏn-cûr'-rent, *a.* Agreeing in the same act.

cŏn-dĕnse', *v. t.* To make more compact.

cŏn-sĕe'-ū-tive, *a.* Following in the same order.

cŏn'-se-quent, *a.* Following as a result.

cŏn-sŏl'-i-dāte, *v. t.* To unite.

cŏn-spic'-ū-oùs, *a.* Easy to be seen.

LESSON 30.

STATIONERS' GOODS.

Books are the true levelers. They give to all who faithfully use them, the society, the spiritual presence, of the greatest and best of our race.—*Channing.*

al'-bum, *n.* A blank book in which to insert autographs.

blŏt'-ting-pā-per, *n.* A kind of paper serving to imbibe wet ink, and thus prevent blots.

cärd'-bōard, *n.* A stiff paper or pasteboard for making cards, etc.

dū-o-dĕç'-i-mo, *n.* A book in which a sheet is folded in twelve leaves.

ĕn'-vel-ōpe or ĕn-vĕl'-op, *n.* A wrapper; a cover, especially of a document, as a letter.

fō'-li-o, *a.* Formed of sheets folded so as to make two leaves.

fount'-ain-pĕn, *n.* A pen with a reservoir furnishing a continuous supply of ink.

lĕad'-pĕn-çil, *n.* An instrument for drawing or making lines, made of black lead.

ma-nil'-la, *n.* A very durable and firm kind of brown paper, made of Manilla hemp.

mĕm-o-răn'-dŭm-bŏŏk, *n.* A book in which memoranda are written down.

mū'-çi-lage, *n.* An aqueous solution of gum.

ŏe-tā'-vo, *n.* A book composed of sheets folded so as to make eight leaves.

pāste'-bōard, *n.* A stiff, thick kind of paper, formed of several single sheets pasted one upon another.

prō'-gram or prō'-grämme, *n.* A brief outline of the order of the subjects embraced in any public exercise.

quar'-to, *a.* Formed of sheets so as to make four leaves.

stā'-tion-er-y, *n.* The articles usually sold by a stationer, as paper, ink, etc.

tăb'-lets, *n. pl.* A kind of pocket memorandum book.

văl'-en-tine, *n.* A love letter sent by young persons to each other on Valentine's day, February 14th.

věl'-lum, *n.* A fine kind of parchment rendered clear and white for writing.

wrăp'-ping-pā-per, *n.* A coarse paper for tying up parcels.

LESSON 31.

DICTATION EXERCISE.

Ah me! the while I stop to think
What Shakespeare did with pen and ink!
I wonder how his ink was made—
If blue or purple was the shade;
His pen—broad-nibbed and rather stiff,
Like this, or fine? I wonder if
He tried a "Gillott," thirty-nine,
Or used a "Spencerian," like mine?
Or was it brains? No ink, I know,
Will really make ideas flow,
Nor can the most ingenious pen
Make wits and poets of dull men.
So this the miracle explains,
He used his pen and ink with brains.
Mine is the harder task, I think,
To write with only pen and ink.—*Century.*

LESSON 32.

WORDS PERTAINING TO WRITING.

The tongue is not the only way
Through which the active mind is heard,
But the good pen as well can say,
In tones as sweet, a gentle word.—*P. R. Spencer.*

bil'-let-doux (bĭl'-le-dōō), *n.* A love note or letter.

eăl'-i-graph, *n.* A writing machine.

eăl-lĭg'-ra-phy or ea-lĭg'-ra-phy, *n.* Fair or elegant penmanship.

ehi-rŏg'-ra-phy, *n.* The art of writing.

eŏr-re-spŏnd', *v. i.* To communicate by writing letters.

erăy'-on, *n.* A pencil.

e-pĭs'-tle, *n.* A letter.

e-răṣ'-ūre, *n.* A scratching out.

ĕs'-eri-toire (-twôr), *n.* A writing desk.

hi-ĕ-rō-glўph'-Ie, *n.* A mystical symbol in ancient writing.

Il-lĕg'-i-ble, *a.* Incapable of being read.

in-serĭp'-tion, *n.* That which is written or engraved on a solid substance.

lĕg'-i-ble, *a.* Capable of being read.

măn'-ū-serĭpt, *n.* A written as distinguished from a printed document.

pĕn'-man-shĭp, *n*.   The art of writing; manner of writing.

scrawl, *n*.   Bad writing.

scrĭb'-bling, *n*.   The act of scribbling, or writing hastily.

ste-nŏg'-rä-pher, *n*.   One skilled in stenography.

ste-nŏg'-rä-phy, *n*.   The art of writing in shorthand.

tȳpe'-wrī-ter, *n*.   A writing machine.

LESSON 33.

HOMOPHONOUS WORDS.

"Candor is the seal of a noble mind, the ornament and pride of man, the sweetest charm of woman, the scorn of rascals, and the rarest virtue of sociability."

bĕat, *v. t.*   To strike.

bĕet, *n*.   A vegetable.

bĕech, *n*.   A kind of tree.

bĕach, *n*.   The shore of the sea.

bĕer, *n*.   A malt liquor.

biĕr, *n*.   A litter for carrying the dead.

bōld'-er, *a*.   More bold.

bōwl'-der, *n*.   A large stone.

bōle, *n*.   A kind of fine earthy clay.

bŏll, *n*.   The pod of a plant, as of flax.

bōwl, *n*.   A concave vessel.

bŏr'-ōugh (bŭr'-rō,) *n*.   An incorporated town that is not a city.

bŭr'-rōw, *n*.   A hole in the ground made by certain animals, for habitation.

bōurne, *n*.   A point aimed at.

bōrne, *p. p. of bear*.   Carried.

bôrn, *p. p. of bear*.   Brought into life.

bur'-y, *v. t.*   To cover out of sight.

bĕr'-ry, *n*.   A small kind of fruit.

brĭd'-al, *n*.   Marriage.

brī'-dle, *n*.   A curb; a check.

LESSON 34.

GROCERIES.

"Let not thy table exceed the fourth part of thy revenue; too much is a vanity; enough is a feast."

all'-spĭçe, *n*.   A spice of a mildly pungent taste.

bĭs'-cuĭt, *n*.   Unfermented bread.

eāy-ĕnne' pĕp-per, *n*.   A very pungent pepper.

chŏe'-o-late, *n*.   A paste used for making a beverage.

çĭn'-na-mon, *n*.   The inner bark of a tree growing in Ceylon.

eŏf'-fee, *n*.   A drink made from the roasted berry of the coffee tree.

gĕl'-a-tīne, *n*.   A concrete animal substance.

grĕase, *n*.   Animal fat in a soft state.

grō'-çer-y, *n*.   A grocer's store.

hŏm'-i-ny, *n*.   Corn, prepared for food by boiling.

ĭn'-dĭ-ḡo, *n*.   Blue coloring matter.

mäe-a-rō'-nĭ, *n*.   An article of food composed of paste.

mo-läs'-sĕs, *n*.   The syrup which drains from sugar.

säl-e-rä'-tus, *n*.   A bicarbonate of potash.

sĭr'-up or sȳr'-up, *n*.   Sweetened liquid of any kind.

suḡ'-ar (shŏŏḡ'-ar), *n*.   A sweet crystalline substance.

tắp-i-ŏ'-eả, *n.* A coarsely granular substance obtained from the roots of a plant found in Brazil.

to-băe'-eo, *n.* A plant much used for chewing and smoking.

vẽr-mĭ-çĕl'-lĭ, *n.* The flour of a hard, small-grained wheat made into dough.

yẽast, *n.* Preparation for raising dough for bread or cakes.

LESSON 35.

FISH AND FOWL.

Master, I marvel how the fishes live in the sea.
Why, as men do a-land : the great ones eat up the little ones.—*Shakespeare.*

ăn-chŏ'-vy, *n.* A small fish of the Herring family, caught in the Mediterranean Sea.

eăn'-vas-băck, *n.* A species of sea duck, highly esteemed for the delicacy of its flesh.

ēel, *n.* A snake-like fish.

gu̇in'-ea-fowl, *n.* A fowl of a dark grey color, variegated with white spots.

hăd'-dŏek, *n.* A sea fish, a little smaller than a cod, which it resembles.

hăl'-i-bŭt, *n.* A large sea fish, some weighing 400 or more pounds.

hẽr'-ring, *n.* A small fish.

lŏb'-ster, *n.* A marine shell-fish.

măck'-er-el, *n.* A marine fish found in the North Atlantic.

mŭs'-kal-lŏnge, *n.* A large kind of pike found in the Northern Lakes, St. Lawrence and Ohio rivers.

oys'-tẽṛ, *n.* A mollusk with a bivalve shell, extensively used for food.

phĕas'-ant, *n.* A wild fowl, the flesh of which is used for food.

pĭek'-er-el, *n.* A fresh water fish belonging to the pike family.

pĭg'-eon, *n.* A small bird of several species.

sălm'-on (săm'-un), *n.* A fish of a yellowish red color.

smĕlt, *n.* A small fish of a silvery white color.

stŭr'-geon (-jŭn), *n.* A large fish.

tŭr'-bot, *n.* A flat fish with a body nearly circular. It grows to the weight of 20 or 30 pounds, and is much esteemed by epicures.

tŭr'-key, *n.* A large fowl, the flesh of which is valued for food.

tŭr'-tle, *n.* A sea tortoise, the flesh of which is esteemed as a great delicacy.

LESSON 36.

PERTAINING TO FOOD.

A fig for your bill of fare ; show me your bill of company.—*Swift.*

ăl-bŭ'-men, *n.* White of eggs.

eŭ'-li-na-ry, *a.* Relating to the kitchen or art of cookery.

çē'-re-al, *n.* Any edible grain, as wheat, rye, etc.

de-lĭ'-çioŭs (-lĭsh'-ŭs), *a.* Affording exquisite pleasure to the taste.

ēat'-a-ble, *n.* Proper for food.

făr-i-nā'-ceoŭs (-shŭs), *a.* Made of meal or flour.

glŭt'-ton-y, *n.* Excess in eating.

hĕalth'-fụl, *a.* Wholesome, serving to promote health.

jũiçe, *n.* The watery part of fruit or vegetables.

lŭs'-cioŭs (lŭsh'-ŭs), *a.* Delicious.

mǎs'-tǐ-eāte, *v. t.* To chew.

nū'-trǐ-mĕnt, *n.* That which nourishes.

nŭ-trǐ'-tioŭs (-trǐsh'-ŭs), *a.* Nourishing.

pǎl'-a-ta-ble, *a.* Agreeable to the taste.

pro-vǐṣ'-ion, *n.* A stock of food.

rǎv'-en-oŭs, *a.* Hungry, even to rage.

rĕl'-ish-a-ble, *a.* Having an agreeable taste.

sā'-tǐ-āte (sā'-shǐ āte), *v. t.* To satisfy the appetite to the full.

sā'-vor-y, *a.* Relishable.

vǐct'-ualṣ (vǐt'-lz), *n.* Sustenance; food.

LESSON 37.

DICTATION EXERCISE.

We may live without poetry, music and art;
We may live without conscience, and live without heart;
We may live without friends; we may live without books;
But civilized man cannot live without cooks.
He may live without books—what is knowledge but grieving?
He may live without hope—what is hope but deceiving?
He may live without love—what is passion but pining?
But where is the man that can live without dining?—*Owen Meredith.*

LESSON 38.

MISCELLANEOUS.

Words are things, and a small drop of ink,
Falling, like dew, upon a thought, produces
That which makes thousands, and perhaps millions, think.—*Byron.*

cŏn'-stǐ-tūte, *v. t.* To make up; to compose.

cŏn-tract', *v. t.* To shorten; to lessen.

cŏn-trǐb'-ūte, *v. t.* To furnish in part.

co-nŭn'-drŭm, *n.* A puzzling question.

cŏn-vēn'-ien-çy, *n.* That which is convenient.

cŏn'-ver-sant, *a.* Well informed.

cŏn-vǐnçe', *v. t.* To satisfy by proof.

cŏr'-o-net, *n.* An inferior crown worn by noblemen.

cŏr-rōde', *v. t.* To eat away by degrees.

cŏs-mět'-ic, *n.* An application to improve the complexion.

co-tǐl'-lion (-yun), *n.* A brisk dance performed by eight persons.

crēat'-ūre, *n.* An animal; a man.

crĕv'-içe, *n.* A narrow opening; a cleft.

crib'-bage, *n.* A game of cards.

crī'-sĭs, *n.* The point of time when anything must terminate or take a new course.

crǐt'-ic-al-ly, *adv.* With nice discernment; in a critical manner.

cro-chet' (cro-shā'), *n.* A netting made with a small hook.

cro-quet' (krō-kā'), *n.* A game played with balls, mallets and hoops or arches.

crouch, *v. i.* To stoop low; to lie close to the ground, as an animal.

crŭmb, *n.* A small fragment or piece of bread or other food.

LESSON 39.

FRUIT.

The native orchard's fairest trees, wild springing on the hill,
Bear no such precious fruits as these, and never will,
Till axe and saw and pruning knife cut from them every bough,
And they receive a gentler life than crowns them now.—Holland.

ăp'-ple, *n.* The fruit of the apple tree.

ä'-prĭ-cŏt, *n.* A fruit of the plum species.

ba-nä'-nå, *n.* A tropical fruit.

căn'-ta-loupe, *n.* A small, round, ribbed variety of muskmelon.

chĕr'-ry, *n.* A fruit of the prune species.

çĭt'-ron, *n.* The fruit of the citron tree, resembling a lemon.

cō'-cōa-nŭt, *n.* The nut or fruit of the cocoa.

gōōse'-bĕr-ry, *n.* The fruit of a small shrub.

hŭck'-le-bĕr-ry or } *n.* The
whor'-tle-bĕr-ry (hwŭrt'-l-), } fruit of a low shrub.

lĕm'-on, *n.* An oval fruit containing an acid pulp.

lïme, *n.* A fruit like the lemon, smaller and more intensely sour.

mŭl'-bĕr-ry, *n.* The fruit of a tree.

mŭsk'-mĕl-on, *n.* A species of melon so called from its musky fragrance.

pēach, *n.* A Persian apple; a tree and its fruit.

pïne'-ăp-ple, *n.* A tropical plant and its fruit.

pŏme-grăn'-ate, *n.* A fruit as large as an orange, of a reddish color and having numerous seeds.

quïnçe, *n.* A fruit with an acid taste and pleasant flavor.

rāi'-sin, *n.* A grape dried in the sun or by artificial heat.

răsp'-bĕr-ry, *n.* A plant and its fruit.

strąw'-bĕr-ry, *n.* The fruit of a small plant.

LESSON 40.

VEGETABLES.

But look at that bin of potatoes! Those are my beautiful Carters;
Every one doomed to be martyrs
To the eccentric desire of Christian people to skin them,
Brought to the trial of fire for the good that is in them.—Holland.

ăs-păr'-a-gŭs, *n.* A garden plant or vegetable.

căb'-bage, *n.* A garden plant.

căr'-rot, *n.* A vegetable having an esculent root.

cąu'-li-flow-er, *n.* A variety of cabbage.

çĕl'-er-y, *n.* A plant of the parsley family.

cū'-cŭm-ber, *n.* A vegetable used unripe as a salad.

găr'-lïc, *n.* A plant having a bulbous root and strong smell.

lĕt'-tuçe (-tĭs), *n.* A plant, the leaves of which are used for salad.

ŏu'-ion (ŭn'-yŭn), *n.* The bulb of a plant used for food.

părs'-ley, *n.* A plant, the leaves of which are used in cooking.

părs'-nĭp, *n.* A plant with a white spindle-shaped root, used for food.

po-tā'-to, *n.* A plant with a farinaceous tuber used for food.

pŭmp'-kin, *n.* A well-known plant and its fruit.

răd'-ĭsh, *n.* A plant, the root of which is eaten raw as a salad.

ru-ta-bā'-gå, *n.* A Swedish turnip.

săl'-sĭ-fў, *n.* Vegetable oyster.

spin'-ach (spin'-ĕj), *n.* A plant whose leaves are used for greens.

to-mā'-to or to-mä'-to, *n.* A plant and its fruit.

tûr'-nip, *n.* A plant with a bulbous root.

vĕg'-e-ta-ble, *n.* A plant used for culinary purposes.

LESSON 41.

WORDS PERTAINING TO AGRICULTURE.

"We must not hope to be mowers and gather the ripe, gold ears,
Until we have first been sowers and watered the furrows with tears."

ā'-ere, *n.* Piece of land containing 160 square rods.

ăg'-ri-eŭlt-ūre, *n.* The art of cultivating the ground.

ăr'-a-ble, *a.* Fit for plowing or tilling.

eŭl'-ti-vāte, *v. t.* To till.

fĕr'-tile, *a.* Rich; fruitful.

fĕr'-ti-lize, *v. t.* To make fertile or enrich.

grăn'-a-ry, *n.* A store-house for grain after it is threshed; a corn house.

hăr'-vest-hōme, *n.* The feast made at the gathering of the harvest.

hôr'-ti-eŭlt-ūre, *n.* Cultivation of a garden.

lōam'-y, *a.* Consisting of sand, clay and carbonate of lime with decaying vegetable matter.

mârsh'-y, *a.* Wet; boggy.

mĕad'-ōw, *n.* A tract of low, level grass land somewhat wet.

ôr'-chard, *n.* An enclosure or assemblage of fruit trees.

păst'-ūr-age, *n.* Land appropriated to grazing.

phŏs'-phate, *n.* A fertilizer formed of phosphoric acid and salt.

plough or plow, *n.* An implement for turning up the soil.

rŭs'-tie-ate, *v.* To live or dwell in the country.

stĕr'-ile, *a.* Producing little or no crop; barren.

tĭll'-a-ble, *a.* Capable of being tilled.

trough (trawf), *n.* A long tray.

LESSON 42.

DICTATION EXERCISE.

The time for toil has passed and night has come—
The last and saddest of the harvest eves;
Worn out with labor, long and wearisome,
Drooping and faint, the reapers hasten home,
Each laden with his sheaves.
My spirit grieves that I am burdened, not so much with grain,
As with a heaviness of heart and brain ;
Behold my sheaves! Few, light and worthless, yet their weight
Through all my frame a weary aching leaves;
For long I struggled with my hopeless fate,
And stayed and toiled till it was dark and late—
Yet well I know I have more tares than wheat—
Brambles and flowers, dry stalks and withered leaves;
Wherefore I blush and weep, as at thy feet
I kneel down reverently and repeat,
"Master, behold my sheaves."—*Elizabeth Akers.*

LESSON 43.

HOMOPHONOUS WORDS.

Thy purpose firm is equal to the deed :
Who does the best his circumstance allows,
Does well, acts nobly ; angels could do no more.— *Young*.

eăl'-en-dar, *n.* An almanac.
eăl'-en-der, *n.* A hot press.

eăn'-non, *n.* A large gun.
eăn'-on, *n.* A church law; a digni-
tary of the church.

eăn'-vas, *n.* A coarse cloth for sails.
eăn'-vass, *v. t.* To solicit something.

eăp-i-tal, *n.* The chief city ; principal.
Eăp'-i-tol, *n.* The building occupied
by the Congress of the U. S.

eāne, *n.* A walking stick.
Eāin, *n.* The first murderer.

çeil, *v. t.* To line the top or roof of.
sēal, *v. t.* To make fast.

çĕll, *n.* A small room, as in a prison.
sĕll, *v. t.* To exchange for money.

çĕl'-lar, *n.* A room under the house.
sĕll'-er, *n.* One who sells.

chōōse, *v. t.* To select.
chews (chōōs), *v. t.* To bite and grind
with the teeth.

elause, *n.* A part of a sentence.
elaws, *n. pl.* Sharp, hooked nails of
animals or birds.

LESSON 44.

ARCHITECTURE.

If cities were built by the sound of music, then some edifices would appear to be constructed by grave, solemn tones, others to have danced forth to light, fantastic airs.— *Hawthorne*.

băl'-us-trāde, *n.* A row of balusters
topped by a rail, serving as an enclosure.
băt'-tle-ment, *n.* A notched or in-
dented parapet.
bāy-wĭn'-dŏw, *n.* A window forming
a bay or recess in the room and projecting outward in different forms.
bou'-doir (bōō'-dwôr), *n.* A lady's
private room.
eăn'-o-py, *n.* A covering over the head.
çeil'-ing, *n.* The upper interior surface
of an apartment.
elŏs'-et, *n.* A small, close room.
eôr'-niçe, *n.* Any molded projection
which finishes the part to which it is
affixed.
eôr'-ri-dŏr, *n.* A gallery or passage-
way.

eū'-po-lå, *n.* A dome-like vault on the
top of an edifice.
dŏm'-i-çĭle, *n.* An abode or permanent
residence.
dôr'-mi-to-ry, *n.* Sleeping quarters or
a bedroom.
ĕx-tē'-ri-or, *n.* The outside part.
gā'-ble, *n.* The vertical triangular end
of a house.
găl'-ler-y, *n.* A long and narrow cor-
ridor.
gŏth'-ĭe, *a.* A style of architecture
with high and sharply-pointed arches,
etc.
in-tē'-ri-or, *n.* The inside part.
kĭteh'-en, *n.* A cook room.
läun'-dry, *n.* The place where clothes
are washed.
läv'-a-to-ry, *n.* A place for washing.

LESSON 45.
Architecture.

Houses are built to live in more than to look on; therefore let use be preferred before uniformity, except where both may be had.—*Bacon.*

môr'-tĭse, *n.* A cavity cut into a piece of timber to receive the end of another piece cut to fit it.

nĭche (nĭch), *n.* A shell-like recess in a wall for a statue, bust, or other erect ornament.

nûrs'-er-y, *n.* A room in the house, appropriated to the care of children.

ŏb-şĕrv'-a-to-ry, *n.* A place from which a view may be commanded.

ō'-ri-el, *n.* A large bay or recessed window projecting outward.

pa-lā'-tial, *a.* Magnificent; like a palace.

păn'-try, *n.* A room where provisions are kept.

pär-tĭ'-tion, *n.* That which divides or separates; an interior wall dividing one part of a house from another.

pa-vĭl'-ion, *n.* A kind of building or turret under a single roof.

pĭ-äz'-zà, *n.* A portico or covered walk supported by arches or columns.

pĭ-läs'-ter, *n.* A square column, usually set in a wall, and projecting only a fourth or fifth of its diameter.

pōr'-ti-eo, *n.* A covered space, enclosed by columns at the front of a building.

ro-tŭn'-dà, *n.* A round building.

seŭl'-ler-y, *n.* A place where culinary utensils are kept.

stēe'-ple, *n.* A tower or turret of a church, ending in a point.

strŭet'-ūre, *n.* A building of any kind.

tăb'-er-na-ele, *n.* A slightly built or temporary dwelling.

tûr'-ret, *n.* A little tower.

vĕs'-tĭ-būle, *n.* A small hall from which doors open into other apartments in the house.

ve-răn'-dà, *n.* A kind of open portico, formed by extending a sloping roof beyond the main dwelling.

LESSON 46.
DICTATION EXERCISE.

The Gothic cathedral is a blossoming in stone, subdued by the insatiable demand of harmony, in man. The mountain of granite blooms into an eternal flower, with the lightness and delicate finish as well as the aerial proportions and perspective of vegetable beauty. Möller, in his essay on Architecture, taught that the building which was fitted accurately to answer its end, would turn out to be beautiful, though beauty had not been intended. I find the like unity in human structures rather virulent and pervasive.—*Emerson.*

LESSON 47.
MISCELLANEOUS.

Like leaves on trees the race of man is found,
Now green in youth, now withering on the ground ;
Another race the following spring supplies ;
They fall successive, and successive rise.—*Homer's Iliad.*

deaf (dĕf or dēf), *a.* Unable to hear sounds.

de-băt'-a-ble, *a.* Disputable.

de-brĭs' (dä-brēe'), *n.* Remains; ruins.

dĕe'-o-rāte, *v.t.* To adorn; to beautify.

de-erẽase', *v. t.* To diminish gradually.

de-gĕn'-er-āte, *v. i.* To grow worse.
de-nōte', *v. t.* To indicate.
de-ō'-dor-īze, *v. t.* To deprive of odor.
de-sīr'-a-ble, *a.* Worthy of desire or longing.
de-tē'-ri-o-rāte, *v. t.* To make worse.
dē'-vi-āte, *v. i.* To go out of one's way; to digress.
dïf'-fi-eŭlt, *a.* Not easy.
di-lăp'-i-dāte, *v. i.* To fall into partial ruin.

dïs-eoûr'-age, *v. t.* To dishearten; to disfavor.
dïs-frăn'-ehīṣe, *v. t.* To deprive of citizenship.
dïs-trïb'-ūte, *v. t.* To divide among several.
dūe'-at, *n.* A European coin, either silver or gold.
ĕf-fāçe', *v. t.* To blot out.
ē'-grĕss, *n.* Departure.
ē-lăs-tïç'-i-ty, *n.* Springiness; rebound

LESSON 48.
DRUGS.

Physic is of little use to a temperate person, for a man's own observation on what he finds does him good and what hurts him, is the best physic to preserve health.—*Bacon.*

ăç'-id, *n.* A sour substance.
ăl'-ka-lï, *n.* A substance which neutralizes acids.
ăm-mō'-nï-à, *n.* An alkali which is gaseous or aeriform in its uncombined state.
a-pŏth'-e-ea-ry, *n.* One who prepares and sells drugs for medicinal purposes.
är'-nï-eâ, *n.* A medicine applied externally as a remedy for sprains or bruises.
är'-se-nïe, *n.* A metal of a steel gray color and brilliant lustre; a poison.
băl'-sam, *n.* An aromatic substance flowing from trees.
bĕl-la-dŏn'-nà, *n.* Deadly nightshade.
bĕn'-zïne, *n.* A light oil of petroleum.
eăl'-o-mĕl, *n.* A preparation of mercury.

eăm'-phor, *n.* A solid white gum or concrete juice.
ea-thär'-tïe, *n.* A purgative.
ehlō'-ro-fôrm, *n.* A medical fluid which when inhaled produces insensibility to pain.
eo-lōgne' (ko-lōn'), *n.* A perfumed liquid.
eŏp'-per-as, *n.* Sulphate of iron.
erē'-o-sōte, *n.* An oily, colorless liquid having the smell of smoke.
dïs-pĕn'-sa-ry, *n.* The place where medicines are prepared.
drŭg'-gïst, *n.* One who deals in drugs.
glŷç'-er-ïne, *n.* A sweet liquid, composed of carbon, hydrogen and oxygen
ïp'-e-eăe, *n.* An emetic.

LESSON 49.
Drugs.

Oh! what avail the largest gifts of heaven,
When drooping health and spirits go amiss?
How tasteless then whatever can be given!
Health is the vital principle of bliss,
And exercise of health.—*Horace Mann.*

lau'-da-nŭm, *n.* Tincture of opium.
lïe'-o-rïçe, *n.* A dark-colored, sweet substance, much used as a remedy for coughs and colds.

măg-nē'-ṣi-à (-nē'-zhï-à), *n.* A white powdered earth, used as a mild cathartic.
mĕr'-eu-ry, *n.* A salt used as a remedial agent.

môr'-phïne, *n.* A vegetable alkaloid extracted from opium.

pär-e-ḡŏr'-ïe, *n.* A medicine that mitigates pain.

pĕp'-per-mïnt, *n.* A liquor distilled from an aromatic and pungent plant.

phär-ma-çeū'tïe, *a.* Pertaining to knowledge of pharmacy.

phär'-ma-çy, *n.* The art of compounding medicines.

pŏi'-ṣon, *n.* That which taints or destroys.

quï'-nïne, *n.* Peruvian bark.

rĕṣ'-in, *n.* A solid, inflammable gum of vegetable origin, soluble in alcohol and in essential oils.

süf'-frou, *n.* A vegetable medicine.

salt-pē'-tre or salt-pē'-ter, *n.* Nitrate of potassia.

sär-sa-pa-rïl'-là, *n.* A medicine distilled from a Mexican plant.

strỹeh'-nïne, *n.* Nightshade, very bitter and poison.

sŭl'-phur, *n.* A simple mineral substance, of a yellow color.

sụ'-mae or sụ'-mäeh (shụ'-mäk), *n.* A plant or shrub used in medicine.

tïṇet'-ūre, *n.* Slight taste or quality added to anything.

tûr'-pen-tïne, *n.* A clear, colorless balsam taken from the pine, fir, larch and other trees.

LESSON 50.

PERTAINING TO PHYSIC.

I think you might dispense with half your doctors, if you would only consult Doctor Sun more, and be more under the treatment of these great hydropathic doctors, the clouds!—*Beecher.*

ăl-lŏp'-a-thy, *n.* Using medicines to produce effects different from those resulting from disease.

ăm-pu-tä'-tion, *n.* Cutting off a member of the body.

çau'-ter-ïze, *v. t.* To burn or sear with fire or a hot iron.

çhär'-la-tan, *n.* A quack.

ehï-rŏp'-o-dïst, *n.* A corn doctor; extracts corns, warts, etc.

dï-aḡ-nō'-sïs, *n.* The determination of a disease by means of distinctive marks.

ĕe-lĕe'-tïe, *n.* Not following any one method or school, but selecting at will from others.

hü-me-ŏp'-a-thy, *n.* Art of curing, founded on resemblances.

hŏs'-pï-tal, *n.* An institution for caring for the sick and infirm.

hỹ-drŏp'-a-thy, *n.* The water-cure.

iu-fïrm'-a-ry, *n.* A hospital where the sick are lodged and nursed.

me-dïç'-ï-nal, *a.* Pertaining to medicine.

nür-eŏt'-ïe, *n.* A medicine which produces sleep.

o'-pi-ate, *a.* Inducing sleep.

ŏp-tï'-cian (-tïsh'-an), *n.* One skilled in the science of vision.

phỹ-ṣï'-cian (fï-zïsh'-an), *n.* One skilled in the art of healing.

spe-çïf'-ïe, *a.* Exerting a peculiar influence over any part of the body.

stïm'-ū-läte, *v. t.* Medicine to produce an exaltation of vital activity.

văe'-çï-näte, *v. t.* To inoculate with kine pox by means of a virus called vaccine, taken from a cow.

vĕt'-ĕr-ï-na-ry, *n.* One skilled in healing domestic animals.

LESSON 51.

HOMOPHONOUS WORDS.

"What shall I do? My boy, don't stand asking;
Take hold of something—whatever you can,
Don't turn aside for the toiling or tasking;
Idle soft hands never yet made a man."

çĕnt, *n.* A coin.
sçĕnt, *n.* Odor; the sense of smell.
sĕnt, *v. i.* Past of send; dispatched.

çīte, *v. t.* To summon.
site, *n.* Local position; situation.
sīght, *n.* The power of seeing.

elĭmb, *v. i.* To rise laboriously.
elĭme, *n.* A climate.

eōarse, *a.* Rude; composed of large parts.
eōurse, *n.* Direction.

eōre, *n.* The center of a fruit.
eōrps (kōr), *n.* A body of men.

eoun'-çĭl, *n.* A deliberative body.
eoun'-sel, *n.* Advice; a legal adviser.

eŭr'-rant, *n.* A small fruit.
eŭr'-rent, *n.* A stream; onward motion.

dēar, *a.* Beloved; costly.
dēer, *n.* An animal.

drȧught (drȧft), *n.* A current; that which is drunk.
drȧft, *n.* A bill of exchange.

LESSON 52.

DISEASES.

He who cures a disease may be the skillfullest, but he who prevents it is the safest physician.—*T. Fuller.*

ăb'-sçĕss, *n.* A tumor filled with purulent matter.
brŏn-chi'-tĭs, *n.* Inflammation of the bronchial membrane.
ea-tȧrrh', *n.* A disease of the head, caused by a cold.
chŏl'-e-rȧ, *n.* A disease.
dĭph-thē'-ri-ȧ, *n.* A disease in which the throat is inflamed, and coated with a leathery membrane.
dĭs-ēase', *n.* Malady or sickness.
dĭz'-zi-ness, *n.* A whirling in the head.
dȳs-pĕp'-si-ȧ, *n.* Difficulty of digestion.
ĕp'-i-lĕp-sy, *n.* Disease of the brain, attended by convulsions.
ĕr-y-sĭp'-e-las, *n.* A disease in which the skin is inflamed.
gȧn'-grēne (gȧng'-), *n.* Mortification of living flesh.

hĭe'-eough (hĭk'-kŭp), *n.* Spasmodic inspiration producing sound.
mēa'-ṣleṣ, *n.* An eruptive disease.
neŭ-rȧl'-ġi-ȧ, *n.* A disease, the chief symptom of which is a very acute pain, seated in a nerve.
pa-rȧl'-y-sĭs, *n.* Loss of voluntary motion with or without loss of sensation.
pleŭ'-ri-sy, *n.* Inflammation of the pleura or the membrane that lines the chest.
pneŭ-mō'-nĭ-ȧ (nū-mō'-), *n.* Inflammation of the lungs.
rheŭ'-ma-tĭṣm (rŭ-), *n.* Painful inflammation of joints and muscles.
serŏf'-ū-lȧ, *n.* A disease of the glands.
tỹ'-phoid, *n.* Typhus fever of a low grade.

LESSON 53.

DICTATION EXERCISE.

" My jolly young fellow," said Health, " now you really
Have lately been drawing on me rather freely.
Who riots with Pleasure by night and by day
Must expect that in time there'll be something to pay.
For the favors you've had, that you may not forget,
Suppose you just give me your note for the debt.
Write as I dictate :

         " ' Twenty years after date
I promise to pay to my health, sure as fate,
For value received, in sin, folly and pleasure,
These prominent parts of estates I should treasure :
My Limbs to be racked with rheumatics and gout ;
My Teeth to decay till they mostly rot out ;
My Eyes to grow dim and my Hair to grow gray,
While dropsy and asthma take turns day by day ;
My Nerves and my Lungs, too, together give way ;
My Stomach to fall to dyspepsia a prey ;
My Taste to forsake me, my Voice to grow weak,
While my Ears cannot hear, save when Conscience shall speak.'
Now sign it. When due you need not waste your breath
For extension. Remember, the protest is Death."

LESSON 54.

PERTAINING TO DISEASE.

Diseases, desperate grown, by desperate appliance are relieved, or not at all.—Shakespeare.

āche, *v. i.* To suffer pain.

a-cūte', *a.* Sharp ; penetrating.

cŏm'-fort-a-ble, *a.* Free from pain.

cŏn-tā'-ġioŭs, *a.* Catching.

cŏn-va-lĕs'-çençe, *n.* Renewal of health.

dĭs'-lo-cāte, *v. t.* To disjoint.

e-mā'-ci-āte (-shĭ-āt), *v. i.* To lose flesh.

ĕp-i-dĕm'-ĭc, *n.* A disease which, arising from a wide-spread cause, affects numbers of people at the same time.

fū'-mi-ġāte, *v. t.* To apply smoke to in cleansing infected apartments.

hăġ'-gard, *a.* Having the expression of one wasted by want or pain.

he-rĕd'-ĭ-ta-ry, *a.* Transmitted from parent to child.

ĭm'-be-çĭle, *n.* One without strength either in body or mind.

lū'-na-tĭc, *n.* A person of unsound mind.

măl'-a-dy, *n.* Sickness or disease of the human body.

ma-lĭġ'-nant, *a.* Tending to produce death.

mŏn-o-mā'-nĭ-ăc, *n.* One whose mind is deranged on a single subject.

păr'-ŏx- y̆sm, *n.* The attack of a disease that occurs at intervals.

re-sŭs'-çi-tāte, *v. t.* To revive from apparent death.

străn-gu-lā'-tion, *n.* The act of destroying life by stopping respiration.

wound (wōōnd or wownd), *n.* A hurt ; an injury.

LESSON 55.

PERTAINING TO THE HUMAN BODY.

"Our body is a well-set clock, which keeps good time; but if it be too much or indiscreetly tampered with, the alarm runs out before the hour."

ăṇ'-kle, *n.* The joint which connects the foot with the leg.

ür'-ter-y, *n.* A vessel that conveys the blood from the heart.

aṇ'-dǐ-to-ry, *n.* Pertaining to the sense of hearing.

brŏṇ'-chi-â, *n.* The two large divisions of the trachea.

eŭl-ĭs-thĕn'-ĭes, *n.* Bodily exercise for strength and graceful movement.

eăp'-il-la-ries, *n. pl.* Small vessels which connect the arteries with the veins.

eär'-ti-lage, *n.* Gristle.

elăv'-i-ele, *n.* The collar bone.

eôr'-ne-â, *n.* The strong membrane which forms the front part of the eye.

erā'-nĭ-ŭm, *n.* The bones which enclose the brain.

eā'-ti-ele, *n.* The outer skin of the body.

dĭ'-a-phrăgm (-frăm), *n.* The muscle separating the chest from the abdomen.

ĕn-ăm'-el, *n.* The hard substance covering the crown of the tooth.

eȳe, *n.* The organ of vision.

fā'-cial (fā'-shăl), *a.* Pertaining to the face.

güst'-a-to-ry, *n.* Nerve of taste.

in-spi-rā'-tion, *n.* Breathing air into the lungs.

knŭck'-le, *n.* The joint of a finger.

lăr'-yṇx, *n.* The upper part of the wind pipe, constituting the organ of voice.

lĭḡ'-a-ment, *n.* A white, inelastic substance serving to bind one bone to another.

LESSON 56.

Pertaining to the Human Body.

God made the human body, and it is by far the most exquisite and wonderful organization which has come to us from the Divine hand. It is a study for one's whole life.—*Beecher.*

mĕ-dŭl'-lâ ŏb-lŏṇ-ḡā'-tâ, *n.* The upper portion of the spinal cord, within the skull.

mĕm'-brāne, *n.* A thin layer of tissue serving to cover some part of the body.

mŭs'-cles, *n. pl.* Organs of motion.

mŭs-tâçhe' (mŭs-tăsh'), *n.* The part of the beard which grows on the upper lip.

ŏl-fāe'-to-ry, *n.* The nerve of smell.

pa-tĕl'-lâ, *n.* The knee pan.

phy-sïque' (fē-sēk'), *n.* Physical structure of a person.

pleŭ'-râ, *n.* The membrane that lines the chest.

pŭl'-mo-na-ry, *n.* Pertaining to the lungs.

pŭl-sā'-tion, *n.* A beat or throb.

rĕt'-i-nâ, *n.* The membranous expansion of the optic nerve in the interior of the eye ball, which receives the impressions resulting in the sense of vision.

sa-lī'-vâ, *n.* Spittle.

shŏul'-der, *n.* The upper part of the back.

stóm'-aeh, *n.* The organ in which the food is digested.

tĕm'-per-a-mĕnt, *n.* Physical and mental character of a person.

tóngue (tŭng), *n* Organ of speech and taste.

tỹm'-pa-nŭm, *n.* The drum of the ear.

vĕr'-te-brà (*pl.* vĕr'-te-brae), *n.* A joint or segment of the back bone.

vĭs'-ion, *n.* Actual sight.

wrĭst, *n.* The joint which unites the hand to the arm, consisting of eight small bones.

LESSON 57.

MISCELLANEOUS.

Procrastination is the thief of time;
Year after year it steals till all are fled,
And, to the mercies of a moment leaves
The vast concerns of an eternal scheme. — *Young.*

ĕl-e-mĕnt'-a-ry, *a.* Simple; consisting of a single element.

ĕm-bĕl'-lish, *v. t.* To adorn; to beautify.

ĕn'-er-ġy, *n.* Life; capacity for acting.

e-nŭ'-mer-āte, *v. t.* To number.

ĕn-vĭ'-ron-ment, *n.* Places that surround another place.

ē'-qua-ble, *a.* Equal and uniform.

e-răd'-i-eāte, *v. t.* To root out.

ĕs-chew', *v. t.* To shun; to avoid.

ĕs-pē'-cial (-pĕsh'-al), *a.* Particular; chief.

ĕs-sĕn'-tial, *a.* Indispensable; important.

e-tĕr'-nal, *a.* Everlasting.

e-văe'-ū-āte, *v. t.* To make empty.

e-văp'-o-rāte, *a.* Dispersed in vapors.

ĕx-hĭb'-it, *v. t.* To present for inspection.

ĕx-hĭl'-a-rāte, *v. t.* To make glad or joyous; to enliven.

ĕx-ĭst'-ençe, *n.* The state of being.

ĕx-pănse', *n.* A wide extent of space.

ĕx-pē'-dĭ-ent, *a.* Desirable; advisable.

ĕx-tĕn'-u-āte, *v. t.* To draw out.

ĕx'-tri-eāte, *v. t.* To disentangle.

LESSON 58.

WORDS USED IN LAW.

Never a law was born that did not fly
Forth from the bosom of Omnipotence,
Matched, wing-and-wing with evil and with good,
Avenger and rewarder—both of God. — *Holland.*

ăb-seŏnd', *v. i.* To retire from public view to avoid a legal process.

ăb-sŏlve', *v. t.* To pardon; to free from.

ăe-çĕs'-so-ry, *n.* Aiding crime, though not present at the perpetration.

ăe-cūṣe', *v. t.* To charge with; to blame.

ăe-knŏwl'-edge, *v. t.* To own; to confess.

ăe-quĭt'-tal, *n.* Formal release from a charge.

ăe'-tion, *n.* Suit at law; an act or thing done.

ăd'-e-quāte, *a.* Equal.

ăd-jūre', *v. t.* To charge on oath.

ăd-mĭn-ĭs-trā'-tor, *n.* A man who manages an intestate estate.

ăd-vĭṣe', *v. t.* To give advice.

ăd'-vo-eāte, *n.*   One who pleads for another.

ăf-fi-dā'-vĭt, *n.*   A written declaration upon oath.

ăf-fĭrm', *v. t.*   To declare positively.

ăg̑-g̑rĕss'-ĭve, *a.*   Making the first attack.

a-g̑rēe'-ment, *n.*   A bargain, compact or contract.

ăl'-ĭ-bī, *n.*   When a person on trial for a crime proves that he was some place else when the act was committed.

ăl'-ien (ăl'-yen), *n.*   A foreigner.

ăl'-ĭ-mō-nў, *n.*   A separate maintenance.

ăl-lēg̑e', *v. t.*   To assert; to affirm.

LESSON 59.
Words used in Law.

"Plate sin with *gold* and the strong lance of Justice, hurtless, breaks; clothe it in *rags*, a pigmy's straw doth pierce it."

a-mē'-na-ble, *a.*   Responsible.

ăm'-nĕs-ty, *n.*   An act of general pardon.

ăn-nū'-i-ty, *n.*   An annual allowance.

ăn-nŭl', *v. t.*   To obliterate.

ăn'-swer (ăn'-ser), *v. t.*   To respond to.

ăp-pēal', *v. t.*   Removal of a cause to a higher court.

ăp-prāiṣ'-al, *n.*   A valuation by authority.

ăr'-bi-tra-ry, *a.*   Despotic; absolute in power.

ar-rāig̑n', *v. t.*   To accuse.

ăt-tĕs-tā'-tion, *n.*   Official testimony.

ăt-tôr'-ney, *n.*   One who is legally appointed by another to transact business for him.

au-thŏr'-i-ty, *n.*   Legal power; warrant; rule.

bāil'-a-ble, *a.*   Capable of being set free after arrest.

be-quĕst', *n.*   Something left by will.

eăt'-e-chiṣe, *v. t.*   To question or examine.

çĕr-tĭf'-i-eate, *n.*   A testimony in writing.

elāim'-ant, *n.*   One who demands something as his right.

elĕm'-en-çy, *n.*   Disposition to treat with favor and kindness.

eli'-ent, *n.*   One who applies to a lawyer for advice on a question of law.

eōde, *n.*   A system of laws.

LESSON 60.
Words used in Law.

"Let us consider the reason of the case, for nothing is law that is not reason."

eŏd'-i-çil, *n.*   Supplement to a will.

eŏu-dĕmn', *v. t.*   To pronounce to be wrong; to doom.

eor-rŏb'-o-rate, *v. t.*   To confirm.

erŏss'-quĕs-tion, *v. t.*   To cross-examine.

de-fĕnd'-ant, *n.*   One who opposes a complaint.

de-pō'-nent, *n.*   One who gives written testimony to be used in court.

dŏe'-ū-ment, *n.*   Anything furnishing proof or evidence.

ĕq'-ui-ta-bly (ĕk'-wĭ-), *adv.*   Justly; impartially.

ĕx-ĕe'-ū-tĭve, *a.*   Carrying into effect.

ĕx-ĕe'-ū-tor, *n.*   One who executes or performs.

ĕx-ĕe'-u-trĭx, *n.*   A female executor.
ĕx'-pĭ-āte, *v. t.*   To atone for.
fī'-ăt, *n.*   A decree.
ḡăl'-lŏws, *n.*   A frame for the execution of criminals.
ḡuärd'-ĭ-an, *n.*   One in charge of property or person of a minor.

ḡuïlt'-y, *a.*   Wicked; evincing guilt.
hẹi'-noŭs, *a.*   Enormous; odious.
hĕr'-ĭt-aḡe, *n.*   Inheritance.
ĭḡ-no-mĭn'-ĭ-oŭs, *a.*   Shameful; dishonorable.
ĭl-lē'-ḡal, *a.*   Unlawful.

LESSON 61.

Words used in Law.

"Law and equity are two things which God hath joined, but which man hath put asunder."

ĭm'-plĭ-eāte, *v. t.*   To bring into connection with.
ĭn-hĕr'-ĭt, *v. t.*   To receive by birth.
ĭn-ĭq'-uĭ-ty (ĭn-ĭk'-wĭ-tỹ), *n.*   A sin or crime.
ĭn-jŭs'-tĭçe, *n.*   Violation of the rights of a person.
ĭn-tĕs'-tate, *a.*   Without a will.
ĭn-văl'-ĭd, *n.*   Of no force.
ĭn-vĕs'-tĭ-gāte, *v. t.*   To inquire into.
jŭdḡ'-ment, *n.*   Decision of a court.
ju-dĭ'-cial (-dĭsh'-al), *a.*   Ordered by a court.
jū-rĭs-dïe'-tion, *n.*   The limit within which power may be exerted.

jŭs'-tĭçe, *n.*   Merited reward or punishment.
lạw'-yer, *a.*   A practitioner of law.
lĕḡ'-a-çy, *n.*   A bequest.
lē'-ḡal-lỹ, *adv.*   According to law.
lĕḡ-a-tēe', *n.*   One to whom a legacy is bequeathed.
le-ḡĭt'-ĭ-mate, *a.*   In accordance with law.
lē'-nĭ-ent, *a.*   Merciful; acting without severity.
lī'-a-ble, *a.*   Responsible.
lī'-bel, *v. t.*   To defame.
lī'-çense, *n.*   A written document by which permission is granted.

LESSON 62.

Words used in Law.

They are the best laws, by which the king hath the greatest prerogative, and the people the best liberty.—*Bacon.*

lī'-en, *n.*   A legal claim.
lĭt'-ĭ-ḡāte, *v. t.*   To contest in law.
măḡ'-ĭs-trāte, *n.*   A public civil officer.
môrt'-ḡaḡe (môr'-ḡej), *n.*   The state of being pledged.
môrt-ḡa-ḡēe' (môr-), *n.*   One to whom a mortgage is given.
môrt'-ḡa-ḡer (môr-), *n.*   The one who conveys property as security for the payment of debt.
nō'-ta-ry, *n.*   A public officer who certifies deeds and other writings.

nŭl'-lĭ-fỹ, *v. t.*   To make void; to deprive of legal force.
pĕn'-al-ty, *n.*   Punishment for crime or offense.
pĕn-ĭ-tĕn'-tia-ry (-sha-rỹ), *n.*   A house of correction where offenders are confined for punishment, and made to labor.
pĕr'-ju-ry, *n.*   False swearing.
pĕt'-ĭt (pĕt'-ỹ), *a.*   Small; little.
plāint'-ĭff, *n.*   The person who commences a suit.

plēa, *n.* That which is alleged by a party in support of his cause.

prō'-bate, *n.* Official proof.

rāt'-a-ble, *a.* Liable by law to taxation.

re-lēase', *v. t.* To give liberty to.

rĕt-ri-bū'-tion, *n.* Reward and punishment.

seăf'-fold, *n.* An elevated platform for the execution of a criminal.

sĭg'-na-tūre, *n.* One's name written by his own hand.

LESSON 63.

Words used in Law.

"The greatest attribute of Heaven is mercy ;
And 'tis the crown of justice, and the glory,
Where it may kill with right, to save with pity."

shĕr'-iff, *n.* The officer of the county, who executes the laws.

so-lĭç'-ĭt-or, *n.* An attorney or advocate.

sub-poē'-nä (-pē-), *n.* A writ commanding the attendance in court of the person on whom it is served, as a witness.

sūe, *v. t.* To seek justice by legal process.

tĕch-ni-căl'-i-ty, *n.* That which is peculiar to any profession, etc.

tĕs'-ta-ment, *n.* A will.

tĕs'-ti-mo-ny, *n.* Proof of some fact.

trĕs'-pass, *n.* Voluntary transgression of the moral law.

tri-bū'-nal, *n.* A court of justice.

văl'-id, *a.* Having legal strength or force.

vĕn'-ūe, *n.* A neighborhood or near place.

vĕr'-dict, *n.* Decision ; judgment.

vĕr'-i-fȳ, *v. t.* To prove to be true.

vē'-to, *n.* An authoritative prohibition.

vĭn'-di-eāte, *v. t.* To defend with success.

void, *a.* Of no legal effect whatsoever.

vouch, *v. t.* To make good a warranty of title.

vouch-ēe', *n.* The one who is called into court to make good his warranty of title.

vouch'-er, *n.* One who vouches to anything.

wrŏng, *n.* That which is not right.

LESSON 64.

DICTATION EXERCISE.

The quality of mercy is not strained,—
It droppeth as the gentle rain from Heaven
Upon the place beneath ; it is twice blessed,—
It blesseth him that gives and him that takes :
It becomes the throned monarch better than his crown ;
But mercy is above this sceptered sway,—
It is an attribute to God himself ;
And earthly power doth then show likest God's,
When mercy seasons justice.—*Shakespeare.*

LESSON 65.

CRIMES AND CRIMINALS.

" Oh how many deeds of deathless virtue and immortal crime,
The world had wanted, had the actor said,
' I will do this tomorrow.' "

ăb-dŭçt', *v. t.* To take away surreptitiously.

ăs-săs'-sĭn, *n.* One who tries to kill by secret assault.

bûrḡ'-lar, *n.* One who breaks into a house to steal.

cŏn-spĭr'-a-çy, *n.* A combination of men for an evil purpose.

crĭm'-i-nal, *n.* One guilty of crime.

fĕl'-on, *n.* A person guilty or capable of crime.

frăt'-ri-çĭde, *n.* One who kills a brother.

hŏm'-i-çĭde, *n.* A person who kills another.

im-pŏs'-tor, *n.* A pretender.

in-çĕn'-di-a-ry, *n.* One who secretly sets fire to a building.

lär'-çĕ-ny, *n.* Theft.

rŏb'-ber-y, *n.* Plunder; theft.

rōgue, *n.* A cheat.

rŭf'-flan (-yan), *n.* A brutal fellow.

smŭḡ'-ḡler, *n.* To export or import goods secretly without paying duty.

stĭḡ'-mà, *n.* Any mark of infamy.

sū'-i-çĭde, *n.* Self-murder.

thĭĕv'-er-y, *n.* Theft.

vā'-ḡran-çy, *n.* Wandering without a settled home.

vĭl'-laĭn, *n.* A wicked, vile person.

LESSON 66.

HOMOPHONOUS WORDS.

One crowded hour of a glorious life
Is worth a world without a name.—*Walter Scott.*

dew (dū), *n.* Moisture in the atmosphere condensed.

dūe, *a.* Time for payment.

dŏne, *a.* Completed.

dŭn, *v. t.* To urge payment; (*a.*) a brown color.

die, *v. i.* To cease to live.

dÿe, *v. t.* To color.

dū'-al, *a.* Consisting of two.

dū'-el, *n.* A combat between two.

dÿ'-ing, *n.* The act of expiring; loss of life; death.

dÿe'-ing, *n.* Coloring.

ĕarn, *v. t.* To gain by labor.

ûrn, *n.* A vessel for earth or ashes.

ewe (yų), *n.* A female sheep.

yew, *n.* A kind of tree.

fäir, *a.* Just; beautiful.

fâre, *n.* Food; the sum paid for conveying a person from one place to another.

fāte, *n.* Doom.

fęte, *n.* A feast.

flĕa, *n.* A small insect.

flĕe, *v. i.* To run away.

LESSON 67.

GOVERNMENT.

For forms of government let fools contest;
Whatever is best administered is best;
For modes of faith let graceless zealots fight;
His can't be wrong whose life is in the right.—*Pope.*

ăb'-so-lūte, *a.* Without limit.

ăl-lē'-ġlançe, *n.* The duty of fidelity to a king, government, or state.

ăm-băs'-sa-dor, *n.* The representative of one sovereign at the court of another.

ăn'-ärch-y, *n.* Want of government.

Çŏn'-ġrĕss, *n.* The Legislature of the United States.

eŏn-stĭ-tŭ'-tion-al, *a.* Regulated by the constitution.

eŏn'-sul, *n.* A person commissioned to reside in a foreign country as an agent or representative.

Czär, *n.* Title of the emperor of Russia.

ġŏv'-ĕrn-ment, *n.* Exercise of authority; restraint.

ġŏv'-ĕrn-or, *n.* One who is invested with supreme authority in a state.

lĕġ'-ĭs-lā-tūre, *n.* The supreme power of a state.

mo-närçh'-ĭ-al, *a.* Vested in a single ruler.

nä'-tion-al, *a.* Common to a whole people or race.

pär'-lia-ment, *n.* The supreme council.

prĕs'-ĭ-den-çy, *n.* Office of president.

quō'-rŭm, *n.* The number of members of any body competent by law to transact business.

re-pŭb'-lĭe, *n.* A country governed by men chosen by the people.

rĕp-re-ṣĕnt'-a-tīve, *n.* A member of the lower house in a State Legislature or in the National Congress.

sĕn'-a-tor, *n.* A member of a senate.

sŏv'-er-eĭgn, *n.* Supreme in power.

LESSON 68.

DICTATION EXERCISE.

We, the People of the United States, in order to form a more perfect union, establish justice, insure domestic tranquillity, provide for the common defence, promote the general welfare, and secure the blessings of liberty to ourselves and posterity, do ordain and establish this Constitution for the United States of America.

This Constitution, and the laws of the United States which shall be made in pursuance thereof, and all treaties made, or which shall be made, under the authority of the United States, shall be the supreme law of the land, and the Judges in every State shall be bound thereby, anything in the Constitution or laws of any State to the contrary notwithstanding.—*From Constitution United States.*

LESSON 69.

PERTAINING TO AUTHORITY.

Obedience is nobler than freedom. What's free ?
The vex'd straw on the wind, the frothed spume on the sea ?
The great ocean itself, as it rolls and it swells,
In the bonds of a boundless obedience dwells.—Owen Meredith.

ăe-quĭ-ĕsçe′, *v. i.* To comply; to agree to.

ąu-thĕn′-tĭ-ęāte, *v. t.* To establish by proof.

băn′-ĭsh, *v. t.* To drive away.

be-sēech′, *v. t.* To entreat; to implore.

eărte-blăuçhe′ (kärt-blänsh′), *n.* Unlimited authority.

eŏm-pĕl′, *v. t.* To urge by force; to oblige.

eŏm-plĭ′-ançe, *n.* A disposition to yield to others.

eŏn-çĕs′-slon, *n.* The act of yielding.

çŏn-fôrm′, *v. i.* To obey; to yield to.

eŏn-jūre′, *v. t.* To implore earnestly.

eŏn-trŏl′, *v. t.* To govern.

erĭ-tē′-rĭ-ou, *n.* A standard of judging.

dē-çĭ̧′-ion, *n.* Unwavering firmness.

dĭe-tă′-tor, *n.* One invested with absolute authority.

dŏm-ĭ-nēer′, *v. i.* To rule with insolence; overbearing.

ĕn-fôrçe′, *v. t.* To compel.

ĕx-ŏu′-er-āte, *v. t.* To clear of an accusation.

fôr-băde′, *v. t.* To prohibit.

ĭm-pĕr′-a-tĭve, *a.* Commanding.

ĭm-por-tūne′, *v. t.* To request with urgency.

LESSON 70.

Pertaining to Authority.

Man, proud man, dressed in a little brief authority,
Plays such fantastic tricks before high heaven,
As make the angels weep.—Shakespeare.

ĭn-dŭl′-ġençe, *n.* A favor granted.

ĭn′-flu-ençe, *n.* Controlling power quietly exerted.

lĭm′-ĭt-a-ble, *a.* Restrained.

măn′-dāte, *n.* An official command.

nō′-tĭ-fy, *v. t.* To give notice to.

o-bey′, *v. t.* To be ruled by.

ŏp-prĕs′-sion, *n.* The state of being oppressed; severity.

păr′-dou-a-ble, *a.* Admitting of excuse.

pĕr′-ĕmp-to-ry, *a.* Absolute; positive; decisive.

pĕr-mĭs′-sĭ-ble, *a.* Allowable.

pĕr-suāde′ (-swād), *v. t.* To influence by argument.

prĕ′-çĕpt, *n.* A direction to be followed.

pro-hĭb′-ĭt, *v. t.* To forbid.

re-fŭ̧′-al, *n.* Denial of anything demanded or offered for acceptance.

re-mĭs′-sĭ-ble, *a.* Capable of being remitted or forgiven.

rĕp′-rĭ-mănd, *n.* Severe reproof for a fault.

re-sĭgn′, *v. t.* To yield to another.

re-strāint′, *n.* That which restrains or hinders any action, physical, moral or mental.

rĭ̧′-or-oŭs, *a.* Exact; severe.

săṇe′-tion, *v. t.* To give validity or authority to.

LESSON 71.

Pertaining to Authority.

"All government, all exercise of power, no matter in what form, which is not based in love and directed by knowledge, is a tyranny."

sěrv'-ant, *n.* One who labors for his master or employer.

sěrv'-ice, *n.* Labor performed for another.

se-vēre', *a.* Very strict.

se-věr'-i-ty, *n.* Extreme strictness; harshness.

slāv'-er-y, *n.* Bondage.

stěrn'-ness, *n.* Severity.

strĭet'-ness, *n.* Exactness in the observance of rules.

strĭn'-ǵent, *a.* Making severe requirements.

sŭb-jēe'-tion, *n.* Bringing under the dominion of another.

sŭb-mĭs'-sion, *n.* Meekness; obedience.

sŭb-ôr'-di-nāte, *a.* Holding a lower position.

sŭp'-pli-eāte, *v. i.* To implore.

su-prěm'-a-çy, *n.* Higher authority.

sûr-vĕil'-lançe, *n.* Inspection; watch.

te-năç'-i-ty, *n.* Firmness.

thwąrt, *v. t.* To frustrate or defeat.

tȳ-răn'-nǐe-al, *a.* Severe in government.

ŭm'-pire, *n.* One who decides a controversy.

ŭn-çěr'-tain-ty, *n.* Doubtfulness.

yĭēld, *v. i.* To give up to the contest; to submit.

LESSON 72.

WORDS USED IN POLITICS.

"If you can climb to the top without falling,
Do it. If not, go as high as you can.
Man is not honored by business or calling;
Business and calling are honored by man."

ăp-point-ēe', *n.* A person appointed.

bǎl'-lot, *n.* A printed ticket used in voting; the act of voting by ticket.

eăm-pāign', *n.* The time an army keeps the field.

eăn'-di-date, *n.* One who seeks an office or is proposed for the same.

děl'-e-ǵate, *n.* A representative.

děm'-a-ǵôǵue, *n.* An artful political orator.

ē-lĕe-tion-ēer', *v. i.* To use arts to secure an election.

ěl'-i-ǵǐ-ble, *a.* Proper to be chosen.

fěd'-er-al, *a.* Pertaining to a league or contract.

lēaǵue, *n.* A union of persons.

ma-jŏr'-i-ty, *n.* More than half.

mi-nŏr'-i-ty, *n.* The smaller number.

nŏm-i-nā'-tion, *n.* The power of naming for an office.

nŏm-i-nēe', *n.* One who has been named for an office.

ŏf-fī'-cial (-fĭsh'-al), *a.* Pertaining to an office or public trust.

plu-răl'-i-ty, *n.* A greater number; the excess of votes cast for one individual over those cast for anyone of several competing candidates.

po-lĭt'-ǐe-al, *a.* Relating to state affairs.

pŏl-i-tī'-cian (-tĭsh'-an), *n.* One versed in politics.

prē'-çǐnet, *n.* A district within certain boundaries.

u-năn'-i-moŭs, *a.* Of one mind.

LESSON 73.

MISCELLANEOUS.

Be good, my dear, let who will be clever;
Do noble things, not dream them all day long;
And so make life, death, and the vast forever,
One grand, sweet song.—*Charles Kingsley.*

făb'-u-lous, *a.* Not real; fictitious.

făl'-li-ble, *a.* Liable to fail or mistake.

făst'-en (făs'-n), *v. t.* To fix firmly.

fĕa'-si-ble, *a.* Capable of being done.

fẽr-mĕnt', *v. t.* To set in motion.

fĭe-tĭ'-tious (-tĭsh'-ŭs), *a.* Not genuine; false.

fĭl'-ial (fĭl'-yăl), *a.* Bearing the relation of a child to parents.

fĭ'-nĭte, *a.* Having a limit.

flĕx'-i-ble, *a.* Yielding to pressure; pliable.

flĭm'-sy, *a.* Without strength; of loose structure.

fo-mĕnt', *v. t.* To apply warm lotions to.

fôrt'-ŭ-nate, *a.* Lucky.

fŏs'-sil, *a.* Changed into stone.

frăg'-ĭle, *a.* Easily broken.

frăg'-ment, *n.* A small detached portion.

hẽr-mĕt'-ĭe-al-ly, *adv.* Perfectly close.

hĭd'-e-ous, *a.* Dreadful to behold.

hŏr'-ri-ble, *a.* Terrible.

hȳ-mĕn-ē'-al, *a.* Pertaining to marriage.

hȳ'-phen, *n.* A mark for joining two syllables.

LESSON 74.

PERTAINING TO SCHOOLS.

I call a complete and generous education, that which fits a man to perform justly, skillfully and magnanimously, all of the offices, both private and public, of peace and war.—*Milton.*

ab'-sençe, *n.* State of being absent.

a-ĕad'-e-my, *n.* A school of arts and sciences; or one holding a place between common schools and colleges.

Ăl'-ma Mä'-ter, *n.* College or seminary where one is educated.

băe-ea-lau'-re-ate, *n.* Bachelor of arts.

eăt'-a-lŏgue, *n.* Register of names.

elăs'-sie-al, *a.* One of the first rank in literature or art.

eŏl'-lege, *n.* A school for study and instruction.

eŏm-mĕnçe'-ment, *n.* The day when degrees are conferred by colleges upon students.

eûr-rĭe'-ŭ-lŭm, *n.* A course of study.

de-lĭn'-quent, *a.* Failing in duty.

de-pärt'-ment, *n.* One of the divisions of instruction.

dis-çi-plin-ā'-ri-an, *n.* One who enforces rigid discipline.

ĕd'-ŭ-ea-tor, *n.* One who educates.

ĕn-rōll', *v. t.* To record.

ĕx-ăm'-ine, *v. t.* To inquire into; to scrutinize.

ĕx'-er-çise, *v. t.* To set in action to develop.

făe'-ul-ty, *n.* A body of men to whom any specific right is granted.

grăd'-ŭ-ate, *v. t.* To mark with degrees.

in'-stĭ-tŭte, *n.* An institution.

in-strŭe'-tion, *n.* Furnishing with knowledge.

LESSON 75.

Pertaining to Schools.

Mercy is the fruit of knowledge, cruelty, of ignorance.—Chas. Reade.

ĭn-ter-mĭs'-sĭon, *n.* A temporary pause.

knŏwl'-edge, *n.* Information.

lȳ-çē'-um, *n.* An association for literary improvement.

pūreh'-ment, *n.* The skin of a sheep or goat prepared for writing on.

pĕd'-a-gŏḡue, *n.* A school master.

rĕç-ĭ-tū'-tion, *n.* The rehearsal of a lesson by pupils before their teacher.

rĕḡ'-ĭs-ter, *n.* A roll; an official enumeration.

rĕḡ-ū-lăr'-ĭ-ty, *n.* Conformity to rule.

re-vĭew' (-vū), *n.* A looking over.

sehŏl'-ar-ship, *n.* Learning.

sçĭ-en-tĭf'-ĭe, *a.* Used in science.

sĕm'-ĭ-na-ry, *n.* A school, academy, college or university.

sēn'-ior (sēen'-yur), *n.* One in the fourth year of his collegiate course, or third year at a professional school.

sŏph'-o-mōre, *n.* One belonging to the second of the four classes in college.

stū'-dĭ-oŭs, *a.* Given to study.

stu-pĭd'-ĭ-ty, *n.* Extreme dullness of understanding.

sū-per-ĭn-tĕnd'-ent, *n.* One who oversees anything, with power of direction.

tēaeh'-a-ble, *a.* Apt to learn.

tu-ĭ'-tion, *n.* Money paid for instruction.

văl-e-dĭe'-to-ry, *n.* An address spoken at commencement of a college, by one of the class who receive the degree of bachelor of arts.

LESSON 76.

DICTATION EXERCISE.

Knowledge and wisdom, far from being one,
Have oft times no connection. Knowledge dwells
In heads replete with thoughts of other men;
Wisdom in minds attentive to their own.
Knowledge—a rude, unprofitable mass,
The mere materials with which Wisdom builds,
Till smoothed, and squared, and fitted to its place—
Does but encumber whom it seems to enrich.
Knowledge is proud that he has learned so much;
Wisdom is humble that he knows no more.—*Cowper.*

LESSON 77.

ORATORY.

He is the eloquent man who can treat subjects of an humble nature with delicacy, lofty things impressively, and moderate things temperately.—Cicero.

ad-drĕss', *n.* A formal discourse either written or verbal.

ăr-tĭe'-ū-late, *a.* Distinctly uttered.

eā'-dĕnçe, *n.* Regular fall or modulation of sound.

dĭ'-a-lĕet, *n.* Form of speech.

e-jāe'-ū-lāte, *v. t.* To utter by sudden impulse.

ĕl-o-eū'-tion, *n.* The power of expression by words.

ĕl'-o-quent, *a.* Speaking with fluency and elegance.

ĕm'-pha-sĭs, *n.* Force impressed by pronunciation.

ĕx-tĕm-po-rā'-ne-oŭs, *a.* Without previous study ; off-hand.

flū'-ent, *a.* Gliding ; easily moving.

gĕs-tie'-ū-lāte, *v. i.* To make motions ; to act.

gŭt'-tur-al, *a.* Formed in the throat.

ha-răṇgue', *n.* A noisy or pompous speech.

ĭm-prŏmp'-tū, *n.* Without previous study.

lĕet'-ūre, *n.* A discourse on any subject.

nā'-ṣal, *a.* Spoken through the nose.

o-rā'-tion, *n.* An elaborate discourse.

pro-nŭn-cĭ-ā'-tion (-shĭ-a'-shŭn), *n.* Utterance.

pŭṇet-ū-ā'-tion, *n.* The art of pointing a writing or discourse.

rhe-tŏr'-ĭc-al, *a.* Oratorical.

LESSON 78.

HOMOPHONOUS WORDS.

" Not all who seem to fail have failed indeed,
Not all who fail have therefore worked in vain ;
For all our acts to many issues lead."

fēat, *n.* An exploit.

fēet, *n.* Plural of foot.

flūe, *n.* An air passage, especially that of a chimney.

flew, *v. i.* Past of fly.

flour, *n.* Finely ground grain.

flow'-er, *n.* A blossom.

fōrt, *n.* A fortified place.

fōrte, *n.* That in which one excels.

fōrth, *adv.* Forward.

fōurth, *n.* One of four equal parts : (*a.*) next following third.

foul, *a.* Filthy.

fowl, *n.* A bird ; poultry.

frănk, *a.* Free ; candid.

frāne, *n.* A French coin.

frēeze, *v. t.* To congeal.

frieze, *n.* A coarse cloth.

gāit, *n.* Manner of walking.

gāte, *n.* An entrance.

gĭlt, *n.* Appearing like gold.

guilt, *n.* Crime.

LESSON 79.

SCIENCES.

" Science, when well digested, is nothing but good sense and reason."

a-eoŭs'-tĭes (-kow'-stĭks), *n.* The science of sounds.

ăs-trŏn'-o-my, *n.* The science of the heavenly bodies.

bĭ-ŏl'-o-ġy, *n.* The science of life.

ehĕm'-ĭs-try, *n.* The science showing the nature and properties of bodies.

ĕn-to-mŏl'-o-ġy, *n.* The science which treats of insects.

ĕth-nŏl'-o-ġy, *n.* The science that treats of the races of men.

ĕt-y-mŏl'-o-ġy, *n.* Treats of the derivation of words.

gās-trŏn'-o-my, *n.* The science of good eating.

ġe-ŏl'-o-ġy, *n.* The science which treats of the structure of the earth.

ġe-ŏm'-e-try, *n.* The science of quantity and mensuration.

ġrăm'-mar, *n.* The science of language.

hȳ'-ġi-ēne, *n.* That part of medical science which treats of the preservation of health.

phī-lŏs'-o-phy, *n.* The science of effects by their causes.

pho-tŏg'-ra-phy, *n.* The science of the action of light on bodies.

phȳs-ĭ-ŏl'-o-ġy, *n.* The science which treats of organs and their functions, in animals and plants.

po-mŏl'-o-ġy, *n.* Science of fruits.

sta-tĭst'-ĭes, *n.* The science which collects and classifies facts.

te-lĕg'-ra-phy, *n.* The science of communicating by means of telegraphs.

the-ŏl'-o-ġy, *n.* The science of God and his relations to his creatures.

thē'-o-ry, *n.* An exposition of the general principles of any science.

LESSON 80.

DICTATION EXERCISE.

I value science—none can prize it more,
It gives ten thousand motives to adore
Be it religious, as it ought to be.
The heart it humbles, and it bows the knee
What time it lays the breast of nature bare,
Discerns God's fingers working everywhere.
In the vast sweep of all embracing laws,
Finds Him the real and only Cause ;
And in the light of clearest evidence
Perceives Him acting in the present tense ;
Not as some claim, once acting, but now not,
The glorious product of His hands forgot—
Having wound up the grand autŏm'aton
Leaving it, henceforth, to itself to run.—*Abraham Coles.*

LESSON 81.

PERTAINING TO SCIENCE.

When man seized the load-stone of science, the load-star of superstition vanished in the clouds.—*W. R. Alger.*

ăp-pa-rā'-tŭs, *n.* A set of instruments for performing scientific experiments.

ba-rŏm'-e-ter, *n.* An instrument for determining the weight of the atmosphere.

eru'-çi-ble, *n.* An earthen pot for melting metals.

frĭe'-tion, *n.* The effect of rubbing, or the resistance which a body meets with from the surface on which it moves.

fŭse, *v. t.* To dissolve by heat; to melt.

găl'-va-nĭsm, *n.* Current electricity.

hȳ-drǎul'-ĭe, *a.* Pertaining to fluids in motion.

hȳ'-dro-ġen, *n.* A gas which constitutes one of the elements of water.

lăb'-o-ra-to-ry, *n.* The work-room of a chemist.

mĭ'-ero-seōpe, *n.* An optical instrument for magnifying objects.

nĭ'-tro-ġen, *n.* A gaseous element without taste, odor or color.

ŏx'-y-ġen, *n.* A gas without smell, taste or color.

ō'-zōne, *n.* Oxygen in a condensed form.

phō'-no-grăph, *n.* An instrument for the mechanical registration and reproduction of sounds.

sŭe'-tion, n. The act of drawing by exhausting the air.

tĕl'-e-phōne, n. An instrument for reproducing articulate speech at a distance, by the aid of electricity.

tĕl'-e-seōpe, n. An optical instrument for viewing distant objects.

ther-mŏm'-e-ter, n. An instrument for measuring temperature.

vŭe'-ū-ŭm, n. A space empty or devoid of all matter.

ve-lŏe'-i-ty, n. Rate of motion.

LESSON 82.

MISCELLANEOUS.

Perseverance is a Roman virtue
That wins each god-like act, and plucks success
Even from the spear-proof crest of rugged danger.—*Havard.*

ĭ'-çi-ele, n. A pendant mass of ice.

ĭd'-i-o-çy, n. Natural absence or marked deficiency of sense and intelligence.

ĭm-ma-tē'-rĭ-al, a; Unimportant.

ĭm-mŏv'-a-ble, a. Firmly fixed; steadfast.

ĭm-pâir', v. t. To weaken; to make worse.

ĭm-pàss'-a-ble, a. Incapable of being passed.

ĭm-pĕde', v. t. To hinder.

ĭm-pĕn'-e-tra-ble, a. Cannot be entered.

ĭm-pĕr'-feet, a. Defective in quantity or quality.

Im'-ple-ment, n. An instrument or utensil as supplying a requisite to an end.

ĭn-ăp-prŏ'-pri-ate, a. Unsuitable.

ĭn-au'-gu-rāte, v. t. To make a public exhibition for the first time.

ĭn-eàr'-çer-ate, v. t. To confine in jail or prison.

ĭn'-çi-dent, n. An event; a circumstance.

ĭn-eŏg'-nĭ-to, n. In disguise or under an assumed character.

ĭn-eo-hĕr'-ent, a. Unconnected; inconsistent.

ĭn-eŏn-sĭst'-ent, a. At variance.

ĭn-eŭl'-eāte, v. t. To impress by frequent admonitions.

ĭn-dĕf'-i-nĭte, a. Having no certain limits.

ĭn-ĕv'-i-ta-ble, a. Unavoidable.

LESSON 83.

ARITHMETIC.

Application is the price to be paid for mental acquisition. To have the harvest we must sow the seed.—*Bailey.*

ăb'-sträet, a. Numbers used without application to things.

ăd-dĭ'-tion, n. Anything added; writing numbers.

a-mount', n. The sum total or result.

a-năl'-y-sĭs, n. To resolve into its elements.

ăn'-a-lȳze, v. t. To separate into first principles.

a-rĭth'-me-tĭe, n. The science of numbers.

ăv'-er-age, n. A mean proportion

ăv-oir-du-pois' (av-er-), n. A system of weights for coarser commodities.

bā'-sĭs, n. The first principle.

eăl'-eu-lāte, v. t. To reckon; to compute.

eăr'-at, n. Weight of four grains.

çi'-pher, n. A character that by itself expresses nothing, but placed at the right of a number increases its value ten-fold.

dĕç'-ĭ-mal, *n.*   Having ten-fold increase or decrease.

dĕf'-ĭ-çĭt, *n.*   Deficiency in amount.

dĕm'-on-strāte, *v. t.*   To make evident or plain.

de-nŏm-i-nā'-tion, *n.*   A name.

dĭg'-ĭt, *n.*   One of the nine figures; any number to ten.

dĭm-ĭ-nū'-tion, *n.*   Making or growing less.

dĭs'-eount, *n.*   Payment in advance of interest upon money loaned.

dĭv'-ĭ-dend, *n.*   A number divided.

LESSON 84.
Arithmetic.

"The mind, like all other things, will become impaired, the sciences are its food,—they nourish, but at the same time they consume it."

di-vĭ§'-ion, *n.*   Separating into parts.

dŏl'-lar, *n.*   A silver coin of the U. S. weighing about 412½ grains; also gold coin weighing 25$\frac{8}{10}$ grains standard gold, or 23$\frac{2}{10}$ grains pure gold.

drăm,
drăchm } *n.* ⅛ oz. apothecary's weight.

dū-o-dĕç'-i-mal, *a.*   Proceeding by twelves.

e-quĭv'-a-lent, *n.*   Equal in value.

ĕv-o-lū'-tion, *n.*   The extraction of roots.

ĕx-ăm'-ple, *n.*   A pattern or copy; a sample.

ĕx-pō'-nent, *n.*   That which points out or represents.

ĕx-trăe'-tion, *n.*   The act of drawing out.

frūe'-tion, *n.*   A portion.

fŭn-da-mĕnt'-al, *n.*   Essential part.

grōss, *n.*   Twelve dozen; *a.* coarse.

gāin, *n.*   Profit; benefit.

găl'-lon, *n.*   A measure containing four quarts.

gāuġe, *v. t.*   To measure; to estimate.

hălve, *v. t.*   To divide into two equal parts.

in-sur'-auçe, *n.*   Premium paid for insuring property.

ĭn'-te-ġral, *n.*   A whole number.

ĭn'-ter-est, *n.*   Premium paid for use of money.

in-vo-lū'-tion, *n.*   The multiplication of a number into itself a given number of times.

LESSON 85.
Arithmetic.

The sciences are of a sociable disposition, and flourish best in the neighborhood of each other; nor is there any branch of learning but may be helped and improved by assistance drawn from other arts.—*Blackstone.*

măth-e-ma-tĭ'-cian, *n.*   One versed in mathematics.

măx'-i-mŭm, *n.*   The greatest quantity or value attainable.

mĕas'-ūre, *n.*   Estimated extent or limit.

mĭn'-i-mŭm, *n.*   The least quantity possible in a given case.

mĭn'-ū-ĕnd, *n.*   The number from which another is to be subtracted.

naught, *n.*   Nothing.

nine'-ti-eth, *n.*   One of ninety equal parts.

no-tā'-tion, *n.*   Any method of using signs, symbols, etc.

nŭ-mer-ā'-tion, *n.*   The act of numbering.

nŭ'-mer-al, *n.*   A figure or character used to express a number

quąd'-ru-ple, *n.*   A four-fold amount.

quạn'-ti-ty, *n.* Measure; amount.

quō'-tient (kwō'-shent), *n.* The number resulting from dividing one number by another.

re-çip'-ro-cal, *n.* The quotient arising from dividing any quantity by unity.

rā'-ti-o (-shĭ-ō), *n.* Fixed regulation of numbers.

rĕek'-on, *v. t.* To compute.

re-māin'-der, *n.* Anything left after removal of part.

seȧle, *n.* Basis for a numeral system.

ŭn'-der-wrī-ter, *n.* One who insures; an insurer.

ū'-ṣū-ry, *n.* Illegal interest.

LESSON 86.

LINES AND FORMS.

"Right is the center of a circle, 'about right' its circumference; the circumference may be drawn to any size, but the center always remains the same."

ăe'-me, *n.* The highest point.

ăl'-tĭ-tūde, *n.* Height.

ăṇ'-ġle, *n.* A point where two lines meet.

ȧre, *n.* A segment of a circle.

ā'-re-ȧ, *n.* Any plane surface.

çĕn'-tral, *a.* Near the center.

çir'-cle, *n.* A plane figure bounded by a single curved line, every point of which is equally distant from a point within called the center.

çir-cŭm'-fer-ençe, *n.* The line that bounds a circle.

cŏl'-umn, *n.* A cylindrical support for a roof; a perpendicular set of lines.

cŏn'-cȧve, *a.* Hollow.

cŏn'-vĕx, *a.* Regularly protuberant or bulging.

crĕs'-çent, *n.* The figure of the new moon.

cū'-bĭe, *a.* Having the form of a cube.

cŭr'-vȧ-tūre, *n.* A continued bending.

çȳ'-cle, *n.* A circle.

çȳl'-ĭn-der, *n.* A long, circular body of uniform diameter.

di-ăġ'-o-nal, *n.* The line joining two not adjacent angles of a quadrilateral.

di-ăm'-e-ter, *n.* A straight line through the center.

height, *n.* Altitude; elevation.

hĕx'-a-ġŏn, *n.* A plane figure of six sides and six angles.

LESSON 87.

Lines and Forms.

" Curved is the line of beauty,
Straight is the line of duty :
Follow the last and thou shalt see
The other ever following thee."

hŏr-ĭ-zŏn'-tal, *a.* Parallel to the horizon; on a level.

hȳ-pŏt'-e-nūse, *n.* The longest side of a right-angled triangle.

ir-rĕġ'-ū-lar, *a.* Not uniform.

ŏb-lique' (-lēek or -lĭk), *a.* Slanting.

ŏb-tūse', *n.* An angle greater than a right angle.

ȯe'-ta-ġŏn, *n.* A plane figure of eight sides and eight angles.

pȧr'-al-lel, *n.* Lines equidistant from each other, proceeding in the same direction.

pĕr-pen-dĭc'-ū-lar, *n.* Exactly upright.

pŏl'-y-ġŏn, *n.* A plane figure with more than four sides.

pȳr'-a-mĭd, *n.* A solid body terminating in a point at the top.

py-răm'-ĭ-dal, *a.* Tapering to a point.

quạd'-răn-ġle, *n.* A plane figure with four sides.

quạd-ri-lăt'-er-al, *n.* A figure having four sides and four angles.

rā'-dĭ-ŭs, *n.* Half the diameter of a circle.

rēet'-ăn-ġle, *n.* A figure having four sides and four right angles.

so-lĭd'-ĭ-tȳ, *n.* Density.

sphēr'-ĭc-al, *a.* Round.

tri-ăn'-ġu-lar, *a.* Having three angles.

vĕr'-tĭe-al, *a.* Upright.

zē'-nĭth, *n.* The point in the heavens directly over head.

LESSON 88.

DICTATION EXERCISE.

" If upright or horizontal, or obliquely I incline,
Whether straight or curved you see me, I am what is called a line.
Like railroad tracks or telegraph wires or many things that I could tell,
Which side by side extend so even, are lines which we call parallel.
Should two of us be joined together at one end, and then we take
Different directions, wholly, 'tis an angle that we make.
When the lines are perpendicular, a right angle you will find ;
Acute is smaller, obtuse is larger, here is one of every kind.
Draw these lines as I will show you ; count them—one, two, three,
And because there are three angles, 'tis a triangle you see.
Very many kinds there may be, rightangled, acute, obtuse,
I-sŏs-çe-lĕṣ and equilateral ; let not these names your mind confuse.
If we have four sides all equal, four rightangles where they meet,
And have drawn our figure neatly, we shall have a square complete."

LESSON 89.

HOMOPHONOUS WORDS.

A man can bear a world's contempt,
When he has that within which says he's worthy.—*Alexander Smith.*

găm'-bol, *v. i.* To play; to frolic.
găm'-ble, *v. t.* To play for money.

guĕssed, *v. t.* Conjectured.
guĕst, *n.* A visitor.

hâre, *n.* A small animal.
hâir, *n.* The covering of part of the head.

hĕar, *v. t.* To perceive by the ear.
hēre, *adv.* In this place.

hĕel, *n.* The back part of the foot.
hĕal, *v. t.* To effect a cure.

heȧrt, *n.* A vital organ.
hȧrt, *n.* A wild animal.

hew (hū), *v. t.* To cut roughly.
hūe, *n.* A tint; a color.

hĕard, *v. t.* Past of hear.
hĕrd, *n.* A number of beasts assembled together.

hĭm, *pron.* Objective case of he.
hȳmn, *n.* A song of devotion.

hōle, *n.* An opening.
whōle, *a.* All of anything.

GEOGRAPHY.

Weep not that the world changes; did it keep
A stable, changeless state, 'twere cause indeed to weep.—Bryant.

ăb-o-rĭg'-ĭ-nal, *a.* First; primitive; original.

a-byss', *n.* A bottomless depth or gulf.

ăt'-mos-phēre, *n.* The air that surrounds the earth.

Au-rō'-rá Bŏr-ē-ā'-lĭs, *n.* The northern lights.

eăt'-a-răet, *n.* A large waterfall.

ehăsm, *n.* A deep opening caused by rupture.

eŏl'-o-ny, *n.* A settlement.

erä'-ter, *n.* The mouth of a volcano.

e-quā'-tor, *n.* A great circle which divides the earth into the northern and southern hemispheres.

ē'-qui-nŏx, *n.* The time when days and nights are equal in length.

frŏnt-iēr', *n.* The part of a country that borders on another.

ḡeȳ'-ser, *n.* A boiling fountain.

ḡe-ŏḡ'-ra-phy, *n.* The science which treats of the earth and its inhabitants.

ḡlä'-çier, *n.* A field of ice or snow moving slowly down a mountain side.

hĕm'-i-sphēre, *n.* A half sphere.

ho-rī'-zon, *n.* The apparent junction of earth and sky.

ĭsl'-and (īl'-and), *n.* A body of land surrounded by water.

lăt'-i-tūde, *n.* Distance either north or south of the equator.

lŏn'-ġi-tūde, *n.* Distance either east or west of some given meridian.

me-rĭd'-i-an, *n.* An imaginary great circle passing around the earth, and through the poles.

Geography.

" I believe this earth is but the vestibule to glorious mansions, through which a moving crowd forever press."

mē'-te-or, *n.* A transient, fiery body seen in the atmosphere.

me-trŏp'-o-lĭs, *n.* The chief city of a state or country.

mi-räġe' (-räzh), *n.* An optical illusion.

ō'-a-sĭs, *n.* A fertile spot in a desert.

ō-çe-ăn'-ĭe (-she-ăn'-), *a.* Found or formed in the ocean.

peu-ĭn'-sū-lá (-sū-, or -shu-), *n.* Land almost surrounded by water.

plä-teau' (-tō), *n.* A level area of land in an elevated position.

prāi'-rĭe, *n.* An extensive tract of land without trees.

prĕç'-ĭ-pĭçe, *n.* A very steep descent.

ra-vīne' (ra-vēn'), *n.* A gorge.

sçĕn'-er-y, *n.* Combination of natural views.

sĕe'-tĭon, *n.* A division; a portion.

sō'-lar, *a.* Pertaining to the sun.

sŭb-ter-rā'-ne-oŭs, *a.* Under ground.

sûr'-fáçe, *n.* The outside.

tŏr'-rent, *n.* A stream running rapidly, as down a precipice.

tĕr'-ri-to-ry, *n.* Extent of country not yet admitted as a State into the Union, but has a separate Legislature of its own.

trŏp'-ĭe-al, *a.* Pertaining to the tropics.

ŭn'-du-lä-ting, *p. a.* Rising and falling like waves; rolling.

văl'-ley, *n.* Space between hills or mountains.

LESSON 92.

DICTATION EXERCISE.

"The strange current of human existence is like the Gulf Stream : three-score and ten years long, it bears each and all of us with a strong, steady sweep away from the Tropics of childhood, enameled with verdure and gaudy with bloom, through the temperate regions of manhood and womanhood, on to the frigid, lonely shores of dreary old age, snow-crowned and ice-veined. Individual destinies seem to resemble the tangled drift on those broad, bounding billows, driven hither and thither, some to be scorched by equatorial heats, some to perish with polar perils, a few to take root and flourish, and many to stagnate in the long, inglorious rest of a Sargasso Sea."

LESSON 93.

MISCELLANEOUS.

"To have the taste of a gentleman and the purse of a beggar is about the height of human misery."

ĭn-făt'-ū-āte, *v. t.* To inspire with foolish passion.

ĭn'-fĭ-nĭte, *a.* Unlimited.

ĭn-flĕx'-ĭ-ble, *a.* Unalterable.

ĭn-grā'-tĭ-āte (-shĭ-āte), *v. t.* To bring into favor.

ĭn-grē'-dĭ-ent, *n.* A component part.

ĭn-ĭ'-tial (-ĭsh'-al), *n.* The first letter of a word.

ĭn-ĭ'-tĭ-āte (-shĭ-āte), *v. t.* To begin ; to introduce into a society or organization.

ĭn-sĭg-nĭf'-ĭ-eant, *a.* Without meaning ; unimportant.

ĭn-sta-bĭl'-ĭ-ty, *n.* Want of firmness in purpose.

ĭn'-stru̇-ment, *n.* That by which work is performed or anything effected.

ĭn-tăn'-gĭ-ble, *a.* That which cannot be touched.

ĭn-tĕn'-sĭ-fy̆, *v. t.* To render more intense.

ĭn-ter-çĕpt', *v. t.* To stop on the way.

ĭn-ter-fēre', *v. i.* To take part in the concerns of others ; to intermeddle.

ĭn-tĕr'-nal, *a.* Inward ; interior.

ĭn-ter-nă'-tion-al, *a.* Pertaining to the relation of two or more nations.

ĭn'-tri-eate, *a.* Complicated ; obscure.

ĭr-re-spŏn'-sĭ-ble, *a.* Not to be trusted.

ĭ'-vo-ry, *n.* The tusks of an elephant.

jū'-ve-nĭle, *a.* Young.

LESSON 94.

PERTAINING TO MOTION.

There is a medium between velocity and torpidity ; the Italians say it is not necessary to be an antelope, but we should not be a tortoise.—*Disraeli.*

ăe-çĕl'-er-āte, *v. t.* To quicken.

ăe-tĭv'-ĭ-ty, *n.* Agility.

ăg'-ĭle, *a.* Quick of motion.

ăn'-ĭ-māte, *v. t.* To quicken ; to give life to.

çe-lĕr'-ĭ-ty, *n.* Rapidity of motion.

erạwl, *v. i.* To creep.

ĕx-pe-dĭ'-tioŭs, *a.* Quick.

hăs'-ten (hăs'-n), *v. t.* To hurry.

nĭm'-bly, *adv.* With light, quick motion.

noiṣe'-less, *a.* Silent ; without noise.

pro-grĕs'-sion, *n.* Moving forward.
quĭek'-ness, *n.* Rapidity of motion.
ra-pĭd'-i-ty, *n.* Swiftness.
re-äe'-tion, *n.* Movement in a contrary direction.
re-mŏv'-al, *n.* Change of place.

sprĭght'-ly, *a.* Lively; brisk.
stăg'-nant, *a.* Motionless.
stä'-tion-a-ry, *a.* Not moving.
swĭft'-ness, *n.* Rapid motion.
vē-lŏç'-i-ty, *n.* Quickness of motion.

LESSON 95.

PERTAINING TO LAZINESS AND FATIGUE.

Go to the ant, thou sluggard, learn to live,
And by her busy ways reform thine own.—*Smart.*

en-nuï' (ŏng-nwē'), *n.* A feeling of weariness and disgust.

fa-tïgue', *n.* Exhaustion of strength.

In-ĕr'-tĭ-à (-shĭ-à), *n.* That property of matter by which it tends when at rest to remain so, and when in motion to continue in motion.

in-de-făt'-i-ga-ble, *n.* Not yielding to fatigue.

in'-do-lenςe, *n.* Indisposition to labor.

la-bŏ'-ri-oŭs, *a.* Toilsome; tiresome.

lăn'-guish, *v. i.* To sink away; to pine.

lăn'-guor (lăng'-gwur), *n.* Listlessness.
lăs'-si-tüde, *n.* Weariness; dullness.
lä'-zi-ness, *n.* Indolence.
lĕth'-ar-ġy, *n.* Dullness; inaction.
loi'-ter, *v. i.* To linger on the way.
slŏv'-en-ly, *a.* Disorderly; not neat.
slŭg'-gard, *n.* A lazy person.
squä'-lôr, *n.* Foulness; filthiness.
tē'-di-oŭs or tĕd'-yus, *a.* Wearisome.
tire'-sóme, *a.* Tedious; fatiguing.
toil'-sóme, *a.* Laborious.
tôr'-por, *n.* Loss of motion; inactivity.
wēa'-ri-ness, *n.* Exhaustion of strength.

LESSON 96.

DICTATION EXERCISE.

" Oh friend, grown weary with the painful climbing
   Up Fame's high mount which ever upward slopes;
On whose sad ear Fate's bells are ever chiming
   The funeral knell of thy most cherished hopes;
Hast thou drunk deep of Marah's bitter fountain?
Has thy bright gold changed into useless dross?
Remember! One before thee climbed a mountain,
   And gained upon its summit—*but a cross.*"

LESSON 97.

WORDS PERTAINING TO MUSIC.

The man that hath no music in his soul,
And is moved not by concord of sweet sounds,
Is fit for treasons, stratagems, and spoils.—*Shakespeare.*

ean-tä'-tä, *n.* A musical composition comprising choruses and solos, arranged in a somewhat dramatic manner.

ehoir (kwir), *n.* A company of singers in church service.
ehŏr'-is-ter, *n.* One who leads a choir.

eŏn-dŭet'-or, *n.* The leader or director in a musical performance.

eŏn-trăl'-tô, *n.* The part sung by the highest male or lowest female voice.

çȳm'-bal, *n.* A musical instrument of brass.

gui-tär', *n.* A stringed musical instrument.

här'-mo-ny, *n.* A just adaptation of parts to each other.

mū-şĭ'-çian (-zish'-an), *n.* A skillful performer of music.

ŏp'-er-å, *n.* A musical drama.

ŏr-a-tō'-rĭ-o, *n.* A sacred composition of music, the subject of which is generally taken from the Scriptures.

ôr'-ehes-trȧ, *n.* A band of instrumental musicians.

pĭ-ä'-no, *n.* A musical instrument.

quạr-tĕt', quạr-tĕtte', } *n.* A piece of music with four parts, each sung or played by a single person.

şchŏt'-tĭsche (shŏt'-teesh), *n.* Music appropriate to a kind of dance.

sĕr-e-nȧde', *n.* Music in the open air at night.

so-prä'-no, *n.* The highest female voice.

sȳm'-pho-ny, *n.* An instrumental and vocal composition of music.

vŏl'-un-ta-ry, *n.* The organ playing at the opening of church.

zĭth'-ern, *n.* A musical instrument with twenty-eight strings.

LESSON 98.
HOMOPHONOUS WORDS.

Do what thou dost as if the stake were heaven,
And that thy last deed ere the judgment day.—*Kingsley.*

ï'-dle, *a.* Lazy.

ï'-dol, *n.* A person or thing much loved or adored.

ï'-dyl, *n.* A short, pastoral poem.

In-dict', *v. t.* To charge with crime.

In-dite', *v. t.* To compose.

kĭll, *v. t.* To deprive of life.

kĭln, *n.* A large oven.

knĕad, *v. t.* To work together.

nĕed, *v. t.* To be in want of.

knĭght, *n.* A brave horseman; a title.

nĭght, *n.* Time of darkness.

knew (nū), *v. t.* Past of know; to have been aware of.

gnū, *n.* A south African animal.

new, *a.* Of late origin.

knŏt, *v. t.* To tie; to perplex.

nŏt, *adv.* A word expressing denial.

lĕs'-sen, *v. t.* To diminish.

lĕs'-son, *n.* That which is to be learned.

lĕv'-ee, *n.* An assembly.

lĕv'-y, *v. t.* To raise or collect by assessment.

LESSON 99.
DICTATION EXERCISE.

The following is an illustration of pronunciation and spelling in the use of wrong words which have the same pronunciation as the right words, and which properly read, would sound right. In copying from dictation, the student is to write the *right* word.

A rite suite little buoy, the sun of a grate kernel, with a rough about his neck, flue up the road swift as eh dear. After a thyme he stopped at a gnu house and wrung the belle. His tow hurt hymn and he kneaded wrest. A feint mown of pane rows from his lips. The made who herd the belle was about to pair a pare, but she through it down and ran with all her mite, for fear her guessed would not weight. Butt, when she saw the little won, tiers stood in her ayes at the site. "Ewe poor deer! Why due yew lye hear? Are yew dyeing?" "Know," he said, "I am feint too thee corps." She bore him inn her arms, as she aught, too a room where he might bee quiet, gave him bred and meet, held cent under his knows, tide his choler, rapped him warmly, gave him some suite drachm from a viol, till at last he went fourth hail as a young horse. His eyes shown, his cheek was as read as a flour, and he gambled a hole our.

LESSON 100.

FIRE AND FUEL.

Fire! fire! it sets me in a craze
To see a first-class building all ablaze;
A burning house resembles, when I'm nigh,
Some old acquaintance just about to die.—*Carleton.*

ăn'-thra-çite, *n.* A hard variety of mineral coal.

bēa'-con, *n.* A signal fire to notify the approach of an enemy.

bĭ-tū'-mi-noŭs, *a.* Compounded with bitumen and mineral pitch.

bŏn'-fĭre, *n.* A fire made to express public joy, or for amusement.

bûrn'-ĭng, *n.* Fire; flame.

căn'-nel-cōal, *n.* A kind of mineral coal that burns with a clear, yellow flame, and has been used as a substitute for candles.

cär'-bon, *n.* Pure charcoal.

chär'-cōal, *n.* Coal made by charring wood.

cōke, *n.* Mineral coal charred.

com-bŭs'-ti-ble, *a.* Capable of burning.

cŏn-fla-grā'-tion, *n.* Fire on a great scale.

făg'-ot, *n.* A bundle of sticks or twigs for fuel.

găs'-o-lïne, *n.* A fluid obtained from bituminous coal.

hŏl'-o-cȧust, *n.* Completely consumed by fire.

ĭn-can-dĕs'-çent, *a.* White or glowing with heat.

ĭn-flăm'-ma-ble, *a.* Capable of being set on fire.

kĕr'-o-sēne, *n.* Oil extracted from bituminous coal.

kĭn'-dlĭng, *n.* Material for commencing a fire.

pēat, *n.* A kind of vegetable substance, dried, used for fuel.

pe-trō'-le-ŭm, *n.* A liquid, inflammable, bituminous oil.

LESSON 101.

FURNITURE.

"Home's not merely four square walls,
Though with pictures hung and gilded;
Home is where affection calls,
Filled with shrines the heart hath builded."

bĕd'-stĕad, *n.* A frame for supporting the bed.

bŏŏk'-cȧse, *n.* A case with shelves for holding books.

brie'-a-brȧe, *n.* A miscellaneous collection of antiquarian or artistic curiosities.

bū'-reau (bū'-rō), *n.* A chest of drawers.

eúb'-in-et, *n.* A piece of furniture with drawers, shelves and doors.

çhăn-de-liẽr', *n.* A frame with branches to hold a number of lights for illumination.

çhif-fon-iẽr' (shĭf-fon-ēer'), *n.* A movable and ornamental piece of furniture.

eŭp'-board (kŭb'-urd), *n.* A small closet in a room, with shelves for dishes.

eŭsh'-ion, *n.* Any stuffed or padded surface.

dĭ-văn', *n.* A movable sofa.

ēa'-ṣel, *n.* A frame on which pictures are placed.

lounġe, *n.* A small sofa.

ŏt'-to-man, *n.* A stuffed seat without a back.

pĕd'-es-tal, *n.* The part on which an upright work stands.

portiere (pŏr-tī-ễr'), *n.* A curtain, hanging across the opening for a door.

rä'-di-ā-tor, *n.* The part of a heating apparatus the use of which is to radiate heat.

re-frĭg'-er-ā-tor, *n.* A box for keeping things cool by means of ice.

side'-bōard, *n.* A piece of cabinet-work, with compartments for dishes.

sō'-fȧ, *n.* A long, cushioned seat, used as a piece of furniture.

tẹte'-ȧ-tẹte (tāt'-ȧ-tāt), *n.* A form of sofa for two persons.

LESSON 102.

PERTAINING TO PICTURES.

Every man carries in his own head more pictures than are to be found in all the galleries of the world.—*Beecher.*

ăm'-bro-tȳpe, *n.* A picture taken on prepared glass.

da-gŭẽrre'-o-tȳpe, *n.* A picture on a plate of copper.

dū'-plĭ-eate, *n.* An exact copy.

ĕf'-fĭ-ġy, *n.* An imitative figure.

fȧe-sĭm'-ĭ-le, *n.* An exact counterpart or copy.

im-i-tā'-tion, *n.* Likeness.

like'-ness, *n.* That which resembles or copies.

lĭth'-o-grȧph, *n.* A print from a drawing on stone.

min'-ĭ-a-tūre, *n.* A painting in colors on a reduced scale.

nĕg'-a-tĭve, *n.* A picture on glass, used for producing photographs.

ō'-le-o-grȧph, *n.* A picture produced in oils, by a process similar to lithographic printing.

pāint'-ĭng, *n.* A colored resemblance of anything.

phō'-to-grȧph, *n.* A picture obtained by photography.

pĭet-ūr-ĕsque', *a.* Fitted to form a good or pleasing picture.

pŏr'-trait, *n.* An exact likeness of a person.

rĕp-re-ṣen-tā'-tion, *n.* A picture, model or other fac-simile.

re-ṣĕm'-ble, *v. t.* To be alike or similar to.

sĭm-i-lãr'-i-ty, *n.* Close likeness.

si-mil'-i-tūde, *n.* Likeness; resemblance.

xȳ-lŏg'-ra-phy (zi-lŏg'-), *n.* Wood engraving.

MISCELLANEOUS.

> A little learning is a **dangerous** thing;
> Drink deep, or taste not the Pierian spring.
> There shallow draughts intoxicate the brain,
> **And** drinking largely, sobers us again.—*Pope.*

lā'-bel, *n.* A slip of paper affixed to anything, denoting its contents.

lŏ-ço-mō'-tĭve, *n.* A steam engine on wheels.

lon-ġĕv'-ĭ-ty, *n.* Length of life.

lũ'-brĭ-eāte, *v. t.* To make smooth or slippery.

măt'-rĭ-mo-ny, *n.* Marriage.

mĕs'-mer-ĭṣm, *n.* The art of inducing a state of the nervous system in which the actor claims to control the actions, and communicate directly with the mind of the recipient.

mŏd'-ern-ize, *v. t.* To cause to conform to recent or present usage or taste.

mŏd'-ĭ-fȳ, *v. t.* To give new form to.

mo-mĕnt'-oŭs, *a.* Of great consequence.

mŏn'-o-grăm, *n.* A character composed of two or more letters interwoven.

mo-nŏt'-o-noŭs, *a.* Continued with dull uniformity.

năt'-ũ-ral, *a.* Not artificial nor exaggerated.

nĕç'-es-sa-ry, *a.* Essential.

neigh'-bor-hŏŏd, *n.* Adjoining district.

neũ'-tral, *a.* Not decided or pronounced; indifferent.

nŏm'-ĭ-nal, *a.* Existing in name only.

nôr'-mal, *a.* Performing proper functions.

no-tō'-rĭ-oŭs, *a.* Manifest to the world.

nŏv'-el-ty, *n.* Recentness of introduction; a new or strange thing.

nŭp'-tial, *n.* Pertaining to marriage.

LESSON 104.

PERTAINING TO THE MIND.

> " Were I so tall to reach the pole,
> Or grasp the ocean with my span,
> I must be measured by my soul,
> The mind's the standard of the man."

ăn-tĭç'-ĭ-pāte, *v. t.* To have a previous view or impression.

ăp-prē'-ci-āte (-shĭ-āt), *v. t.* To estimate justly; to value.

ăp-pre-hĕnd', *v. t.* To understand; to believe.

ăs-çer-tāin', *v. t.* To make certain; to assure.

ăs-sĭd'-ũ-oŭs, *a.* Constant in application or attention.

be-lĭēve', *v. t.* To regard as true.

eŏḡ'-nĭ-zant (eoḡ'- or çon'-), *a.* Having knowledge of.

eŏm-pli-eā'-tion, *n.* Perplexity; entanglement.

eŏm-pre-hĕnd', *v. t.* To understand.

eŏn-jĕet'-ũre, *n.* Probable inference; surmise.

eŏn'-science (kŏn'-shens), *n.* The moral sense.

eŏn'-scioŭs (kŏn'-shŭs), a. Possessing the faculty or power of knowing one's own thoughts or mental operations.

eŏn'-strue, v. t. To interpret; to understand.

eŏn'-tem-plāte or eŏn-tĕm'-plāte, v. t. To meditate on; to study.

ere-dū'-li-ty, n. A disposition to believe on slight evidence.

eū-ri-ŏs'-i-ty, n. Disposition to inquire, investigate or seek after knowledge.

de-çi'-pher, v. t. To unravel; to find out so as to make known the meaning of.

dĕs'-ig-nāte, v. t. To mark out and make known.

de-tĕr'-mine, v. t. To ascertain definitely.

de-vĕl'-op, v. t. To unfold gradually.

LESSON 105.

Pertaining to the Mind.

Talk not of talents; what hast thou to do?
Thy duty, be thy portion five or two.
Talk not of talents; is thy duty done?
Thou hadst sufficient, were they ten or one.—*Montgomery*.

dī-grĕss', v. i. To wander from the main subject of attention in writing or speaking.

dil'-i-ġent, a. Steady and devoted in application.

dis-a-grēe', v. t. To differ in opinion.

dis-çĕrn'-ment, n. The faculty of the mind which distinguishes one thing from another.

dis-erē'-tion, n. Prudence; judgment.

dis-erim'-i-nate, v. t. To distinguish; to select.

dis-tiṇ'-guish, v. t. To recognize or discern.

ĕn-dĕav'-or, n. An exertion of intellectual or physical strength.

e-niġ'-mà, n. A statement, the hidden meaning of which is to be discovered or guessed.

ĕx-pĕet'-ant, a. Looking for; waiting.

făth'-om, v. t. To get to the bottom of.

fĕign (făn), v. t. To pretend; to imagine.

ġĕn'-ius (jĕn'-yŭs), n. Distinguished mental superiority.

i-dē'-al, a. Existing in thought.

i-dĕn'-ti-fy, v. t. To establish the identity of.

im-ăġ-i-nā'-tion, n. Image-making power; conception.

im-pro-vise', v. t. To bring about on a sudden, off-hand, or without previous preparation.

in-eli-nā'-tion, n. Leaning of the mind, feelings, preferences, or will.

in-erĕd'-i-ble, a. Impossible to be believed.

in-de-pĕnd'-ençe, n. Free from dependence on others.

LESSON 106.

Pertaining to the Mind.

Each, after all, learns only what he can;
Who grasps the moment as it flies,
He is the real man.—*Goethe*.

in-dis-erim'-i-nate, a. Not making any distinction.

in'-fer-ençe, n. A conclusion.

in-fē'-ri-or, a. Lower in place, rank, or excellence.

in-ġe-nū'-i-ty, n. Power of ready invention.

in-quir'-y, *n.* Research; investigation.

in'-stinct, *n.* Inward impulse.

in'-tel-lect, *n.* The power to judge and comprehend.

in-ter'-pret, *v. t.* To make clear; to explain the meaning of.

in-ter'-ro-gāte, *v. i.* To ask questions.

in-tu-ī'-tion (-ish'-un), *n.* An act of immediate knowledge, as in perception or consciousness.

lŏg'-ie-al, *v. t.* According to reason.

ŏb-jĕe'-tion, *n.* Reason or argument against.

ŏb-lĭv'-i-on, *n.* Forgetfulness.

ŏb'-sti-nate, *a.* Not yielding to reason.

o-pīn'-ion (-yŭn), *n.* A mental conviction on any point of knowledge.

ŏp'-tion (-shŭn), *n.* The power of choosing.

pĕr-çēive', *v. t.* To discern; to behold.

per-vĕr'-si-ty, *n.* Obstinacy.

prĕf'-er-ençe, *n.* Choice.

prŏs-e-eū'-tion, *n.* Pursuits by effort of body or mind.

LESSON 107.
Pertaining to the Mind.

Our whitest pearl we never find;
Our ripest fruit we never reach;
The flowering moments of the mind,
Drop half their petals in our speech.—*Holmes.*

pro-spĕet'-ĭve, *a.* Looking forward in time.

rā'-tion-al (răsh'-un-al), *a.* Having reason.

rē'-al-īze, *v. t.* To impress upon the mind as real; to accomplish.

rĕe'-og-nīze, *v. t.* To allow that one knows.

rĕe-ol-lĕet', *v. t.* To remember.

rĕf'-er-ençe, *n.* One who or that which is referred to.

re-flĕe'-tion, *n.* Meditation.

re-mĕm'-brançe, *n.* Memory; recollection.

rĕt'-ro-spĕet, *v. i.* A contemplation of things past.

sa-ḡū'-cioŭs, *a.* Shrewd; wise.

skĕp'-ti-çĭsm, *n.* An undecided, inquiring state of mind.

spĕe'-ū-lāte, *v. i.* To contemplate; to consider.

sto-lĭd'-i-ty, *n.* Dullness of intellect.

sū-pĕr-fī'-cial (-fĭsh'-al), *a.* Not deep nor profound.

sŭp-po-ṣī'-tion, *n.* The act of imagining what is not proved to be true.

tāl'-ent-ed, *a.* Possessing skill or talent.

ŭn-der-stănd', *v. t.* To have knowledge of; to comprehend; to know.

ŭn-rēa'-ṣon-a-ble, *a.* Not agreeable to reason.

văç'-il-lāte, *v. i.* To fluctuate in mind or opinion; to waver.

va-gū'-ry, *n.* A wandering of the thoughts.

LESSON 108.
DICTATION EXERCISE.

Our minds are seventy-year clocks. The Angel of Life winds them up once for all, then closes the case and gives the key into the hands of the Angel of the Resurrection. Tic-tac! tic-tac! go the wheels of thought; our will cannot stop them; they cannot stop themselves; sleep cannot still them; madness only makes them go faster; death alone can break into the case, and, seizing the ever-swinging pendulum, which we call the heart, silence at last the clinking of the terrible escapement we have carried so long beneath our wrinkled foreheads.—*Oliver W. Holmes.*

HOMOPHONOUS WORDS.

Truth crushed to earth will rise again ;
The eternal years of God are hers :
But Error, wounded, writhes in pain,
And dies amid his worshipers.—*Bryant.*

lăx, *a.* Not severe, rigid or strict; loose.

lăeks, *v. t.* Wants; needs.

li'-ar, *n.* One who falsifies.

lÿre, *n.* A musical instrument.

lie, *n.* A falsehood.

lÿe, *n.* Solution made by water passing through ashes.

lĭnks, *n.* Rings or parts of a chain.

lÿṇx, *n.* An animal that has a brilliant eye, and prowls about at night.

lōan, *n.* That which is lent.

lōne, *a.* Solitary.

lŏch (lŏk), *n.* A lake.

lŏck, *n.* A fastening for doors, trunks, etc.

māil, *n.* Mailed matter, as letters, papers, etc.

māle, *a.* Masculine.

māde, *v. t.* Completed.

māid, *n.* An unmarried woman.

māne, *n.* Long hair on the neck of an animal.

māiṇ, *a.* Chief.

māze, *n.* Perplexity.

māize, *n.* Indian corn.

LITERATURE.

It is the masterful will that compresses a life-thought into a pregnant word or phrase, and sends it ringing through the centuries.—*Mathews.*

a-erŏs'-tie, *n.* A poem whose initial letters spell a word or words.

ăd'-age, *n.* An old saying; a maxim.

ăl'-le-go-ry, *n.* Description of one thing under the image of another.

ăl'-ma-năe, *n.* A book containing a calendar of days, weeks and months.

ăm-bi-gū'-i-ty, *n.* Uncertainty of signification.

ăn'-nals, *n.* A series of historical events.

a-nŏn'-y-moŭs, *a.* Without the real name of the author.

ạu-to-bi-ŏg'-ra-phy, *n.* One's life written by one's self.

ăx'-i-om, *n.* A self-evident truth; a maxim.

bĕlles-lĕt'-tres (bĕl-lĕt'-ter), *n.* Polite or elegant literature.

bi-ŏg'-ra-phy, *n.* History of one's life and character.

eŏm'-men-ta-ry, *n.* A book of explanations on the work of any author.

dĕf-i-nī'-tion, *n.* An explanation of the meaning of a word or term.

de-tāil', *v. t.* To report minutely.

die'-tion-a-ry (-shŭn-), *n.* A book containing words arranged alphabetically, with explanations of their meaning.

ĕn-çÿ-elo-pē'-di-ă, *n.* A general survey of human knowledge.

ĕr-rō'-ne-oŭs, *a.* Liable to mislead.

ĕs'-sāy, *n.* A composition treating of any particular subject.

fā'-ble, *n.* A feigned story intended to instruct or amuse.

fĭg'-ū-ra-tĭve, *a.* Not literal.

Literature.

Books, we know, are a substantial world, both pure and good;
Round these, with tendrils strong as flesh and blood,
Our pastime and our happiness will grow.— *Wordsworth.*

glŏss'-a-ry, *n.* A limited dictionary.

hĭs'-to-ry, *n.* Record of past events.

ĭl-lĭt'-er-ate, *a.* Ignorant of books; unlearned.

ĭl-lŭs'-trāte, *v. t.* To ornament and explain by pictures.

ĭn'-dex, *n.* A table for facilitating reference to topics.

lĕ'-ģend or lĕġ'-end, *n.* Any story handed down from early times.

lĭt'-er-a-ry, *n.* Pertaining to literature.

lўr'-ĭe, *n.* A poem which expresses the individual emotions of the poet.

mĕm'-oir (-wor), *n.* A written memorial of an individual.

năr'-ra-tĭve, *n.* A story.

nō-men-clāt'-ūre, *n.* A list of the more important words in a language, with their signification.

păm'-phlet, *n.* A small book stitched together, but not bound.

păr'-a-ble, *n.* A fable from which a moral is drawn.

păr'-a-grăph, *n.* A short sentence or passage.

păr'-o-dy, *n.* A writing by which the words of the author are, with slight alterations, adapted to a different purpose.

per-sŏn'-i-fӯ, *v. t.* To treat as a person.

pĭe-tō'-ri-al, *a.* Illustrated by pictures.

plā'-ģia-rĭst, *n.* One who purloins the writings of another, and puts them off as his own.

plau'-sĭ-ble, *a.* Apparently right.

pō'-et-ry, *n.* Metrical composition; verse.

LESSON 112.

Literature.

It is the glorious doom of literature, that the evil perishes and the good remains.— *Bulwer Lytton.*

prē'-ăm-ble, *n.* An introductory portion; a preface.

prĕf'-açe, *n.* An introduction to a book.

pro-vĕrb'-ĭ-al, *a.* Resembling or suitable to a proverb.

quo-tā'-tion, *n.* The part of a book or writing named, repeated as an illustration.

rhӯme (rīm), *n.* A word answering in sound to another word; harmony of language.

rhӯthm (rĭthm), *n.* Harmonious flow of vocal sounds.

ro-mănçe', *n.* An extravagant story.

săt'-īre, *n.* An invective poem.

sa-vant' (sä-vŏng'), *n.* One versed in literature or science.

sĕn-sā'-tion-al, *a.* Fitted to excite great interest.

sĕn'-sĭ-ble, *a.* Containing sense or reason.

sĕn-ti-mĕnt'-al, *a.* Having or containing sentiment.

sē'-quel, *n.* A succeeding part.

sē'-ri-al, *n.* A work appearing in a series or a succession of parts.

stăn'-ză, *n.* Part of a poem.

stē'-re-o-tȳpe, *v. t.* To compose a book in fixed types.

sŭp'-plē-ment, *n.* That which completes something already arranged.

sȳn-ŏn'-y-moŭs, *a.* Conveying the same idea.

tra-dī'-tion-al, *a.* Transmitted from age to age without writing.

vo-eăb'-ū-la-ry, *n.* A list of words arranged alphabetically and explained.

LESSON 113.

DICTATION EXERCISE.

"It may be glorious to write thoughts that shall glad the two or three high souls, like those far stars that come in sight once in a century, but better far it is to speak one simple word, which now and then shall waken the free nature in the weak and friendless sons of men.

To write some earnest verse or line, which seeking not the praise of art, shall make a clearer faith, and manhood shine in an untutored heart.

He who doeth this, in verse or prose, may be forgotten in his day, but surely shall be crowned at last with those who live and speak for aye."

LESSON 114.

MISCELLANEOUS.

Nothing ever happens but once in this world. What I do now I do once for all. It is over, it is gone, with all its eternity of solemn meaning.—*Carlyle.*

ŏb-li-gā'-tion, *n.* The binding power of a vow, promise, etc.

ŏb-lit'-er-āte, *v. t.* To erase or blot out.

ŏb'-sta-ele, *n.* Anything that hinders progress.

ŏb'-vi-āte, *v. t.* To prevent by interception.

ŏe-eā'-ṣion, *n.* A favorable opportunity

ŏe-eu-pā'-tion, *n.* The principal business of one's life; possession.

ŏf'-fer-to-ry, *n.* The act of offering or the thing offered.

ŏf-fĭ'-ei-āte (-fĭsh'-ĭ-āte), *v. i.* To perform the appropriate business of an office or public trust.

ō'-ġle, *n.* A side glance or look.

o-mis'-sion, *n.* The act of leaving out.

ŏp'-po-ṣite, *a.* Facing; contrary.

ôr'-di-na-ry, *a.* Customary; common.

ôr-gan-i-zā'-tion, *n.* An organized existence.

ō-ri-ĕnt'-al, *a.* Pertaining to the orient or east.

o-riġ'-i-nal, *n.* Commencement; source.

ôr'-na-ment, *n.* That which adds grace or beauty.

ôr'-phan, *n.* A child who is bereaved of both father and mother.

os-tĕn'-si-ble, *a.* Manifest; apparent.

ō-ver-whĕlm', *v. t.* To overspread or crush.

ō-ver-wrôught', *v. i.* Labored to excess.

LESSON 115.

PERTAINING TO WAR OR MILITARY SERVICE.

" Whether on the scaffold high,
Or in the battle's van,
The fittest place where man can die
Is where he dies for man."

ăd'-ver-sa-ry, *n.* A member of a hostile party; an enemy.

aid'-de-eamp (ād'-de-kŏng), *n.* An officer who conveys the general's orders, and represents him in correspondence and in directing movements.

ăl-lī'-ançe, *n.* A union or connection of interests.

ăl-lȳ', *n.* A confederate.

ăn-nī'-hi-lāte, *v. t.* To reduce to nothing.

ăn-tăg'-o-nīze, *v. t.* To act in opposition.

är-tĭl'-ler-y, *n.* Offensive weapons of war; cannon.

băy'-o-net, *n.* A dagger attached to a musket.

bĭv'-ouăe (-wăe), *n.* The watch or guard of a whole army; an encampment for the night without tents or covering.

brăv'-er-y, *n.* Fearlessness of danger.

brĭg-a-dier'-gĕn'-er-al, *n.* An officer next above a colonel.

eär'-bine, *n.* A fire-arm between the pistol and musket in length and weight, used by mounted troops.

eär'-tridge, *n.* A case containing a charge for a fire-arm.

eăv'-al-ry, *n.* Mounted troops.

ehăl'-lenge, *n.* An invitation to a contest.

ehăp'-lain, *n.* A clergyman of the army.

ehief'-tain, *n.* A captain or leader

ehĭv'-al-ry, *n.* Valor; knight errantry.

eolonel (kûr'-nĕl), *n.* The commander of a regiment.

eŏn-dī'-tion-al, *a.* Made or granted on certain terms.

LESSON 116.

Pertaining to War or Military Service.

Were half the power that fills the world with terror,
Were half the wealth bestowed on camp and courts,
Given to redeem the human mind from error,
There were no need of arsenals and forts.— Longfellow.

eŏn'-fĭs-eāte or eŏn-fĭs'-eāte, *v. t.* To appropriate, as a penalty, to the public use.

eŏn'-quer-or (kŏnk'-er-ur), *n.* One who gains a victory.

eŏr'-po-ral, *n.* A military officer.

eoŭr'-age, *n.* Boldness; valor.

dĭ-plō'-ma-çy, *n.* Skill in securing advantage.

dȳ'-na-mīte, *n.* Nitro glycerine.

ex-ploit', *n.* A great or noble achievement.

fĭ-nĕsse', *n.* To use stratagem.

fŏr'-age, *v. i.* To ravage; to feed on spoil.

fŏr'-mi-da-ble, *a.* Exciting fear.

frā'-eas, *n.* A noisy quarrel.

găl'-lant, *a.* Brave; courageous.

hăz'-ard-oŭs, *a.* Dangerous.

hŏs'-tile, *a.* Unfriendly.

ĭn'-fant-ry, *n.* A body of soldiers on foot.

ĭn-vĭn'-çĭ-ble, *a.* Incapable of being conquered.

knăp'-săck (năp'-), *n.* A soldier's sack in which to carry clothing.

măs'-sa-ere (-ker), *n.* A cold-blooded destruction of life.

mĭ-lĭ'-tĭ-à (-lĭsh'-à), *n.* National military force.

mū'-tĭ-ny, *n.* Insurrection against authority.

LESSON 117.

Pertaining to War or Military Service.

Many a shaft at random sent,
Finds mark the archer little meant!
And many a word at random spoken,
May soothe, or wound, a heart that's broken.—*Scott.*

pā-trĭ-ŏt'-ĭe, *a.* Full of love for one's country.

quĭ-vĭve (kē-vēv). On the alert, like a sentinel.

rē-bĕl', *v. i.* To take up arms traitorously against the state or government.

re-bĕll'-ioňs (-yŭs), *a.* Traitorously renouncing the authority of the government to which allegiance is due.

re-eruit', *n.* A newly enlisted soldier.

re-pĕl', *v. t.* To drive back.

re-șist'-auçe, *n.* Opposition.

se-çēdž', *v. i.* To withdraw, as a State from the Union.

se-çĕs'-sion (-sĕsh'-un), *n.* The withdrawal or attempt to withdraw from the National Union.

sĭēġe, *n.* Continued attempt to gain possession.

skĭr'-mĭsh, *n.* A contest; a slight fight in war.

slaugh'-ter, *v. t.* To slay in battle; to visit with great destruction of life.

sŏl'-dier (sŏl'-jĕr), *n.* One who serves in the army.

străt'-e-ġem, *n.* A plan or scheme for deceiving an enemy.

tär'-ġet, *n.* A mark for marksmen to fire at.

trăĭ'-tor-oŭs, *a.* Guilty of treason; faithless.

trēa'-șon, *n.* Disloyalty.

văl'-iant (văl'-yŭnt), *a.* Heroic; brave.

văl'-or-oŭs, *a.* Brave; courageous.

văn'-quish (vănk'-wĭsh), *v. t.* To conquer.

LESSON 118.

WORDS DENOTING CONFUSION.

Times of general calamity and confusion have ever been productive of the greatest minds. The purest ore is produced from the hottest furnace, and the brightest thunderbolt from the darkest storm.—*Colton.*

ăġ'-ĭ-tāte, *v. t.* To disturb.

bā'-bel, *n.* Confusion.

bois'-ter-oŭs, *a.* Noisy; rough; acting with noisy turbulence.

ehạ-ŏt'-ĭe, *a.* Confused.

eŏm-mō'-tion, *n.* Civil or public disturbance.

eŏn-fū'-șion, *n.* Disorder; tumult.

dis-ŏr'-der, *n.* Confusion; disarray.

dis-sĕn'-sion, *n.* Strife; discord.

dis-tûrb'-auçe, *n.* Violent disorder.

ĕx-çĭte'-ment, *n.* Agitation.

hŭb'-bŭb, *n.* A great noise.

hûr'-lў-bûr-lў, *n.* Confusion.

hŭs'-tle, *v. i.* To move hastily and in confusion.

rămp'-age, *n.* A state of excitement or passion.

rī'-ot-oŭs, *a.* Unrestrained; engaging in riot.

rough (rŭf), *a.* Tempestuous; not smooth.

stôrm'-y, *a.* Proceeding from violent agitation or fury.

tem-pĕst'-ū-oŭs, *a.* Violent; stormy.

tu-mŭlt'-ū-oŭs, *a.* Greatly agitated; confused.

tûr'-bu-lent, *a.* In violent commotion.

LESSON 119.

DICTATION EXERCISE.

"Then came the mad retreat; the whirlwind snows
Sweeping around them, merciless as man;
The stiffening hand, the pulseless heart and eye,
The frozen standard and the palsied arm;
The unfrequent watch-fires rising like red sparks
Amidst the illimitable snows; the crowds
Of spectral myriads shuddering around them,
Frozen to statues; scathed by the red flames
Or speared by howling savages; until
Winter, less merciful than they, threw o'er them
Her winding sheet of snows, deep burying
Armies whose presence vanished like a dream."

LESSON 120.

HOMOPHONOUS WORDS.

"Count that day lost whose low descending sun,
Views from thy hand no worthy action done."

măn'-tel, *n.* The shelf over a fireplace, in front of the chimney.

măn'-tle, *n.* A loose wrap.

măn'-ner, *n.* Mode of action.

măn'-or, *n.* The land belonging to a lord or nobleman.

meet, *v. t.* To encounter.

meat, *n.* Flesh used for food.

mete, *v. t.* To limit; to allot; to measure.

mĕd'-al, *n.* A reward of merit.

mĕd'-dle, *v. i.* To interfere; to take part in a thing with which one should have nothing to do.

mĕt'-al, *n.* A lustrous mineral.

mĕt'-tle, *n.* Excitable temperament.

mean, *a.* Low; vile; intermediate.

mien, *n.* Appearance; manner.

min'-er, *n.* One who works in a mine.

min'-or, *n.* One under age. (*a.*) less.

moan, *v. i.* To bewail.

mown, *v. t.* Cut with a scythe, etc.

oar, *n.* An instrument for rowing.

ore, *n.* The compound of a metal and some other substance.

o'er, *prep.* Contraction of over.

LESSON 121.

WORDS DENOTING ANNOYANCE.

" Men are born to trouble at first, and exercised in it all their days, yet it will not hurt you unless it makes you sour, narrow and skeptical."

ăn-noy'-ançe, *n.* Causing trouble.

çha-grïn' (shȧ-g̃rïn'), *n.* Vexation ; mortification.

dĭs-ad-vȧn'-tage, *n.* Unfavorable circumstance.

dĭs-trĕss', *v. t.* To cause pain to ; to afflict.

ĕx-erÿ'-çi-āte (-shĭ-āt), *a.* Tortured ; tormented.

hăr'-ass, *v. t.* To tease ; to perplex.

in-con-vēn'-ien̄çe (-yen̄çe), *n.* Trouble; disadvantage.

mĭs'-chiev-oŭs, *a.* Troublesome ; inclined to do harm.

mĭs-fôrt'-ūne, *n.* Ill luck ; harm ; disaster.

nūi'-sançe, *n.* That which annoys or gives trouble.

ôr'-de-al, *n.* Severe trial.

per-plĕx', *v. t.* To tease; to distract.

plāg̃ue, *v. t.* To vex ; to trouble.

prĕj'-ū-diçe, *n.* Damage; prejudgment.

tăn'-ta-lize, *v. t.* To tease ; to torment.

tēase, *v. t.* To vex with importunity; to annoy.

tôr-mĕnt'-er or tôr-mĕnt'-or, *n.* One who torments.

tôrt'-ūre, *v. t.* To pain extremely.

troŭb'-le-sóme, *a.* Giving trouble.

vex-ā'-tioŭs, *a.* Teasing ; annoying.

LESSON 122.

DENOTING INJURY.

Is it worth while that we battle to humble
  Some poor fellow creature down in the dust ?
Time will soon tumble all of us together,
  Humbled indeed, down into the dust.—*Joaquin Miller.*

ea-lŭm'-nĭ-āte, *v. t.* To accuse falsely.

con-tăm'-i-nāte, *v. t.* To pollute.

cor-rŭpt', *v. t.* To debase ; to defile.

dē-môr'-al-ize, *v. t.* To corrupt the morals of.

de-rōg̃'-a-to-ry, *a.* Injurious.

dĕt-ri-mĕnt'-al, *a.* Hurtful.

im-po-şĭ'-tion, *n.* An excessive exaction.

in-jū'-ri-oŭs, *a.* Harmful.

lăç'-er-āte, *v. t.* To tear; to rend.

mū'-ti-lāte, *v. t.* To destroy an essential part of.

per-nĭ'-cioŭs (-nĭsh'-ŭs), *a.* Ruinous; destructive.

pĕr'-se-eūte, *v. t.* To pursue in a manner to injure.

pĕr-vĕr'-sion, *n.* Change to something worse.

poi'-şon-oŭs, *a.* Corrupting ; impairing soundness or purity.

rū'-in-oŭs, *a.* Destructive.

seŭn'-dal-ize, *v. t.* To defame.

slăn'-der-oŭs, *a.* Containing defamation.

sŭb'-tle (sŭt'-l), *a.* Sly in design.

sŭr-rep-tĭ'-tious (-tish'-ŭs), *a.* Made or introduced fraudulently; done by stealth.

vĭ'-o-len̄çe, *n.* Vehemence ; unjust force.

LESSON 123.

PERTAINING TO DISASTER.

Disasters come not singly, but as if they watched and waited,
Scanning one another's motions. When the first descends the others
Follow, follow, gathering flock-wise round their victim sick and wounded,
First a shadow, then a sorrow, till the air is dark with anguish.—*Longfellow.*

ăe-çi-dĕnt'-al, *a.* Happening by chance.

ăd-vĕnt'-ûre, *n.* Hazard; a remarkable occurrence.

ăd-vĕr'-si-ty, *n.* Calamity.

ănx'-ioŭs (ănk'-shŭs,) *a.* Painful suspense.

en-lăm'-i-ty, *n.* Misfortune.

eăṣ'-ū-al-ty, *n.* An accident.

ea-tăs'-tro-phe, *n.* A final event of a disastrous nature.

eol-liṣ'-ion, *n.* The act of striking together.

eŏn-tĭu'-ġen-çy, *n.* That which comes without being foreseen.

dău'-ġer-oŭs, *a.* Unsafe; full of risk.

di-lĕm'-mà or di-lĕm'-mà, *n.* A state of things in which it is difficult to tell what to do.

dis-ăs'-ter, *n.* An unfortunate event.

e-mĕr'-ġen-çy, *n.* An unforeseen occurrence.

jĕop'-ard-y, *n.* Danger; peril.

pĕr'-il-oŭs, *a.* Full of risk; dangerous.

quan'-da-ry, *n.* Doubt; uncertainty.

quar'-an-tīne (kwŏr-), *v. t.* To compel to remain at a distance.

sĕ'-ri-oŭs, *a.* Attended with danger.

so-lĭç'-ĭt-oŭs, *a.* Anxious to avoid; concerned.

sus-pĕnse', *n.* State of uncertainty.

LESSON 124.

DICTATION EXERCISE.

Let Fate do her worst; there are relics of joy,
Bright dreams of the past, which she cannot destroy;
And which come in the night-time of sorrow and care,
To bring back the features that joy used to wear;
Long, long be my heart with such memories filled;
Like the vase in which roses have once been distilled,
You may break, you may ruin the vase if you will,
But the scent of the roses will hang round it still.—*Thomas Moore.*

LESSON 125.

MISCELLANEOUS.

Among the pitfalls in our way,
The best of us walk blindly;
So man, be wary, watch and pray,
And judge your brother kindly.—*Alice Cary.*

păç'-i-fỹ, *v. t.* To tranquilize; to allay.

păl'-li-āte, *v. t.* To cover with excuse.

păr-tĭ-ăl'-i-ty (-shi-ăl'-), *n.* Inclination to favor one side of the question, or one party.

par-tĭç'-i-pāte, *v. t.* To share; to partake.

păss'-a-ble, *a.* That can be passed; acceptable.

pe-eūl'-iar (-kūl'-yar), *a.* Unusual; singular.

pĕud'-ū-loŭs, *a.* Hanging; swinging.

pĕn'-e-trāte, *v. t.* To enter into.

pĕr'-fo-rāte, *v. t.* To make a hole or holes through.

pĕr'-ish-a-ble, *a.* Subject to decay.

pĕr'-me-āte, *v. t.* To penetrate and pass through without causing rupture.

pĕr'-pe-trāte, *v. t.* To commit; to be guilty of.

pĕr-se-vēr'-ançe, *n.* Continued pursuit.

pĕt'-ri-fȳ, *v. t.* To convert to stone.

pho-nĕt'-ĭe, *a.* Representing sounds.

phȳṣ'-ĭe-al, *a.* Relating to natural or material things.

piĕrçe'-a-ble, *a.* Capable of being pierced.

pin'-ion (-yun), *n.* A feather or wing.

pŏst'-age, *n.* The price paid for the conveyance of all mailable matter.

prāe'-tiçe, *n.* Actual performance, not theory.

LESSON 126.

PERTAINING TO TRAVELING.

It's quite the thing to travel nowadays
And see if distant ground in general looks
As mentioned in the papers and in books.—*Carleton.*

bäg'-gage, *n.* Trunks, valises, etc., containing clothing which a traveler carries with him on his journey.

çir-eu-lā'-tion, *n.* Going about from place to place.

çir-en'-i-toŭs, *a.* Going round about or indirect.

de-pōt' (de-pō' or dē'-po), *n.* A railway station.

dĕs-ti-nā'-tion, *n.* End of a journey.

ĕm'-i-grāte, *v. i.* To move from one state or country to another.

ĕx-eur'-sion, *n.* A trip for pleasure or health.

ĕx'-o-dŭs, *n.* Departure from a place.

joŭr'-ney, *n.* Travel from one place to another.

mi'-gra-to-ry, *a.* Regularly moving from one place to another.

pe-dĕs'-tri-an, *n.* One who travels or journeys on foot.

pōrt-män'-teau (-män'-tō), *n.* A bag of leather for carrying clothing on journeys.

route (rōōt or rowt), *n.* The way traveled.

sāch'-el also sătch'-el, *n.* A small sack or bag.

tĕr'-mi-nŭs, *n.* The extreme point at either end of a piece of railway.

toŭr'-ist, *n.* One who journeys in a circuit.

trăns-por-tā'-tion, *n.* Removal; conveyance.

trăv'-el-er, *n.* One who travels.

va-līse', *n.* A traveling bag.

wạn'-der, *v. t.* To travel without a certain course.

LESSON 127.

DICTATION EXERCISE.

Tell me gentle traveler, who through the world hast gone,
And seen the sweetest roses blow,
And brightest gliding rivers flow,
Of all thine eyes have looked upon, which is the fairest land?

Child, shall I tell where Nature has best and fairest flowers?
It is where those we love abide;
Though small that space it is more wide   ,
Than kingdoms; though a desert bare,
The river of the gods is there,
And there are the enchanted bowers.—*From a Persian Poem.*

LESSON 128.

VEHICLES.

" For a restorative to a weary brain, bracing to weary muscles, exhilaration for the blues, a smoothing out of tangled nerves, and for an exercise that strengthens while it does not exhaust, pumping fresh red blood vigorously to the very finger tips, ride a bicycle."

ăm'-bu-lançe, *n.* A kind of movable hospital; a vehicle for conveying injured persons to a hospital.

ba-rouche' (ba-rōōsh'), *n.* A four-wheeled carriage with falling top, and seat outside for driver.

bï'-çy-ele, *n.* A two-wheeled velocipede.

bŭg'-gy, *n.* A light carriage.

eăr'-riage, *n.* A vehicle, especially for pleasure or passengers.

çhāise (shāz), *n.* A two-wheeled carriage, with a calash top, and the body hung on leather straps.

chăr'-i-ot, *n.* A four-wheeled state carriage, with one seat.

eŏn-vẹy'-ançe, *n.* The means of carrying anything from place to place.

eou-pẹ' (kōō-pā'), *n.* A four-wheeled close carriage for passengers.

hăn'-som, *n.* A light, low, two-wheeled street carriage, with the driver's seat elevated behind.

ŏm'-nï-bŭs, *n.* A large, four-wheeled carriage, conveniently arranged for carrying many people.

phā'-e-tŏn, *n.* An open carriage.

sleigh, *n.* A vehicle moved on runners.

stāge'-eōach, *n.* A coach that runs regularly from one place to another, for the convenience of passengers.

sŭr'-rey, *n.* A two-seated carriage.

trï'-çy-ele, *n.* A three-wheeled velocipede.

vē'-hï-ele, *n.* A conveyance.

ve-lŏç'-ï-pēde, *n.* A two-wheeled carriage for a single person, and propelled by his feet.

vïe-tō'-rï-à, *n.* A four-wheeled carriage designed for two persons, with a driver's seat.

wăg'-on, *n.* A vehicle on four wheels, especially used for carrying freight.

LESSON 129.

PERTAINING TO NAVIGATION.

No man ever sailed over exactly the same route that another sailed before him. Every man who starts on the ocean of life arches his sails to an untried breeze.—*William Mathews.*

a-bŏard', *adv.* Within a ship or boat.

ăneh'-or, *n.* An iron instrument for holding a boat at rest in the water.

bärġe, *n.* A large boat for conveying passengers or goods.

Bĕth'-el, *n.* A house of worship for seamen.

eạ-nọe', *n.* A small boat made of a tree or bark.

eäp'-stan, *n.* A strong column of timber with levers, for heaving in cables, as raising the anchor.

flo-til'-lä, *n.* A fleet of small vessels.

gäl'-ley, *n.* A low, flat built boat with one deck, navigated with sails and oars.

gŏn'-do-lä, *n.* A long, narrow, flat-bottomed pleasure boat used in Venice, Italy, on the canals.

gŏn-do-liër', *n.* A man who rows a gondola.

lär'-board, *n.* Left-hand side of a ship when looking forward.

ma-rīne', *a.* Pertaining to navigation or the sea.

mär'-i-tĭme, *a.* Pertaining to the ocean; marine.

nạu'-tĭe-al, *a.* Pertaining to seamen or art of navigation.

näv'-i-gä-tor, *n.* One who navigates or sails.

nāv-i-gä'-tion, *n.* Passing on water in ships or other vessels.

nä'-vy, *n.* The whole of the ships of war belonging to a nation.

sehŏŏn'-er, *n.* A small, sharp-built vessel with two or three masts, and fore and aft sails.

stär'-bōärd, *n.* Right-hand side of a ship when looking forward.

yạeht (yŏt,) *n.* A pleasure vessel.

LESSON 130.
DICTATION EXERCISE.

With white wings spread she bounded o'er the deep,
Home from the tossing of a stormy sea,
Where waves had yawned, and winds howled fearfully;
And where the harbor's waters seemed to sleep
In breezeless calm, and deep, untroubled rest,
She glided in, furling her weary wing,
Dropping her anchor down, and like a living thing,
Settling securely on the water's breast.
So, Oh, my God! from the rough sea of life,
Driven by doubt and fear and haggard care,
Let me my worn and weary spirit bear,
Far from its rage, and noise and stormy strife,
Into the haven of Thy sheltering love,
And find an anchorage no storm can move.—*Mary A. Livermore.*

LESSON 131.
PERTAINING TO WIND AND WEATHER.

The day is cold, and dark, and dreary;
It rains, and the wind is never weary;
The vine still clings to the mouldering wall,
But at every gust the dead leaves fall,
And the day is dark and dreary.—*Longfellow.*

eälm'-ness, *n.* Quietness.

eŏn-ḡeal', *v. t.* To freeze.

çy'-elōne, *n.* A rotary hurricane.

drīz'-zle, *v. i.* To fall in small drops.

drought (drout), *n.* Dry weather.

ē-lĕe-trĭç'-i-ty, *n.* The electric fluid identical with lightning.

ē-qui-nŏe'-tial, *a.* Pertaining to the time when the sun enters the equinoctial points.

fŏg'-ġy, *a.* Damp; misty; cloudy.

frĭg'-ĭd, *a.* Cold.

hŭr'-rĭ-eāne, *n.* A violent storm, with wind.

ĭn-elĕm'-en-çy, *a.* Storminess; roughness.

pē-rĭ-ŏd'-ĭe-al, *a.* Happening at fixed intervals.

sĭ-mōōn', *n.* A hot, dry wind, generated by the extreme heat of the parched desert, or sandy plains.

tem-pĕst'-ū-oŭs, *a.* Stormy; violent.

thŭn'-der-elŏud, *n.* A cloud that produces lightning and thunder.

tor-nā'-do, *n.* A hurricane.

tôr'-rĭd, *a.* Violently hot.

tȳ-phōōn', *n.* A violent whirlwind that rushes up from the earth, whirling clouds of dust.

whīrl'-wĭnd, *n.* A violent wind, moving in a circle, and having a progressive motion.

zĕph'-yr, *n.* Any soft, mild, gentle breeze.

LESSON 132.

HOMOPHONOUS WORDS.

Habits are soon assumed, but when we strive
To strip them off, 'tis being flayed alive.—*Cowper.*

one (wŭn), *n.* A single thing.

wŏn, *v. t.* Obtained; conquered.

our, *pro.* Belonging to us.

hour, *n.* Sixty minutes.

pāle, *a.* White; not bright.

pāil, *n.* A vessel with a bail.

pāne, *n.* A plate of glass for a window.

pāin, *n.* Suffering.

păl'-ate, *n.* The roof of the mouth.

păl'-let, *n.* A small and poor or rude bed.

pâir, *n.* Two things of a kind.

peâr, *n.* A kind of fruit.

pēal, *n.* A loud sound.

pēel, *v. t.* To remove the skin.

pēaçe, *n.* Calmness.

piēçe, *n.* A part of anything.

pēak, *n.* The summit.

pīque (pēk), *n.* Wounded pride.

pēer, *n.* A nobleman; an equal.

pīer, *n.* Support of a bridge.

LESSON 133.

TIME.

We live in deeds, not years; in thoughts, not breaths;
In feelings, not in figures on a dial;
We should count time by heart throbs. He most lives
Who thinks most, feels the noblest, acts the best.—*Bailey.*

ăft'-er-ward, *adv.* In time subsequent.

au'-tŭmn, *n.* Third season of the year; decline.

çēase'-less, *a.* Without pause or end.

çĕnt'-ū-rȳ, *n.* A period of a hundred years.

eŏn-tĭn'-ū-al, *a.* Perpetual; never ceasing.

dē̆e'-ade, *n.* The sum or number of ten, as ten years.

dĭ-rĕet'-lȳ, *adv.* Immediately; without delay.

dĭ-ûr'-nal, *a.* Daily.

e-lâpse', *v. i.* To pass away silently, as time.

e-phĕm'-e-ral, *a.* Beginning and ending in a day.

êre-lŏng', *adv.*   Before long ; soon.

frē'-quen-çy, *n.*   Occurrence oft repeated.

Im-mē'-di-ate-ly, *adv.*   Without delay ; instantly.

In-stan-tā'-ne-oŭs, *a.*   Done in an instant.

lēap'-yēar, *n.*   Every fourth year, containing 366 days.

lēi'-ṣure, *n.*   Time free from employment.

mĭn'-ute (mĭn'-ĭt), *n.*   Sixty seconds of time.

mō'-ment-a-ry, *a.*   Lasting a very short time.

noe-tûr'-nal, *a.*   Occurring or done at night.

ŏft'-en (ŏf'-n), *adv.*   Frequent.

LESSON 134.

Time.

"The years have linings, just as goblets do;
The old year forms the lining of the new;
Filled with the wine of pleasant memories,
The golden *was* doth line the silver *is*."

ŏp·por-tūne', *a.*   Seasonable; timely.

ŏp-por-tū'-ni-ty, *n.*   Fit or convenient time.

per-ĕn'-ni-al, *a.*   Perpetual; never-failing.

pĕr'-ma-nen-çy, *n.*   Duration; continuance in the same state or place.

per-pĕt'-ū-al, *a.*   Never ceasing.

prē'-vi-oŭs, *a.*   Happening before.

pro-erăs'-ti-nate, *v. t.*   To put off till to-morrow, or from day to day; to postpone.

rē'-çent-ly, *adv.*   Not long since.

re-eŭr'-rent, *a.*   Returning from time to time.

sēa'-ṣon-a-ble, *a.*   Opportune; timely.

sĕc'-ond, *n.*   The sixtieth part of a minute of time.

si-mul-tā'-ne-oŭs, *a.*   At the same time.

sŭb'-se-quent, *a.*   Following in time.

sŭm'-mer, *n.*   The second season of the year.

tür'-di-ly, *adv.*   Slowly.

tĕm'-po-ra-ry, *a.*   Lasting for a time only.

trăn'-sient (-shĕnt), *a.*   Of short duration.

ŭn-ū'-ṣu-al, *a.*   Not occurring often; uncommon.

ūṣ'-ū-al, *a.*   Occurring often; customary.

yēar'-ly, *adv.*   Happening or coming every year.

LESSON 135.

DICTATION EXERCISE.

"O a wonderful stream is the river Time
   As it runs through the realm of tears,
With a faultless rhythm and a musical rhyme,
And a broader sweep and a surge sublime,
   As it blends in the ocean of years.
How the winters are drifting like flakes of snow,
   And the summers like buds between,
And the year in the sheaf, how they come and they go
On the river's breast with its ebb and flow,
   As it glides in the shadow and sheen."

MISCELLANEOUS.

" From torch reversed, the flame
Still streameth, rising straight ;
So struggleth up the brave man
Stricken down by fate."

pre-dŏm'-i-nant, *a.* Prevalent over others ; superior in strength, influence or authority.

prĕp-a-rā'-tion, *n.* Anything which makes ready or prepares the way.

prĕv'-a-lençe, *n.* General existence or extension.

prĭv'-i-lĕge, *n.* A peculiar benefit or advantage.

prŏb'-a-ble, *a.* Likely; having more evidence for than against.

pro-çĕd'-ūre, *n.* An act performed.

prŏc-la-mā'-tion, *n.* An official or general notice.

pro-dū'-çi-ble, *a.* Capable of being brought forth.

prŏm-e-nāde' or prŏm-e-nädte', *v. i.* To walk for amusement or exercise.

prŏm'-i-nençe, *n.* Conspicuous.

pro-mĭs'-çu- oŭs, *a.* Mingled.

pub-lĭç'-i-ty, *n.* Notoriety ; being public.

pŭl'-ver-ize, *v. t.* To reduce to fine powder.

pŭnçt'-ūre, *v. t.* To pierce with a small pointed instrument.

pûr-sū'-ant, *a.* Following.

pûr-vey', *v. t.* To furnish or provide.

qua-drĭlle' (kwa- or ka-), *n.* A kind of dance.

răd'-i-cal, *a.* Extreme ; unsparing.

râis'-a-ble, *a.* That can be raised.

răn'-çĭd, *a.* Having a rank smell.

WORDS USED IN SOCIETY.

" Like as a plank of drift-wood, tossed on the watery main,
Another plank encounters, meets, touches, parts again ;
So, meeting and parting ever, on life's unresting sea,
Men meet, and greet, and sever, parting eternally."

ae-quăint'-ançe, *n.* One well known.

as-sĕm'-ble, *v. i.* To meet or come together.

as-sō'-çi-āte (-shi-āt), *n.* A companion.

aux-ĭl'-ia-ry (-ya-rў), *n.* Helping ; assisting.

e-clät', *n.* Brilliancy of success ; splendor.

e-lite' (ā-lēet'), *n.* A choice or select body.

in-fôrm'-al, *a.* Not in the usual established form.

ĭn'-ter-view, *n.* A conference.

ĭn'-ti-ma-çy, *n.* Nearness in friendship.

in-tro-duçe', *v. t.* To make known by formal announcement.

ĭs'-o-lāte, *v. t.* To place by oneself, or itself.

mūt'-ū-al, *a.* Interchanged ; common.

ŏs'-tra-çize, *v. t.* To banish from society.

pĕr'-son-al, *a.* Belonging or pertaining to a person.

rou-tīne', *n.* A round of business or pleasure often pursued.

se-clū'-sion, *n.* Separation from society.

so'-cia-ble (-sha-bl), *a.* Fond of companions.

so-çi'-e-ty, *n.* An association for mutual benefit, pleasure or usefulness.

soir-ee' (swä-rä'), *n.* An evening party.

sŏl'-i-tūde, *n.* State of being alone.

LESSON 138.

NAMES APPLIED TO MEN.

"To thine own self be true,
And it must follow, as the night the day,
Thou canst not then be false to any man."

băch'-e-lor, *n.* An unmarried man.

bĕn'-e-dĭet, *n.* A married man.

brĕth'-ren, *n.* Used in Scriptural language in place of brothers.

chăn'-çĕl-lor, *n.* A judicial officer of high rank.

chŭrl, *n.* A surly, ill-bred fellow.

fō'-ġy, *n.* A dull old fellow.

fra-tĕr'-nal, *a.* Brotherly.

ġī'-ant, *n.* A man of extraordinary bulk or stature.

ĭ-tĭn'-er-ant, *n.* One who travels from place to place, particularly a preacher.

măs'-eu-lĭne, *a.* Not feminine; strong; robust.

Môr'-phe-ŭs, *n.* The god of dreams.

nĕph'-ew, *n.* The son of a brother or sister.

pro-fĕss'-or, *n.* One who professes to teach any science or branch of learning.

pū'-ġil-ĭst, *n.* One who fights with his fists.

seŭlp'-tor, *n.* One whose occupation is to carve images or figures.

swāin, *n.* A country gallant or lover.

tū'-tor, *n.* A private or public teacher.

ŭn'-ele, *n.* The brother of one's father or mother.

vĕt'-er-an, *n.* One grown old in service.

vīe'-ar, *n.* The incumbent of an appropriated benefice.

LESSON 139.

DICTATION EXERCISE.

"Many men have been obscure in their origin and birth, but great and glorious in life and death. They have been born and nurtured in villages, but have reigned and triumphed in cities. They were first laid in the mangers of poverty and obscurity, but afterwards have become possessors of thrones and palaces. Their fame is like the pinnacle which ascends higher and higher, until at last it becomes a most conspicuous and towering object of attraction. It is not good for human nature to have the road of life made too easy. So it is a common saying that the men who are most successful in business are those who begin the world in their shirt sleeves, while those who begin with fortunes generally lose them."

LESSON 140.

NAMES APPLIED TO WOMEN.

"A woman is too slight a thing
To trample the world without feeling its sting."

bru-nĕtte', *n.* A woman of dark complexion.

eŏ-quĕtte', *n.* A jilt; a flirt.

daugh'-ter, *n.* A female descendant.

dow'-a-ġer, *n.* A title given in England to a widow, to distinguish her from the wife of her husband's heir bearing the same name.

ĕm'-press, *n.* The consort or wife of an emperor.

fĕm'-i-nine, *n.* Womanly.

gŏd'-dess, *n.* A female god.

hĕr'-o-ine, *n.* A woman of brave spirit.

maid'-en, *n.* An unmarried woman.

mam-mä', *n.* Mother.

ma-tĕr'-nal, *a.* Motherly.

mä'-tron, *n.* The female head of a household.

Mi-nĕr'-và, *n.* The goddess of wisdom, of war, and of the liberal arts.

niēçe, *n.* The daughter of a brother or sister.

pre-çĕp'-tress, *n.* A female teacher.

queen, *n.* A female monarch.

shĕp'-herd-ess (-erd-), *n.* A woman that tends sheep.

si'-ren, *n.* An enticing or alluring woman.

sul-tä'-nà or sul-tä'-nà, *n.* The wife of a sultan.

tĕr'-ma-gant, *n.* A boisterous, brawling woman.

. LESSON 141.

NAMES APPLIED TO PERSONS.

The heights by great men reached and kept
Were not attained by sudden flight,
But they, while their companions slept,
Were toiling upward in the night.—*Longfellow.*

a-dŭlt', *n.* A person grown up.

ăp'-pli-cant, *n.* One who makes request.

ăs-pir'-ant, *n.* One who aspires or seeks with eagerness.

ăs-sĕss'-or, *n.* One who determines the taxes.

bĕg'-gar, *n.* One who begs.

big'-ot, *n.* One unreasonably devoted to a party or creed.

blŏnde, *n.* A person with fair complexion.

çăn'-ni-bal, *n.* One who eats human flesh.

çhăp'-er-ōn, *n.* One who attends a lady in public places as a guide and protector.

çit'-i-zen, *n.* An inhabitant of a city, state or country.

eŏl'-lēague, *n.* A partner or associate in some civil office.

eŏl-lĕet'-or, *n.* An officer appointed and commissioned to receive taxes, duties, tolls or customs.

eŏn-nois-seur' (kŏn-nis-sur'), *n.* One well versed in any subject.

eō-tĕm'-po-rä-ry, *n.* One who lives at the same time as another.

eoŭs'-in (kŭz'-n), *n.* The child of an uncle or aunt.

de-pŏs'-i-tor, *n.* One who deposits.

dĕp'-ū-tȳ, *n.* An assistant empowered to act in the officer's name.

ĕp'-i-eūre, *n.* One who indulges in the luxuries of the table.

fa-năt'-ie, *n.* One extravagant in opinion.

fū'-gi-tive, *n.* One who flees from danger.

LESSON 142.

Names Applied to Persons.

"Some murmur when their sky is clear and wholly bright to view,
If one small speck of dark appear in their great heaven of blue;
And some with thankful love are filled if but one streak of light—
One ray of God's good mercy—gild the darkness of the night."

fūne'-tion-a-ry, *n.* One who holds an office.

gȳp'-sy, *n.* One of a vagabond race, of a roving disposition; a dark-colored person.

hĕr'-mit, *n.* A recluse; one who retires from society and lives in solitude.

ig-no-rä'-mus, *n.* An ignorant person.

in-eŭm'-bent, *n.* The person in present possession of an office.

ĭn-dĭ-vĭd′-ū-al, *n.* A person.

ĭn-hăb′-ĭt-ănt, *n.* One who has a legal settlement in a town, city or parish.

ĭu′-stĭ-gä-tor, *n.* A tempter.

mē′-nĭ-al, *n.* A servant.

mẽr′-chant, *n.* One who buys goods to sell again.

mĕs′-sen-ġer, *n.* One who bears a message or an errand.

mĭ′-ṣer, *n.* An extremely covetous and stingy person.

no-vĭ′-ti-ate (-shĭ-ate), *n.* One who is going through a period of probation.

op-pō′-uent, *n.* One who opposes; an adversary.

pēo′-ple, *n.* The population, or part of it.

re-çĭp′-i-ent, *n.* One who receives.

rĕṣ′-i-dent, *n.* One who resides or dwells in a place for some time.

shĭrk, *n.* One who seeks to avoid duty.

sŭb′-stĭ-tūte, *n.* One who or that which is put in place of another.

trăns-ġrĕss′-or, *n.* One who violates any known principle of rectitude.

LESSON 143.

NATIONS.

National progress is the sum of individual industry, energy and uprightness, as national decay is of individual idleness, selfishness and vice.—*Samuel Smiles.*

Ăf′-ri-ean, *n.* A native of Africa.

A-mẽr′-i-ean, *n.* A native of America.

Bĕd′-ou-ĭn, *n.* One of the tribe of nomadic Arabs, who live in tents.

Ĉau-eã′-sian, *n.* Any one belonging to the Indo-European race, and the white races originating near Mt. Caucasus.

E-ġȳp′-tian, *n.* A native or naturalized inhabitant of Egypt.

Ĕs′-qui-mau (ĕs′-kĭ-mō), *n.* An inhabitant of arctic America and Greenland.

Eū-ro-pē′-an, *n.* An inhabitant of Europe.

Ġĕn′-tĭle, *n.* The nations at large as distinguished from the Jews.

Ġrē′-eian (-shan), *n.* A native of Greece; a Greek.

Hē′-brew (-brụ), *n.* An Israelite; a Jew.

Hĭn′-dŏō, *n.* A native of Hindostan.

Ĭu′-diau (ĭnd′-yan), *n.* One of the aboriginal inhabitants of America.

I-tăl′-ian (-yau), *n.* A native of Italy.

Jăp-a-nēṣe′, *n.* A native of Japan or the people of that country.

Lăp′-land-er, *n.* A native of Lapland.

Mŏu-ġō′-li-au, *n.* A native of Mongolia.

Nôr-wē′-ġi-an, *n.* A native of Norway.

Pŏr′-tu-ġuēṣe, *n.* An inhabitant of Portugal.

Rŭs′-sian (rŭsh′-au or rụ′-shan), *n.* A native of Russia.

Si-bē′-ri-an, *n.* A native of Siberia.

LESSON 144.

DICTATION EXERCISE.

Breathes there a man with soul so dead,
Who never to himself hath said,
"This is my own, my native land!"
Whose heart hath ne'er within him burned,
As home his footsteps he hath turned,
From wandering on a foreign strand?

If such there breathe, go, mark him well:
For him no minstrel raptures swell,
High though his titles, proud his name,
Boundless his wealth as wish can claim;
Despite those titles, power and pelf,
The wretch concentrated all in self,
Living, shall forfeit fair renown,
And, doubly dying, shall go down
To the vile dust from which he sprung,
Unwept, unhonored, and unsung.—*Walter Scott.*

LESSON 145.

HOMOPHONOUS WORDS.

Though the mills of God grind slowly, yet they grind exceeding small,
Though with patience he stands waiting, with exactness grinds he all.—*Longfellow.*

pauşe, *v. i.*   To cease for a time.
pawş, *n. pl.*   Feet of an animal.

pĕd'-al, *n.*   Used by or belonging to
the feet.
pĕd'-dle, *v. t.*   To sell from house to
house.

plŭm, *n.*   A small fruit.
plŭmb, *a.*   Perpendicular.

pōle, *n.*   A long, round piece of wood.
pŏll, *n.*   A head ; a place for voting.

pōre, *n.*   A small opening ;   (*v. i.*) to
study.
pōur, *v. t.*   To send forth.

prāy, *v. i.*   To beseech.
prey, *n.*   Booty ; plunder.

prĭn'-çĭ-pal, *a.*   Chief.
prĭn'-çĭ-ple, *n.*   A rule of action ; a
fundamental truth.

prŏf'-it, *n.*   Gain ; valuable results.
prŏph'-et, *n.*   A religious teacher ; one
who foretells events.

quarts, *n. pl.*   Plural of quart, the
fourth part of a gallon.
quartz, *n.*   A mineral.

rāişe, *v. t.*   To lift up.
rāyş, *n.*   Lines of light.

LESSON 146.

PERTAINING TO MANNERS.

What a rare gift is that of manners !   Better for one to possess them than wealth, beauty or
talent; they will more than supply all.—*Bulwer Lytton.*

a-bū'-sĭve, *a.*   Offering harsh words
and ill treatment.
ăf'-fa-ble, *a.*   Easy of manners or conversation.
ā'-mi-a-ble, *a.*   Worthy of love.
ăr'-ro-ğançe, *n.*   Proud contempt for
others.
awk'-ward, *a.*   Clumsy ; ungraceful
in manner.

be-hāv'-ior (-yur), *n.*   Manner of conducting one's self.
brăğ'-gart, *a.*   Boastful.
blŭn'-der-er, *n.*   A careless person.
ea-prī'-cioŭs (-prĭsh'-ŭs), *a.*   Whim-
sical.
eâre'-fŭl-ness, *n.*   Heedfulness.
eâre'-less, *a.*   Heedless.

eau'-tioŭs (-shŭs), a. Timorous; over prudent.

eŏm-plä'-çen-çy, n. Satisfaction.

eŏm-pŏṣ'-ure, n. Calmness; tranquility.

eŏn-de-sçĕnd', v. i. To relinquish dignity of character.

eŏn-fī-dĕn'-tial, a. Secret; trustworthy.

eŏn-ġē'-ni-al, a. Sympathetic; of the same nature.

eŏn-sçi-ĕn'-tioŭs (-shĭ-ĕn'-shŭs), a. Influenced by conscience.

eŏn-tĕmpt', n. Disdain.

eôr'-di-al or eôrd'-ial, a. Sincere; affectionate.

LESSON 147.
Pertaining to Manners.

*" Many young persons believe themselves natural
When they are only impolite and coarse."*

eoûrt'-e-sy, n. Politeness of manners.

eŏv'-et-oŭs, a. Eager to obtain.

eow'-ard-içe, n. Timidity; fear.

erĭt'-ie-al, a. Severe in judging; inclined to find fault.

erŭde'-ly, adv. In an immature or hasty manner; rudely.

de-eŏ'-roŭs or dĕe'-o-roŭs, a. Proper.

de-eŏ'-rum, n. Propriety of manner or conduct.

dĕf-er-ĕn'-tial (-shal), a. Accustomed to defer.

de-lĭb'-er-ate, a. Not sudden or rash.

dĕs'-ul-to-ry, a. Immethodical; inconstant.

dĭf'-fĭ-dent, a. Timid; distrustful.

dĭġ'-ni-ty, n. Manners suited to inspire respect.

doubt'-fui (dout-), a. Hesitating; undetermined.

dū'-bi-oŭs, a. Unsettled or doubtful.

ēa'-ġer, a. Keenly desirous.

ĕar'-nest, a. Ardent in pursuit of an object.

ĕe-çĕn'-trie, a. Odd.

ĕm-băr'-rass, v. t. To confuse; to disconcert.

ĕt-ĭ-quĕtte' (ĕt-ĭ-kĕt'), n. Conventional decorum.

fa-mĭl'-iar (-yar), a. Not formal; unceremonious.

LESSON 148.
Pertaining to Manners.

"Unbecoming forwardness oftener proceeds from ignorance than impudence."

fäs'-çi-nāte, v. t. To charm; to captivate.

fas-tĭd'-i-oŭs, a. Difficult to please.

fe-rŏ'-cioŭs, a. Fierce; savage.

fĭ-dĕl'-i-ty, n. Loyalty.

fĭĕrçe'-ness, n. Fury; violence.

flĭp'-pan-çy, n. Pertness; petulancy.

fŏr'-çi-ble, a. Possessing force.

fŏr-măl'-i-ty, n. Habitual mode.

frĕt'-fui, a. Peevish; irritable.

friv'-o-loŭs, a. Given to trifling.

ġe'-ni-al, a. Sympathetically cheerful and cheering.

ġĕn-tēel', a. Polite; well-bred.

grä'-cioŭs (-shŭs), a. Merciful; kind to the poor.

haŭgh'-ty (hạw'-), a. Disdainful.

hĕṣ-i-tä'-tion, n. Doubt.

ĭd-i-o-sỹn'-era-sy, n. A characteristic of an individual.

ĭm-pär'-tial, a. Not favoring one more than another.

ĭm-pā'-tience (-shĕns), n. Violence of temper.

ĭm-pĕr'-ti-nent, a. Rude in behavior.

ĭm-pĕt'-ū-oŭs, a. Vehement in feeling or action.

LESSON 149.

Pertaining to Manners.

Intelligence and courtesy not always are combined ;
Often in a wooden house a golden room we find.—Longfellow.

Im-pro-pri'-e-ty, *n.* An unsuitable act or expression.

Im'-pu-dent, *a.* Bold, with contempt for others.

im-pŭl'-sive, *a.* Acting momentarily or by impulse.

nĕġ'-li-ġençe, *n.* Heedlessness.

nĕrv'-oŭs, *a.* Easily agitated.

ŏf-fī'-cioŭs (-fĭsh'-ŭs), *a.* Meddlesome.

ŏp-prĕss'-ĭve, *a.* Over-powering ; un-justly severe.

pär-tie'-ū-lar, *a.* Hard to suit ; pre-cise.

pĕt'-ū-lan-çy, *n.* Peevishness ; freak-ish passion.

po-lite'-ness, *n.* Good breeding.

pŏmp'-oŭs, *a.* Boastful.

pre-çĭp'-i-tāte, *v. t.* To hurry rashly.

pre-çĭṣ'-ion (-sĭzh'-un), *n.* The quality of being precise.

pre-eō'-cious (-shŭs), *a.* Too forward.

pre-ṣumpt'-ū-oŭs, *a.* Over-confident ; going beyond bounds of modesty.

pre-tĕn'-tious (-shŭs), *a.* To lay claim to more than is one's due.

prŏmpt, *a.* Quickly and cheerfully performed.

pŭġ-nā'-cious (-shŭs), *a.* Disposed to fight.

pū-sil-lăn'-i-moŭs, *a.* Cowardly.

quȧint'-ness, *n.* Oddness.

LESSON 150.

Pertaining to Manners.

" There is policy in manner. I have heard one not inexperienced in the pursuit of fame, give it his earnest support, as being the surest passport to absolute and brilliant success."

quĕr'-ụ-loŭs, *a.* Quarrelsome.

quĕṣ'-tion-a-ble, *a.* Doubtful ; suspi-cious.

re-lŭe'-tan-çy, *n.* Unwillingness.

rĕt'-i-çent, *a.* Reserved.

sȧu'-çi-ness, *n.* Impudence.

serụ'-pu-loŭs, *a.* Careful ; doubtful.

se-rēne'-ly, *adv.* Calmly.

sĭm-plĭç'-i-ty, *n.* Artlessness of mind.

sĭn-çĕr'-i-ty, *n.* Honesty of mind.

smĭrk, *n.* An affected smile.

ti-mĭd'-i-ty, *n.* The state of being timid.

trȧn'-quĭl-ly, *a.* In a tranquil manner ; quietly.

trĕp-i-dā'-tion, *n.* Involuntary trem-bling, caused usually by terror or fear.

trĭv'-i-al-ly, *adv.* In a trifling manner.

ŭn-eoŭth', *a.* Awkward ; odd.

ûr-băn'-i-ty, *n.* Politeness ; refine-ment.

văn'-i-ty, *n.* Idle show ; pride.

vī-vā'-cioŭs, *a.* Lively ; active.

whĭm'-ṣi-eal, *a.* Full of whims.

zĕal'-oŭs, *a.* Ardent in behalf of an object.

LESSON 151.

PERTAINING TO LINEAGE.

There is certainly something of exquisite kindness and thoughtful benevolence in that rar-est of gifts—fine breeding.—Bulwer Lytton.

ȧn'-çes-try, *n.* A series of ancestors ; lineage.

ȧn'-cient (-shĕnt), *a.* Old.

ȧn-tĭq'-ui-ty (-tĭk'-wĭ-), *n.* Ancient times.

a-rĭs'-to-erȧt or **ȧr'-ĭs-to-erȧt,** *n.* A proud or haughty person.

ăr-ĭs-tŏe'-ra-çy, *n.* The nobility or chief persons in a state.

de-scĕnd'-eut, *a.* Proceeding from an ancestor or source.

fŏre'-fà-ther, *n.* An ancestor.

g̈ĕn-e-ăl'-o-g̈y, *n.* A pedigree.

g̈ĕn'-try, *n.* Rank by birth.

lĭn'-e-ag̈e, *n.* Race; descent.

no-bĭl'-ĭ-ty, *n.* Noble birth.

pär'-ve-nū, *n.* One newly risen into notice.

pa-trĭ'-cian (-trĭsh'-an), *n.* One of noble birth.

pĕd'-ĭ-g̈ree, *n.* Line of ancestors.

ple-bē'-ian (-yan), *n.* One of the common people.

pŏp'-ū-laçe, *n.* The common people.

po-sĭ'-tion, *n.* Social rank.

prĕd-e-çĕs'-sor, *n.* One whom another comes after.

roy̆'-al-ty, *n.* The state of being regal or royal.

yeō'-man, *n.* A plebeian of the most respectable class.

LESSON 152.

DICTATION EXERCISE.

Who are the nobles of the earth, the true aristocrats
Who need not bow their heads to lords, nor doff to kings their hats?
Who are they but the men of toil, the mighty and the free,
Whose hearts and hands subdue the earth, and compass all the sea?
Who are they but the men of toil, who cleave the forest down,
And plant, amid the wilderness, the hamlet or the town,—
Who fight the battles, bear the scars, and give the world its crown
Of name, and fame, and history, and pomp of old renown?
These claim no gaud of heraldry, and scorn the knighting rod;
Their coats of arms are noble deeds, their peerage is from God!
They take not from ancestral graves the glory of their name,
But win, as once their fathers won, the laurel wreath of fame.—*Stewart.*

LESSON 153.

MISCELLANEOUS.

A man should never be ashamed to own he has been in the wrong, which is but saying in other words that he is wiser to-day than yesterday.—*Pope.*

rĕad'-ĭ-ly, *adv.* Without delay or objection.

re-çĕp'-ta-ele, *n.* A receiver or holder.

re-eoil', *v. i.* To take a reverse motion.

rĕe-on-çĭl-ĭ-ā'-tion, *n.* Renewal of friendship.

re-dū'-çi-ble, *a.* That can be reduced.

rē'-g̈iôn, *n.* Vicinity.

re-läpse', *v. i.* To fall back; to return.

re-lĭĕf', *n.* The removal of anything oppressive or burdensome.

re-lĭṇ'-quĭsh, *v. t.* To withdraw from.

re-lŷ', *v. i.* To depend upon.

re-mē'-di-a-ble, *n.* Capable of being remedied or cured.

rĕn'-dez-vous (-de-vōō), *n.* A place appointed for meeting.

re-new'-al (-nū'-), *n.* Commencing again.

re-pâir', *v. t.* To restore to a sound or good state.

rĕp'-a-ra ble, *a.* That can be repaired.

re-pū'-di-āte, *v. i.* To have nothing to do with.

rĕq'-ui-site (-wĭ-), *a.* Something indispensable.

re-tăl'-i-āte, *v. i.* To return like for like.

re-vĕr'-ber-āte, *v. i.* To resound.

ronge (rōōzh), *n.* A cosmetic used to give a red color.

LESSON 154.

PERTAINING TO TEMPER AND DISPOSITION.

In ourselves the sunshine dwells;
From ourselves the music swells;
By ourselves our life is fed
With sweet or bitter daily bread.—*Goldsmith.*

a-grēe'-a-ble, *a.* Pleasing.

chänge'-a-ble, *a.* Fickle; inconstant.

eŏn-tĕnt'-ment, *n.* Satisfaction; without disquiet.

dĭs-po-ṣĭ'-tion, *n.* Acquired aptitude of temper or character; disposal.

dŏç'-ile, *a.* Easily managed or taught.

ĕn-dūr'-ançe, *n.* Patience; a bearing or suffering.

ĕx-ȧs'-per-āte, *v. t.* To enrage; to provoke.

frĕn'-zy, *n.* Madness; rage.

in-dĭg'-nant, *a.* Feeling wrath.

in-fū'-ri-āte, *v. t.* To enrage.

jĕal'-oŭs-y, *n.* Uneasiness from fear of rivalry.

ŏp'-ti-mĭst, *n.* One who thinks everything happens for the best.

păs'-sion-ate, *a.* Easily moved to anger.

pĕs'-si-mĭst, *n.* One who thinks everything is for the worst.

plăç'-ĭd, *a.* Serene; tranquil.

săn'-guine, *a.* Full of hope.

sŭs-pĭ'-cioŭs (-pĭsh'-ŭs), *a.* Apt to imagine without proof.

ŭm'-brage, *n.* Offense.

world'-li-ness (wûrld'-), *n.* Being fond of temporal enjoyments.

wräth, *n.* Violent anger.

LESSON 155.

DENOTING HATRED.

If you hate your enemies, you will contract such a vicious habit of mind as by degrees will break out upon those who are your friends, or those who are indifferent to you.—*Plutarch.*

ȧb-hŏr'-rençe, *n.* Extreme hatred.

a-bŏm'-i-nāte, *v. t.* To hate in the highest degree.

ăn-i-mŏs'-i-ty, *n.* Violent hatred.

ăn-tĭp'-a-thy, *n.* Disgust; repugnance.

a-vĕr'-sion, *n.* Dislike.

dĕs'-pi-ca-ble, *a.* Worthless; to be despised.

ĕn'-mi-ty, *n.* Hatred; ill-will.

hā'-tred, *n.* Very great dislike.

in'-fa-moŭs, *a.* Detestable.

lōath'-sôme, *a.* Exciting disgust or hatred.

ma-lĕv'-o-lençe, *n.* Evil disposition toward another.

ma-lĭ'-cioŭs (-lĭsh'-ŭs), *a.* Proceeding from hatred or ill-will.

ŏb-nŏx'-ioŭs, *a.* Odious; hateful.

ō'-di-oŭs, *a.* Deserving hatred.

răn'-cor, *n.* Inveterate hatred.

re-pŭg'-nançe, *n.* Aversion; dislike.

re-vĕnge'-ful, *a.* Vindictive.

vē'-he-ment, *a.* Furious.

vĕnge'-ançe, *n.* Passionate revenge.

vĕn'-om-oŭs, *a.* Malignant; spiteful.

LESSON 156.

DICTATION EXERCISE.

Life appears to me too short to be spent in nursing animosity or registering wrongs. We are, and must be, one and all, burdened with faults in this world, but the time will come when, I trust, we shall put them off in putting off our corruptible bodies; when debasement and sin will fall from us with this cumbrous frame of flesh. It is a creed in which I delight, to which I cling. It makes eternity a rest, a home—not a terror and an abyss. With this creed, revenge never worries my heart, degradation never too deeply disgusts me, injustice never crushes me too low; I live in calm, looking to the end.—*Charlotte Brontë.*

LESSON 157.

PERTAINING TO INTEMPERANCE.

"I *dare* not drink for my own sake;
I *ought* not to drink for my neighbor's sake."

ăb'-stĭ-nençe, *n.* Voluntary refraining from indulging the appetite, as for strong drink.

ăl'-eo-hol, *n.* Pure or highly rectified spirit.

dĭs-tĭll'-er-y, *n.* A building and works where distilling is carried on.

drŭŋk'-ard, *n.* One who habitually drinks to excess.

ha-bĭt'-u-al, *a.* Acquired by habit.

ĭn-ē'-brĭ-āte, *n.* An habitual drunkard.

ĭn-tĕm'-per-ançe, *n.* Habitual indulgence in drinking spirituous liquors.

lĭq'-uŏr (lĭk'-ur), *n.* Any alcoholic fluid, either distilled or fermented.

mŏd-er-ā'-tĭon, *n.* Freedom from excess.

rĕf-or-mā'-tĭon, *n.* Change from worse to better.

re-mŏn'-strançe, *n.* Act of urging against.

rĕs-o-lū'-tĭon, *n.* Firmness in opinion, act or thought.

rē'-tro-ḡrāde or rĕt'-ro-ḡrāde, *n.* Declining from better to worse.

sa-lōōn', *n.* A place where liquors are sold in small quantities.

so-brī'-e-ty, *n.* Habitual soberness.

tee-tō'-tal-er, *n.* One pledged to entire abstinence from intoxicating drinks.

tĕm'-per-ançe, *n.* Moderation.

tĕm'-per-ate, *a.* Not excessive.

tĕmpt, *v. t.* To try to persuade.

whĭs'-key or whĭs'-ky, *n.* A spirit distilled from grain.

LESSON 158.

WORDS DENOTING KINDNESS.

How far that little candle throws its beams!
So shines a good deed in a naughty world.—*Shakespeare.*

ăe-eŏm'-mo-dāte, *v. t.* To supply with something desired.

ăs-sĭst'-ance, *n.* Help; aid.

be-nĕv'-o-lençe, *n.* Disposition to do good.

be-nĭḡ'-nant, *a.* Kind.

boun'-te-ŏus, *a.* Disposed to give freely.

chăr'-ĭ-ty, *n.* Liberality to the poor.

eŏn-çẽrn', *n.* Solicitude; interest in or care for any person or thing.

eŏn-dō'-lençe, *n.* Expressing sympathy for another.

eŏn-grăt'-ū-lāte, *v. t.* Expressing sympathetic joy.

eŏn-sĭd'-er-ate, *a.* Careful of the rights and feelings of others.

eŏn-sōle', *v. t.* To comfort; to soothe.

ğĕn'-er-oŭs, *a.* Free to give.

gra-tū'-ĭ-ty, *n.* Something given freely.

hu-māne', *a.* Kind; benevolent.

lĭb'-er-al, *a.* Generous; open-hearted.

măg-năn'-i-moŭs, *a.* Not selfish.

mēr'-çi-fŭl, *a.* Tender; not cruel.

phĭ-lăn'-thro-py, *n.* Universal good will.

săe'-rĭ-fice (-fīz), *v. t.* To devote or give up with loss or suffering.

sỹm'-pa-thy, *n.* Fellow feeling.

LESSON 159.
DICTATION EXERCISE.

My heart was heavy, for its trust had been
Abused, its kindness answered with foul wrong;
So, turning gloomily from my fellow men,
One summer Sabbath-day I strolled among
The green mounds of the village burial place,
Where, pondering how all human love and hate
Find one sad level, and how, soon or late,
Wronged and wrong-doer, each with meekened face,
And cold hands folded over a still heart,
Pass the green threshold of our common grave,
Whither all footsteps tend, whence none depart—
Awed for myself, and pitying my race,
One common sorrow like a mighty wave
Swept all my pride away, and trembling, I forgave.—*Whittier.*

LESSON 160.
HOMOPHONOUS WORDS.

On this side, and on that, men see their friends
Drop off, like leaves in autumn; yet launch out
Into fantastic schemes, which the long-livers
In the world's hale and undegenerate days
Could scarce have leisure for.—*Blair.*

rāin, *n.* Water falling in drops from the atmosphere.

reįgn, *v. i.* To rule.

reįn, *n.* A check.

rēed, *n.* A hollow stalk.

rēad, *v. t.* To peruse.

rĕst, *n.* Freedom from everything which wearies.

wrĕst, *v. i.* To take from by force.

riçe, *n.* A kind of grain grown in warm climates, and used for food.

rise (rīs), *n.* An ascent; that which rises or seems to rise.

right, *a.* Just; not wrong; true.

rite, *n.* A ceremony.

wright, *n.* An artisan.

write, *v. t.* To express ideas by letters or characters.

rŏad, *n.* A public highway.

rōde, *v. i.* Past of ride.

rōwed, *v. t.* Past of row.

rōle, *n.* A part played.

rōll, *n.* A list.

rỹe, *n.* Grain used for food.

wrỹ, *a.* Distorted.

LESSON 161.

CONVERSATION.

As it is a characteristic of great wits to say much in few words, so it is of small wits to talk much and say nothing.—*Rochefoucauld.*

a-dieū', *adv.* Farewell.

ăl-lūde', *v. i.* To refer to; to have reference.

ăl-lū'-ṣion, *n.* A hint.

ăl-ter-eā'-tion, *n.* Dispute carried on with heat or anger.

a-pŏl'-o-ġy, *n.* An excuse.

ȧr'-ġūe, *v. t.* To persuade by reasoning.

bȧd'-i-nȧġe (bȧd'-in-äzh), *n.* Light or playful discourse.

băn'-ter, *v. t.* To joke or jest with.

brĕv'-i-ty, *n.* Contraction into few words; conciseness.

çĕn'-sure, *v. t.* To find fault with.

ĕŏl'-lo-quy, *n.* A mutual discourse of two or more.

ĕŏm-mūne', *v. i.* To converse together familiarly.

ĕŏm-plāint', *n.* Finding fault.

ĕŏn-çīse', *a.* Expressing much in few words.

ĕŏn'-fer-ençe, *n.* To consult together.

ĕŏn-tĕn'-tion, *n.* Strife in debate; controversy.

ĕŏn-tra-dīet', *v. t.* To oppose in words.

ĕŏn'-tro-vĕr-sy, *n.* Discussion; dispute.

ĕŏn-vĕr-sā'-tion, *n.* Familiar discourse.

de-bāte', *v. t.* To contend for in words or argument.

LESSON 162.

Conversation.

"The first ingredient in conversation is truth, next good sense, third good humor, and the fourth wit."

dĕe-la-rā'-tion, *n.* Formal expression; publicly announcing.

de-nī'-al, *n.* A contradiction.

de-nounçe', *v. t.* To inform against.

dī'-a-lōgue, *n.* A conversation between two or more persons.

dis-eŭs'-sion, *n.* Examination by argument.

dis-pūte', *n.* Verbal controversy.

ĕx-ăġ'-ġer-āte, *v. t.* To enlarge beyond bounds.

ĕx-plīç'-it, *a.* Plain in language.

ĕx-pŏst'-ū-lāte, *v. i.* To remonstrate.

ġăb'-ble, *v. i.* To talk without meaning.

ġär'-rụ-loŭs, *a.* Very talkative.

ĭn-sĭn'-ū-āte, *v. t.* To hint; to introduce artfully.

lăn'-guaġe, *n.* Human speech.

lĭn'-guĭst, *n.* A master of language.

lo-quā'-cioŭs (-shŭs), *a.* Talkative.

mûr'-mur, *v. i.* To utter sullen discontent; to make a low, continued noise.

năr-rā'-tion, *n.* Telling the particulars of an event.

pre-vär'-i-eāte, *v. i.* To evade telling the truth.

pshȧw (shȧw), *interj.* An exclamation to denote disdain.

räil'-ler-y, *n.* Jesting language.

LESSON 163.

Conversation.

" It is not only difficult to say the right thing in the right place, but, far more difficult still, to leave unsaid the wrong thing at the tempting moment."

rē-en-pĭt'-ū-lāte, *v. t.* To relate in brief.

re-çĭt'-al, *n.* A narration; that which is recited.

re-eount', *v. t.* To tell the particulars of.

re-lāte', *v. t.* To tell over.

rĕp-ar-tēe', *n.* A smart and witty reply.

rĕp-e-tĭ'-tion, *n.* Doing or uttering a second time.

rụ'-mor, *n.* A current story passing from one person to another without any authority for it.

săl-ū-tā'-tion, *n.* Greeting.

sär'-easm, *n.* A taunt; a cutting jest.

sa-tĭr'-ic-al-ly, *adv.* With severity of remark.

serĕam, *v. t.* To cry out with a shrill voice.

shriĕk, *v. t.* To utter sharply and shrilly.

smōōth'-ness, *n.* Easy flow of words; (*a.*) evenness of surface.

so-lĭl'-o-quy, *n.* Talking to one's self.

sŭg-gĕs'-tion (-yŭn), *n.* A hint; an intimation.

ŭt'-ter-ançe, *n.* Vocal expression.

vāgue'-ly, *adv.* Unfixedly; in a vague manner.

vĕr'-bal, *a.* Expressed in words.

wĭt'-ti-çĭṣm, *n.* A witty sentence or phrase.

wĕl'-eŏme, *v. t.* To salute with kindness.

LESSON 164.

DICTATION EXERCISE.

Never shall thy spoken word be again unsaid, unheard ;
Well their work thy lips have wrought, joy or grief or evil thought ;
Though it pierce a poisoned spear through the soul thou holdest dear,
Though it quiver, fierce and deep, through some stainless spirit's sleep,
Once for all the rune is read, once for all the judgment said ;
Offer life and soul and all that one sentence to recall,
Rue it all thy lingering days, hide it deep with love and praise,
All thy travail is in vain, spoken words come not again.—*Christian Union.*

LESSON 165.

MISCELLANEOUS.

Fasten your souls so high, that constantly
The smile of your heroic cheer may float
Above all floods of earthly agonies,
Purification being the joy of pain.—*E. B. Browning.*

sāfe'-ty, *n.* Free from hurt, injury or loss.

sa-lū'-brĭ-oŭs, *a.* Healthful.

seoûrġe (skûrj), *v. t.* To whip severely.

serụ'-ti-nize, *v. t.* To search closely.

sēareh'-a-ble, *a.* That can be searched.

sĕe'-ond-a-ry, *a.* Of second place.

sē'-ere-çy, *n.* Privacy.

sĕd'-i-ment, *n.* Settlings.

sĕs'-sion, *n.* The actual assembly of members of any body.

shiĕld, *v. t.* To protect.

sĭḡ-nĭf'-i-eant, *n.* Standing as a sign or token.

si'-lenҫe, *n.* Absolute stillness.

sin'-gu-lar, *a.* Odd; being alone.

si'-phon, *n.* A bent tube or pipe.

sit-ū-ā'-tion, *n.* Position.

slip'-per-y, *a.* Smooth; unstable.

slough (slou), *n.* A hole full of mire.

sō-bri-quet' (sō-bre-kā'), *n.* A nickname.

sŏl'-ū-ble, *a.* That can be dissolved.

sǫuve-nīr' (sōōv-nēer'), *n.* A keepsake.

LESSON 166.

WORDS DENOTING PRAISE.

His words are bonds, his oaths are oracles;
His love sincere, his thoughts immaculate,
His tears pure messengers sent from the heart;
His heart as far from fraud as heaven from earth.—*Shakespeare.*

ăd'-mi-ra-ble, *a.* Worthy of admiration.

ăd-mire', *v. t.* To regard with love or esteem.

a-dŏr'-a-ble, *a.* Worthy of adoration.

beaū'-ti-fṳl, *a.* Having the qualities which constitute beauty.

brĭll'-iant (brĭl'-yant), *a.* Distinguished by qualities which excite admiration.

eom-mĕn-dā'-tion, *n.* Praise.

eŏm'-pa-ra-ble, *a.* Worthy of comparison.

eŏm'-pli-ment, *n.* Delicate flattery; praise.

erĕd'-it-a-bly, *aav.* With credit; without disgrace.

de-șir'-a-ble, *a.* Worthy of desire, or longing.

ē'-go-tĭst, *n.* One who speaks much of himself, or magnifies his own achievements.

e-lăb'-o-rate, *a.* Finished with great care.

ĕm'-i-nenҫe, *n.* Exaltation; distinction.

ĕn-eō'-mi-ŭm, *n.* Formal praise.

ĕs'-ti-ma-ble, *a.* Worthy of regard.

eū'-lo-ḡize, *v. t.* To praise.

ĕx'-ҫel-lent, *a.* Very good.

ĕx'-em-pla-ry, *a.* Serving as a pattern: commendable.

ĕx'-qui-șite, *a.* Exceedingly nice.

ĕx-tŏl', *v. t.* To eulogize.

LESSON 167.

Words Denoting Praise.

Large was his bounty, and his soul sincere,
    Heaven did a recompense as largely send;
He gave to Misery all he had—a tear;
    He gained from Heaven ('twas all he wished)—a friend.—*Grey.*

fū'-moūs, *a.* Renowned.

fault'-less, *a.* Perfect.

fā'-vor-ite, *a.* Especial esteem or preference.

flăt'-ter-y, *n.* False praise.

ḡĕn'-ū-ine, *a.* Real; natural.

ḡŏr'-ḡeoūs (-jŭs), *a.* Magnificent.

ḡrănd'-eūr, *n.* Splendor of appearance.

hŏn'-or-a-ble (ŏn'-ur-), *a.* Worthy of being esteemed.

Il-lŭs'-tri-oŭs, *a.* Renowned; brilliant.

im-măe'-ū-late, *a.* Without blemish.

In-eŏm'-pa-ra-ble, *a.* Without equal.

lạud, *v. t.* To praise.

lū'-min-oŭs, *a.* Shining.

lŭs'-tre or lŭs'-ter, *n.* Splendor; brightness.

maḡ-nif'-i-çent, *a.* On a grand scale; splendid.

ma-jĕs'-tie, *a.* Of august dignity, stateliness or imposing grandeur; splendid.

mär'-tyr, *n.* One who makes a great sacrifice for the sake of principle.

mĕr-i-tō'-ri-oŭs, *a.* Worthy of honor.

nōt'-a-ble, *a.* Worthy of notice; remarkable.

pär'-a-ḡŏn, *n.* A model of excellence.

LESSON 168.

Words Denoting Praise.

He was the soul of goodness,
And all our praises of him are like streams
Drawn from a spring, that still rise full, and leave
The part remaining, greatest.—*Shakespeare.*

per-fĕc'-tion, *n.* The state of being perfect.

prāiṣe, *n.* Approval of merit.

prĕ'-cioŭs (prĕsh'-ŭs), *a.* Of great value.

pū'-ri-ty, *n.* Innocence.

quin-tĕs'-sençe, *n.* Pure or concentrated essence.

rā'-di-aṇt, *a.* Beaming with brightness.

re-märk'-a-ble, *a.* Uncommon; noticeable.

stĕr'-ling, *a.* Genuine; of excellent quality.

sub-lim'-i-ty, *n.* Being sublime; eminence.

sŭb-stän'-tial, *a.* True.

su-pĕrb', *a.* Grand; elegant.

su-pē-ri-ŏr'-i-ty, *n.* More excellent than any other.

tran-sçĕnd'-ent, *a.* Very excellent.

trŭst'-wor-thȳ (-wûr-), *a.* Worthy of confidence; trusty.

vĕn'-er-a-ble, *a.* Worthy of reverence.

ve-rā'-cioŭs, *a.* Truthful.

vĭg'-i-laṇt, *a.* Watchful; circumspect.

vĭrt'-ū-oŭs, *a.* Blameless; good.

wŏn'-droŭs, *a.* Admirable; astonishing.

wor'-thȳ (wûr-), *a.* Possessing merit.

LESSON 169.

DICTATION EXERCISE.

True to the promise of thy far-off youth,
   When all who loved thee, for thee prophesied
A grand, full life, devoted to the truth,
   A noble cause by suffering sanctified.
True to all beauties of the poet thought
   Which made thy youth so eloquent and sweet;
True to all duties which thy manhood brought
   To take the room of fancies light and fleet.
True to the steadfast walk and narrow way,
   Which thy forefathers of the covenant trod!
True to thy friend in foul or sunny day,
   True to thy home, thy country and thy God !—*All the Year Round.*

LESSON 170.

HOMOPHONOUS WORDS.

Better trust all and be deceived,
  And weep that trust and that deceiving,
Than doubt one heart that, if believed,
  Had blessed one's life with true believing.—*Frances A. Kemble.*

rōōd, *n.* The fourth of an acre.
rụde, *a.* Uncivil.

sāil, *v. i.* To move on the water by means of sails.
sāle, *n.* The transfer of property for money.

sēam, *n.* Two edges joined.
sēem, *v. i.* To appear.

sēa, *n.* A large body of water.
sēe, *v. t.* To perceive.

sērf, *n.* A slave.
sûrf, *n.* The swell of the sea which breaks upon the shore.

sērġe, *n.* A coarse cloth.
sûrġe, *v. i.* To rise high and roll, as waves.

sew (sō), *v. t.* To fasten together with needle and thread.
sōw, *v. t.* To scatter.

sīghs, *n.* Heavy breathing.
sīze, *n.* Bulk; magnitude.

skŭll, *n.* The part of the head which encloses the brain.
seŭll, *n.* A small, narrow boat.

sōle, *n.* The bottom of the foot; (*a.*) only.
sōul, *n.* The spiritual part of man.

LESSON 171.

PERTAINING TO RELIGION.

"Religion is the best armor in the world, but the worst cloak."

bĕn-e-dĭe'-tion, *n.* The short prayer which closes public worship.
blas-phēme', *v. t.* To speak with irreverence of God.
ea-thē'-dral, *n.* The head church in a diocese.
Eăth'-o-lĭe, *n.* An adherent of the Roman Catholic church.
ehris'-ten (krĭs'-n), *v. t.* To give a name, and baptize.
ehris'-tian (krĭst'-yan), *n.* One who professes to believe, or is assumed to believe, in the religion of Christ.
eŏm-mū'-ni-eant, *n.* A church member.
eŏn-gre-gā'-tion, *n.* An assembly of people for the worship of God.
eŏn'-se-erāte, *v. t.* To appropriate to sacred use.

ere-ā'-tion, *n.* The act of bringing the world into existence.
Ere-ā'-tor, *n.* The supreme being.
erų-çi-fĭx'-ion (-fĭx'-shŭn), *n.* The Savior's death upon the cross.
dĕe'-a-lŏgue, *n.* The ten commandments.
dĕd'-ĭ-eāte, *v. t.* To set apart and consecrate.
dĕs'-e-erāte, *v. t.* To divert from a sacred purpose.
dĕv-o-tēe', *n.* One wholly given to religion.
dī'-o-çēse, *n.* The district under a bishop's care.
dĭs-çī'-ple, *n.* A follower.
dŏx-ŏl'-o-ġy, *n.* A hymn of praise.
e-thē'-re-al, *a.* Celestial.

LESSON 172.

Pertaining to Religion.

Never trust anybody not of sound religion, for he that is false to God can never be true to man.—*Lord Burleigh.*

ē-văn'-ġel-ĭst, *n.* One authorized to preach, but who has no special charge.

Ġĕn'-e-sĭs, *n.* The first book in the Bible; formation.

hў-pŏc'-ri-sy, *n.* Feigning to be what one is not.

ĭm'-pi-oŭs, *a.* Not pious; wanting in veneration for God and His authority.

ĭn'-fi-del, *n.* One who does not believe in Christ.

mĭn'-ĭs-ter, *n.* The pastor of a church.

mĭs'-sion-a-ry (mĭsh'-un-), *n.* One who is sent to spread religion.

mŏn'-as-tĕr-y, *n.* A house of religious retirement for Monks.

ôr'-tho-dŏx, *a.* Sound in the Christian faith.

prâyer (prâr), *n.* An earnest supplication to God.

Prĕs-by-tē'-ri-an, *n.* One who belongs to a church governed by presbyters.

priĕst, *n.* One who performs the rites of sacrifice.

prŏt'-est-ant, *n.* A Christian who protests against the doctrines of the Church of Rome.

prŏv-i-dĕn'-tial, *a.* Proceeding from divine providence.

psälm'-ĭst (säm-), *n.* A writer of sacred songs.

re-lĭġ'-ioŭs, *a.* Pious; godly.

re-pĕnt'-ançe, *n.* Sorrow for what one has done or omitted to do.

rĕv'-er-ençe, *n.* Veneration; a title applied to priests and ministers.

Sĕript'-ūre, *n.* The Bible.

sŏl'-emn, *a.* Serious; sacred.

LESSON 173.

DICTATION EXERCISE.

"The Lord is my shepherd; I shall not want. He maketh me to lie down in green pastures; he leadeth me beside the still waters.

He restoreth my soul; he leadeth me in the paths of righteousness for his name's sake.

Yea, though I walk through the valley of the shadow of death, I will fear no evil; for thou art with me; thy rod and thy staff they comfort me.

Thou preparest a table before me in the presence of mine enemies; thou anointest my head with oil; my cup runneth over.

Surely goodness and mercy shall follow me all the days of my life; and I will dwell in the house of the Lord forever."—*Twenty-third Psalm.*

LESSON 174.

DENOTING MYSTERY.

As defect of strength in us makes some weights to be unmovable, so likewise defect of understanding makes some truths to be mysterious.—Bishop Sherlock.

ăp-pa-rĭ'-tion, *n.* A ghost; a preternatural appearance.

ĕn-chånt'-er, *n.* One who deals in spells or sorcery.

ĕx-traôr'-dĭ-na-ry, *a.* Uncommon; wonderful.

ğhōst, *n.* An apparition; the spirit.

ğŏb'-lin, *n.* An evil spirit.

ĭn-ĕx'-plĭ-ĕā-ble, *a.* Cannot be accounted for.

lĕğ-ẽr-de-māin', *n.* Sleight of hand.

ma-ğĭ'-cian, *n.* One skilled in magic.

mär'-vel-oŭs, *a.* Wonderful; astonishing.

mĭr'-a-cle, *n.* A wonder, or wonderful thing.

mĭ-räe'-û-loŭs, *a.* Performed supernaturally.

mys-tē'-rĭ-oŭs, *a.* Impossible to understand.

mys'-tĭe-al, *a.* Governed by mysterious laws.

mys'-tĭ-fȳ, *v. i.* To involve in mystery so as to mislead.

ŏm'-ĭ-noŭs, *a.* Containing an omen.

phe-nŏm'-e-nŏn, *n.* An appearance whose cause is not immediately obvious.

prŏph'-e-çȳ, *n.* A prediction.

prŏph'-e-sȳ, *v. t.* To predict.

sû-pẽr-nät'-û-ral, *a.* Miraculous.

sû-pẽr-stĭ'-tion, *n.* Fear of that which is unknown or mysterious.

LESSON 175.

MISCELLANEOUS.

Show me the man you honor; I know by that symptom better than by any other what kind of a man you are yourself; for you show me what your ideal of manhood is, what kind of a man you long to be.—Carlyle.

sŏp-o-rĭf'-ĭe, *a.* Causing sleep.

spē'-cial, *a.* Different from others.

spĕç'-ĭ-fȳ, *v. t.* To name as a particular thing.

spĕç'-ĭ-men, *n.* A sample.

splğ'-ot, *n.* A pin or peg used to stop a faucet.

splin'-ter, *n.* A thin piece of wood, or other solid substance, rent from the main body.

spŏnğe, *n.* A porous substance capable of imbibing a great quantity of water, found in Southern waters.

spon-tā'-ne-oŭs, *a.* Voluntary; willing.

spû'-rĭ-oŭs, *a.* Not genuine.

squēal, *v. i.* To cry with a sharp, shrill, prolonged sound.

squîrm, *v. i.* To move with writhing or contortions.

sta-bĭl'-ĭ-ty, *n.* Firmness; steadiness.

stăğ'-ğer, *v. t.* To cause to doubt and waver; to shock.

stāin'-less, *a.* Free from reproach or guilt; free from any stain.

stăm-pēde', *n.* A sudden flight in consequence of a panic.

stånch, *v. t.* To stop the flowing of; to extinguish.

stärt'-le, *n.* A sudden shock, caused by an unexpected alarm, surprise, or apprehension of danger.

stĕad'-ĭ-ness, *n.* Steadfastness; constancy.

stĕalth'-y, *a.* Secret; done by stealth.

strĕngth, *n.* Force; power.

LESSON 176.

PERTAINING TO DEATH.

When Death, the great reconciler, comes, it is not of our kindness we repent, but our severity.—*George Eliot.*

bu'-rĭ-al (bĕr'-rĭ-al), *n.* Funeral solemnity.

çĕm'-e-tĕr-y, *n.* Burial place.

eŏf'-fĭn, *n.* The case in which a dead body is buried.

eôrpse, *n.* The dead body of a human being.

eor-rŭpt'-ĭ-ble, *n.* That which may decay or perish ; the human body.

ere-mā'-tion, *n.* The burning of the dead.

dĭrġe, *n.* A funeral hymn.

ĕp'-ĭ-tăph (-tăf), *n.* Inscription on a monument.

fū'-ner-al, *n.* The ceremony of burying a dead human body.

ĭm-môr'-tal, *a.* Not mortal; lasting forever.

me-mō'-rĭ-al, *n.* Anything intended to preserve the memory of a person.

môrġue (môrġ), *n.* A place where the bodies of persons found dead are exposed that they may be claimed by their friends.

môr-tăl'-ĭ-ty, *n.* Subject to death.

o-bĭt'-ū-a-ry, *n.* Notice of the death of a person.

ŏb'-se-quie̮s, *n. pl.* Funeral solemnities.

pĕr-dĭ'-tion, *n.* Future misery or eternal death.

pûr'-ġa-to-ry, *n.* A place where, after death, one may expiate such offenses committed in this life as do not merit eternal damnation.

sĕr'-aph, *n.* An angel of the highest order.

spĭr'-it-ū-al, *a.* Not material; consisting of spirit.

ŭn-der-tāk'-er, *n.* One who takes charge of funerals.

LESSON 177.

DICTATION EXERCISE.

So live, that when thy summons comes to join
The innumerable caravan, that moves
To that mysterious realm, where each shall take
His chamber in the silent halls of death,
Thou go not, like the quarry-slave at night,
Scourged to his dungeon, but, sustained and soothed
By an unfaltering trust, approach thy grave,
Like one who wraps the drapery of his couch
About him, and lies down to pleasant dreams.

—*Wm. Cullen Bryant.*

LESSON 178.

SORROW.

Hearts, like apples, are hard and sour,
Till crushed by Pain's resistless power;
And yield their juices rich and bland
To none but Sorrow's heavy hand.—*Holland*

ăf-flĭe'-tion, *n.* A state of pain, distress or grief.

ăṇ'-guĭsh, *n.* Extreme pain.

dĕp'-re-eāte, *v. t.* To regret deeply.

dĕs'-o-late, *a.* Afflicted; left alone.

dĕs'-per-ate, *a.* Beyond hope.

de-spŏnd'-ent, *a.* Marked by despair.

dĕs'-ti-tūte, *n.* One without friends or comforts.

dĭs-ap-point'-ment, *n.* Defeat of hopes or expectations.

dĭs-ăs'-troŭs, *a.* Unfortunate.

dĭs-eŏn'-so-lāte, *v. t.* Without comfort.

dŏl'-or-oŭs, *a.* Sorrowful; full of grief.

grĭēv'-ançe, *n.* Cause of complaint or grief.

hu-mĭl-ĭ-ā'-tion, *a.* Abasement of pride; mortification.

in-fe-lĭç'-i-ty, *n.* Misery; unhappiness.

mĕl'-aṇ-ehŏl-y, *n.* Gloomy state of mind.

mĭs'-er-a-ble, *a.* Very unhappy.

môr-ti-fi-eā'-tion, *n.* Humiliation or chagrin.

mōurn'-fṳl, *a.* Full of sorrow.

ŏb-sen'-ri-ty, *n.* Darkness; gloom.

pĭt'-e-oŭs, *a.* Mournful; miserable.

LESSON 179.

FINISHED.

" Let me not leave my space of ground untilled;
Call me not hence with mission unfulfilled.
Let me not die before I've done for Thee
My earthly work, whatever that may be."

a-bŏl'-ĭsh, *v. t.* To put an end to.

ăe-eŏm'-plĭsh, *v. t.* To complete.

a-chĭēve', *v. t.* To accomplish.

eŏm-plē'-tion, *n.* Act of finishing.

eŏn-elū'-sive, *a.* Decisive.

eŏn'-sum-māte or eŏn-sŭm'-māte, *v. t.* To bring to completion.

eŭl'-mi-nāte, *v. i.* To reach the highest point.

de-mŏl'-ĭsh, *v. t.* To destroy.

e-vĕnt'-ū-al, *a.* Final; terminating.

ĕx-hạust', *v. t.* To consume entirely.

ĕx-pi-rā'-tion, *n.* Termination.

ĕx-tĕr'-mi-nāte, *v. t.* To destroy utterly.

ĕx-tĭṇet', *a.* Ended; having ceased.

ĕx'-tir-pāte or ĕx-tĭr'-pāte, *v. t.* To root out.

fi-nä'-le (fē-nä'-lā), *n.* The last note or end of a piece of music; close; termination.

frṳ-ĭ'-tion, *n.* Pleasure derived from possession.

fṳl-fĭll', *v. t.* To bring to pass.

qui-ē'-tus, *n.* That which silences; a final discharge.

tĕr-mi-nā'-tion, *n.* Conclusion.

ŭl'-ti-māte, *a.* Final; the last result.

HOMOPHONOUS WORDS.

He liveth long who liveth well!
All else is life but flung away;
He liveth longest who can tell
Of true things only done each day.—H. Bonar.

shoe, *n.* A covering for the foot.
shoo, *v. t.* To drive away.

shone or shone, *v. i.* Did shine.
shown, *v. t.* Caused to see.

shoot, *v. t.* To cause to be driven by force.
chute, *n.* A frame-work for sliding articles from a higher to a lower level.

sleight, *n.* Trick; artifice.
slight, *a.* Slender. (*v. t.*) Neglect.

some, *n.* A portion of.
sum, *n.* The whole amount.

son, *n.* A male child.
sun, *n.* The source of light.

sore, *a.* Painful; bruised.
soar, *v. i.* To fly aloft.

stare, *v. i.* To look with fixed eyes.
stair, *n.* A series of steps for ascent or descent.

steel, *n.* Refined iron.
steal, *v. t.* To take without right or leave.

suck'-er, *n.* A kind of fish.
succ'-cor, *n.* Help; assistance.

WORDS DENOTING JOY.

I sing as sings the bird on yonder branches swinging;
It is not that the song be heard, but for the joy of singing.
And yet if there chance by, or hap to linger nigh,
One who listens to my lay and goes bravely forth to meet the day,
With a heart less troubled, the joy of song is doubled.—Century.

ac-claim', *n.* A joyous shout of applause.
buoy'-ant, *a.* Cheerful; vivacious.
ec'-sta-sy, *n.* Enthusiastic delight.
en-thu'-si-asm, *n.* Ecstasy.
fe-lic'-i-ty, *n.* Being very happy.
grat'-i-fy, *v. t.* To give pleasure to.
grat'-i-tude, *n.* Thankfulness.
hal'-cy-on, *a.* Peaceful; undisturbed.
hi-lar'-i-ty, *n.* Mirth; gayety.
joe'-und, *a.* Merry; lively.
joy'-ous, *a.* Glad; gay.
ju'-bi-lant, *a.* Rejoicing; shouting for joy.

laugh'-ter (laf'-ter), *n.* Convulsive expression of mirth.
peace'-a-ble, *a.* Tranquil; quiet.
pleas'-ure, *n.* Agreeable sensations of emotion.
rapt'-ure, *n.* Extreme joy or pleasure.
re-joic'-ing, *n.* Occasion of joy or gladness.
sat-is-fac'-tion, *n.* Gratification of desire.
tri-umph'-ant, *n.* Rejoicing for victory.
vic-to'-ri-ous, *a.* Winning; triumphant.

LESSON 182.

PERTAINING TO HUMOR.

" Live for to-day ! To-morrow's light
Will bring to-morrow's cares to sight;
Go, sleep like the flowers at night
And Heaven will bless thy morn !"

ăb-sûrd', *a.* Ridiculous.

eär'-ĭ-ea-tūre, *v. t.* To ridiculously exaggerate.

eŏm'-ĭe-nl, *a.* Exciting mirth; droll.

de-ride', *v. t.* To turn to ridicule.

drŏll, *a.* Ludicrous from oddity.

fa-çẽ'-tious (-shŭs), *a.* Given to wit and good humor.

frŏl'-ĭe-sòme, *a.* Full of gayety and mirth.

gäy'-e-ty, *n.* Merry delight; state of being gay.

ĝrĭ-māçe', *n.* A made up face.

ĝro-tĕsque' (-tĕsk), *a.* Ludicrous.

hū'-mor-oŭs (or yŭ'-mur-), *a.* Exciting laughter.

jŏe'-ū-lar, *a.* Given to jesting.

lïugh'-a-ble, *a.* Fitted to excite laughter.

lĕv'-ĭ-ty, *n.* Lightness of temper or conduct.

lū'-dĭ-eroŭs, *a.* Laughable; comical.

mïrth'-fŭl, *a.* Full of mirth or merriment.

plāy'-fŭl-ness, *n.* The state of being playful.

rĭ-díe'-ū-loŭs, *a.* Laughable.

spŏrt'-ĭve, *a.* Gay; frolicsome; playful.

wäĝ'-gïsh, *a.* Roguish in sport or good humor.

LESSON 183.

PERTAINING TO THE THEATRE.

" This life a theatre we well may call,
        Where every actor must perform with art ;
    Or laugh it through, and make a farce of all,
    '   Or learn to bear with grace his tragic part."—*From the Greek.*

äet'-or, *n.* One who acts or performs.

ŭm-a-teŭr', *n.* Not a professional.

a-mūşe'-ment, *n.* Entertainment; recreation.

ạu'-dĭ-ençe, *n.* An assembly of hearers.

bŭr-lĕsque', *n.* A ludicrous representation.

çïr'-eus, *n.* An enclosed place for games, or feats of horsemanship.

eo-mē'-dĭ-an, *n.* An actor or player in comedy.

eŏm'-e-dy, *n.* A dramatic composition of a light and amusing character.

drä'-mä or drä'-mä, *n.* A composition designed to be represented on the stage by several characters.

eŋ-eōre' (ŏŋg-kōr'), *adv.* Once more.

färçe, *n.* A low style comedy.

mïn'-strel-sy, *n.* A collective body of minstrels; singers and musicians.

mu-şē'-um, *n.* A repository for curiosities.

pän'-to-mime, *n.* A theatrical entertainment given in dumb show.

pär-quet' (-kä or -kĕt), *n.* The body of seats on the floor of a theatre nearest the orchestra.

pẽr-fôrm'-ançe, *n.* An exhibition.

täb-lean' (-lō), *n.* A representation of some scene by persons grouped in the proper manner.

thĕ'-a-ter,} *n.* A house for the exhibi-
thĕ'-a-tre,} tion of dramatic performances.

tra-ġē'-di-an, *n.* A tragic actor.

träġ'-e-dy, *n.* A dramatic poem performed by illustrious persons, and generally having a fatal issue.

LESSON 184.

PERTAINING TO FESTIVITY.

Pleasures are like poppies spread,
You seize the flower, its bloom is shed;
Or like the snow flakes on the river,
A moment white, then gone forever.—*Burns.*

ăn-nĭ-vẽr'-sa-ry, *n.* A day on which an event is celebrated annually.

băṇ'-quet (bänk'-wet), *n.* A rich entertainment; a feast.

bär'-be-cūe, *n.* A large animal roasted whole.

bĭrth'-däy, *n.* The anniversary of one's birth.

eär'-ni-val, *n.* A festival of merriment and revelry.

çel-e-brā'-tion, *n.* Honor bestowed by public ceremonies.

çĕn-tĕn'-ni-al, *a.* The hundredth anniversary.

çẽr'-e-mo-ny, *n.* Outward rite.

Chrĭst'-mas, *n.* The festival of the Christian church, observed annually on December 25th, in memory of the birth of Christ.

eŏr-o-nā'-tion, *n.* The act of crowning a sovereign.

fĕs-tĭv'-ĭ-ty, *n.* Gayety; joyfulness.

hŏl'-ĭ-däy, *n.* A day set apart in commemoration of some event.

ĭl-lū-mi-nā'-tion, *n.* Festive decorations of houses or buildings with lights.

jŏl-li-fĭ-cā'-tion, *n.* Noisy festivity and merriment.

jū'-bi-lee, *n.* A season of great joy.

ŏs-ten-tā'-tion, *n.* Pretentious parade; unnecessary display or show.

pàġ'-eant-ry, *n.* Pompous exhibition or display.

pro-çĕs'-sion, *n.* Regular, ceremonious progress.

rĕe-re-ā'-tion, *n.* Entertainment; amusement.

rĕv'-el-ry, *n.* Noisy festivity.

LESSON 185.

DICTATION EXERCISE.

Ring, joyous chords! ring out again!
A swifter still, and a wilder strain!
They are here, the fair face and the careless heart,
And stars shall wane ere the mirthful part.

But I meet a dimly mournful glance,
In a sudden turn of the flying dance;
I heard the tone of a heavy sigh
In a pause of the thrilling melody!
And it is not well that woe should breathe
On the bright spring flowers of the festal wreath!
Ye that to thought or to grief belong,
Leave, leave the hall of song!—*Mrs. Hemans.*

LESSON 186.

MISCELLANEOUS.

"Get into the habit of looking for the silver lining of the clouds, rather than at the leaden gray in the middle. It will help you over many hard places."

sŭb·serĭp′-tion, *n.* To give consent by writing the name.

sŭb-sĭst′-en̦çe, *n.* Means of support.

sŭf′-fo-eāte, *v. t.* To stifle; to smother.

sūit′-a-ble, *a.* Proper; becoming.

sŭre (shūr), *adv.* Without doubt; certainly.

sûr-vey′, *v. t.* To examine.

sy̆m′-bol, *n.* A significant character or letter.

sy̆m-mĕt′-rie-al, *a.* Having parts in due proportion.

sy̆s-tem-ăt′-ie, *a.* According to regular method.

te-nā′-ciou̯s, *a.* Holding fast.

tĕnd′-en-çy, *n.* Drift; direction towards an object.

tĕn′-sion, *n.* The act of stretching or straining.

tĕp′-id, *a.* Moderately warm.

tĕr-rĕs′-tri-al, *a.* Earthly.

tĕr′-ri-ble, *a.* Dreadful.

tĕr-rĭf′-ie, *a.* Causing terror.

thĭrst′-y, *a.* Suffering from thirst.

thŏr′-ough, *a.* Complete; perfect.

tou̯gh (tŭf), *a.* Strong; able to endure hardship.

trĕaeh′-er-ou̯s, *a.* Faithless; false.

LESSON 187.

PERTAINING TO FLOWERS

Life evermore is fed by death,
In earth, and sea and sky;
And that a rose may breathe its breath,
Something must die.—*Holland.*

a-ly̆s′-sum, *n.* A plant belonging to the mustard family, bearing small, white, sweet-scented flowers.

a-nĕm′-o-ne, *n.* Called wind flower, as its leaves are so easily stripped off by the wind.

ar′-bu-tus, *n.* A pale pink flower, found early in spring.

a-zā′-le-a, *n.* A flowering plant.

bou̯-quet′ (bōō-kā′), *n.* A nosegay.

eā′-ly̆x, *n.* The leaf-like envelope of a flower.

eär-nā′-tion, *n.* A species of clove pink.

ehry̆s-ăn′-the-mŭm, *n.* A kind of flower, of many species.

e-lĕm′-a-tĭs, *n.* A climbing plant, with flower.

çy̆′-press, *n.* A flowering vine.

dăf′-fo-dĭl, *n.* A plant with a yellow flower.

dăh'-lià (däl'-yá or dāl'-yä), *n.* A large and beautiful flower.

dän'-de-li-on, *n.* A plant with a yellow flower, and leaves the shape of a lion's tooth.

ĕg'-lan-tine (or -tĭn), *n.* The sweet briar; a species of rose.

fleųr-de-lĭs' (flųr-de-lē'), *n.* A flower of the lily family.

flō'-rĭst, *n.* One who cultivates flowers.

frā'-grant, *a.* Sweet of smell.

fūch'-si-à (fōōk'-sĭ-à), *n.* A flowering plant.

ģe-rā'-ni-ŭm, *n.* A plant and flower.

hē'-li-o-trōpe, *n.* A very fragrant flower.

LESSON 188.

Pertaining to Flowers.

" Leaves have their time to fall,
And flowers to wither at the north wind's breath."

hȳ'-a-çĭnth, *n.* A bulbous plant bearing beautiful spikes of fragrant flowers.

hȳ-drän'-ģe-à, *n.* A plant bearing large heads of showy flowers of a rose color naturally.

ja-pŏn'-i-eä, *n.* A species of camellia bearing beautiful red or white flowers.

jäs'-mine or jäs'-mine, *n.* A climbing plant bearing flowers of a peculiarly fragrant odor.

lĭl'-ȳ, *a.* A beautiful and fragrant flower.

mär'-i-gōld, *n.* A plant bearing yellow flowers.

mign-on-ĕtte' (mĭn-yon-ĕt'), *n.* An annual flowering plant having a delicate odor.

när-çĭs-sus, *n.* A flowering plant with bulbous root.

nas-tûr'-tium, *n.* A climbing plant with yellow flowers.

ō'-dor-oŭs, *n.* Having a sweet odor.

ôr'-chid (ôr'-kĭd), *n.* A species of orchis.

pē'-o-ny, *n.* A large, beautiful, showy flower.

pĕr'-fūme, *n.* Fragrance.

pĕt'-al or pē'-tal, *n.* One of the colored leaves of a flower.

phlŏx (flŏks), *n.* An American flowering plant, having red, white or purple flowers.

rhō-do-dĕn'-dron, *n.* A plant with handsome evergreen leaves and beautiful rose-colored or purple flowers.

sy-rĭṇ'-gä', *n.* A kind of shrub with sweet-scented white flowers.

thĭs'-tle (thĭs'-sl), *n.* A prickly plant with pink or lavender flowers.

vä'-ri-e-gäte, *v. t.* To mark with different colors.

vẽr-bē'-nà, *n.* A beautiful flower.

LESSON 189.

DICTATION EXERCISE.

I cannot despise the cold man of science, who walks with his eyes
All alert through a garden of flowers, and strips
The lilies' gold tongues, and the roses' red lips,
With a ruthless dissection ; since he, I suppose,
Has some purpose beyond the mere mischief he does.

But the stupid and mischievous boy, that uproots
The exotics, and tramples the tender young shoots
For a boy's brutal pastime, and only because
He knows no distinction between heartsease and haws,—
One would wish, for the sake of each blossom so nipped,
To catch the young rascal and have him well whipped.—*Owen Meredith.*

LESSON 190.

COLOR.

"When death's shadows my bosom uncloud,
When I shrink from the thought of the coffin and shroud,
May hope, like the rainbow, my spirit unfold
In her beautiful pinions of purple and gold."

ăz'-ure, *n.* The blue color of the sky.

eür'-mine, *n.* A rich red or crimson color.

eŏl'-or, *n.* Any hue or tint as distinguished from white.

erĭm'-şon, *n.* A deep red color.

ģrãy, *n.* Any mixture of white and black.

lăv'-en-der, *n.* A grayish blue color.

ma-ģĕn'-tà, *n.* A red or crimson color, derived from aniline.

ma-rōōn', *n.* A brownish crimson, or claret color.

mauve (mōv), *n.* A delicate and beautiful purple or lilac.

măz-a-rīne', *n.* A deep blue color.

ō'-eher, **ō'-ehre,** *n.* Pale yellow.

ŏl'-ĭve, *n.* A dark brownish green color.

ŏr'-ange, *n.* Golden yellow.

pûr'-ple, *n.* A color composed of red and blue, much esteemed for its richness and beauty.

sĭ-ĕn'-nà, *n.* A brownish yellow color.

ŭm'-ber, *n.* A blackish brown color.

vērd'-ūre, *n.* Greenness.

vēr-mĭl'-ion (-yun), *n.* A beautiful red color.

vī'-o-lĕt, *n.* Dark blue, inclining to red.

yĕl'-lōw, *n.* A bright, golden color, reflecting the most light of any, after white.

LESSON 191.

TREES.

Mouldering and moss-grown, through the lapse of years, in motionless beauty stands the giant oak, whilst those that saw its green and flourishing youth are gone and are forgotten.—*Longfellow.*

är'-bor vī'-tæ, *n.* An evergreen tree.

äsp'-en, *n.* A species of poplar, whose leaves tremble with the slightest impulse of the wind.

bĭrch, *n.* A tree of several species.

bŭt'-ter-nŭt, *n.* An American tree and its fruit.

ea-tăl'-pà, *n.* A tree having large leaves and white flowers.

çē'-dar, *n.* An evergreen tree.

chĕst'-nŭt (chĕs'-), *n.* A tree, with fruit enclosed in a prickly bur.

eō'-eōa (kō'-kō), *n.* A palm, producing the cocoanut.

ĕb'-on-y, *n.* A wood from Madagascar and Ceylon, which admits of a fine polish; the usual color is black.

ĕlm, *n.* A tree much used in America for shade.

fō'-li-age, *n.* A collection of leaves arranged by nature.

hĭek'-o-ry, *n.* An American tree.

măġ-nō'-li-å, *n.* A tree having large, fragrant flowers, found in the southern parts of the United States.

ma-hŏġ'-a-ny, *n.* A large tree found in tropical America.

păl-mĕt'-to, *n.* A species of palm, growing in the West Indies and southern United States.

pĕr-sĭm'-mon, *n.* An American tree, with fruit like a plum.

săs'-sa-frăs, *n.* A tree whose bark has an aromatic smell and taste.

sȳe'-a-môre, *n.* A large tree found in Egypt and Syria, and is the sycamore of Scripture; in America the button-wood tree is called by this name.

wąl'-nŭt, *n.* A tree, of which there are several species, and its fruit.

wĭl'-lōw, *n.* A tree with slender, pliant branches.

LESSON 192.

HOMOPHONOUS WORDS.

'Tis a very good world that we live in,
To lend, to spend, or to give in ;
But to beg or to borrow, or to get a man's own,
'Tis the very worst world that ever was known.—*Bulwer Lytton.*

stāke, *v. t.* To wager ; (*n.*) A post.
steāk, *n.* A slice of meat.

stile, *n.* Steps over a fence.
stȳle, *n.* Fashion ; manner.

strāit, *n.* A narrow passage of water between two larger bodies of water.
strāight, *a.* Not crooked.

swēet, *a.* Agreeable.
suīte (swēet), *n.* A series; a collection.

tăcks, *n.* Small nails.
tăx, *n.* Tribute to the government.

tēar, *n.* A drop of water from the eye.
tiĕr, *n.* A row.

teâr, *v. t.* To rend.
târe, *n.* A weed; deduction from freight.

tēam, *n.* Two or more horses.
tēem, *v. i.* To be full; to abound.

thrōne, *n.* A chair of state.
thrōwn, *v. t.* Past of throw.

tŏll, *n.* Tax on the highway.
tōle, *v. t.* To cause to follow.

LESSON 193.

ANIMALS.

The motives of conscience, as connected with repentance and the feeling of duty, are the most important differences which separate man from the animal.—*Darwin.*

ăl'-li-gā-tor, *n.* A large reptile living in water or on land.

câr'-cass, *n.* The dead body of an animal.

cha-mē'-le-on, *n.* A lizard-like reptile, whose color changes more or less with the color of the objects about it.

çhăm'-ois (shăm'-mȳ), *n.* A species of antelope living on the highest peaks in Europe.

crŏc'-o-dile, *n.* A large reptile.

drŏm'-e-da-ry, *n.* A camel, with one hump.

ĕl'-e-phant, *n.* One of the largest quadrupeds now in existence.

fawn, *n.* A young deer.

fẽr'-ret, *n.* An animal of the weasel kind.

ġi-räffe', *n.* An African quadruped with short hind legs, long fore legs and long neck.

ġo-ril'-lă, *n.* A large African monkey.

hip-po-pŏt'-a-mŭs, *n.* A large quadruped, native of Africa.

hȳ-ē'-nă, *n.* A wild animal with a bristly mane like a hog; it feeds upon carrion.

kăn-ga-rōō', *n.* An Australian quadruped.

lĕop'-ard, *n.* A yellow or fawn-colored animal with black spots along the back and sides.

men-ăġ'-e-rie (-äzh-), *n.* A place where animals are kept and trained.

mŏnk'-eẏ, *n.* A species of ape.

pôr'-eu-pine, *n.* An animal covered with quills with sharp prickies.

quad'-rn-ped, *n.* Having four feet.

rhi-nŏç'-e-rŏs, *n.* A large and powerful quadruped nearly allied to the elephant.

LESSON 194.

BIRDS.

"What though thy seed should fall by the wayside
And the birds snatch it—yet the birds are fed;
Or they may bear it far across the tide,
To give rich harvest after thou art dead."

bŏb'-o-link, *n.* An American singing bird.

ea-nā'-ry, *n.* A species of singing bird.

eŏek-a-tōō', *n.* A bird of the parrot kind.

eôr'-mo-rant, *n.* A sea raven.

euek'-ōō, *n.* A bird that derives its name from its song.

ēa'-ġle, *n.* A rapacious bird of the falcon family, very large and strong.

fla-min'-ġo, *n.* A bird having long legs and neck.

gŏld'-finch, *n.* A beautiful singing bird, so named for the color of its wings.

hŭm'-ming-bird, *n.* A very small bird, remarkable for the brilliancy of its plumage.

jäek'-daw, *n.* A bird allied to the crows; it is black, with a blue or metallic reflection.

night'-in-ġale, *n.* A small bird that sings at night.

ō'-ri-ōle, *n.* A singing bird having plumage of a golden yellow, mixed with black.

ŏs'-trich, *n.* A large bird, nearly ten feet high, with long plumes instead of feathers; it can surpass horses in speed.

păr'-o-quĕt, *n.* A small bird found in tropical countries.

păr'-rot, *n.* A bird having brilliant plumage, and celebrated for its powers of mimicry.

pĕl'-i-ean, *n.* A web-footed water fowl, larger than a swan, and remarkable for its enormous bill, to the lower edge of which is attached a pouch that will hold many quarts of water.

pĕn'-ġuin, *n.* A web-footed marine bird; it is unable to fly, but swims and dives well; it is found only in the south temperate and frigid regions.

rŏb'-in, *n.*   An American singing bird, having a breast of a somewhat dingy orange red color.

serēech'-owl, *n.*   An owl that utters a harsh cry at night.

wrĕn, *n.*   A small bird.

LESSON 195.

INSECTS.

Not a worm is cloven in vain,
Not a moth with vain desire,
Is shriveled in a fruitless fire,
But subserves another's gain.— *Tennyson.*

bēe'-tle, *n.*   An insect having four wings, the outer pair being stiff cases for covering the others when folded.

bŭt'-ter-flȳ, *n.*   An insect of different species, so called from the color of a yellow species.

eăt'-er-pĭl-lar, *n.*   The worm state of a moth or butterfly.

çĕn'-ti-pĕd (also çĕn'-ti-pēde), *n.*   A many-jointed, wingless insect having many feet.

ehrȳs'-a-lis (krĭs-), *n.*   The form into which the butterfly passes, and from which the perfect insect emerges.

eŏek'-rōach, *n.*   An insect with a long body and flat wings; is very troublesome, infecting houses and ships.

eo-eōōn', *n.*   The oblong case of a silkworm, in which it lies in its chrysalis state.

erĭek'-et, *n.*   An insect with a chirping note.

drăḡ'-on-flȳ, *n.*   An insect having a large head, wings and eyes, and a long body.

glōw'-worm, *n.*   An insect emitting a green light. *

gnăt (năt), *n.*   A small, troublesome insect having lancet-like stings.

grâss'-hŏp-per, *n.*   A jumping insect.

hôr'-net, *n.*   A large, strong wasp of a dark brown and yellow color.

kū'-ty-dĭd, *n.*   An insect of a pale green color, closely allied to the grasshopper.

lō'-eust, *n.*   A jumping insect of the species of the grasshopper.

môs-quī'-to, *n.*   A small insect having a sharp pointed proboscis, by means of which it punctures the skin of animals causing a considerable degree of pain.

sĭlk'-worm, *n.*   The caterpillar which produces silk.

spī'-der, *n.*   An insect remarkable for spinning webs for taking its prey, forming its habitation and holding its food.

ta-răn'-tu-lå, *n.*   A species of spider.

whĭrl'-i-ḡĭg, *n.*   An insect that lives on the surface of the water and moves about with great celerity.

LESSON 196.

DICTATION EXERCISE.

Rubbing her shoulder with rosy palm,
    As the loathsome touch yet seemed to thrill her,
My little girl cried, "I found on my arm
    A horrible, crawling caterpillar!"

And with mischievous smile she could scarcely smother,
  Yet a glance in its daring, half awed and shy,
She added, " While they were about it, mother,
  I wish they'd just finished the butterfly ! "

Ah, look thou largely, with lenient eyes,
  On whatso beside thee may creep or cling,
For the possible glory that underlies
  The passing phase of the meanest thing !

What if God's great angels, whose waiting love
  Beholdeth our pitiful life below
From the holy height of their heaven above,
  Couldn't bear with the worm till the wings should grow.
                 —*Mrs. Whitney.*

LESSON 197.

HOMOPHONOUS WORDS.

I count this thing to be grandly true:
  That a noble deed is a step toward God,
  Lifting the soul from the common sod
  To a purer air and a broader view.—*Holland.*

thêir, *pron.* Belonging to them.
thêre, *adv.* In that place.

thÿme (tim), *n.* A fragrant plant.
time, *n.* Duration.

tìde, *n.* Rise and fall of the sea.
tïed, *a.* Fastened.

tŏŏ, *adv.* Excessively.
tǫ, *prep.* Toward.
twǫ, *a.* Twice one.

tŭn, *n.* A liquid measure.
tŏn, *n.* A weight of 2,000 pounds.

vāle, *n.* A valley.
vçil, *n.* A cover for the face.

vāin, *a.* Proud; fond of praise.
vēin, *n.* A vessel that conveys the blood back to the heart.
vāne, *n.* A weathercock.

vī'-al, *n.* A small bottle.
vī'-ol, *n.* A musical instrument.

vïçe, *n.* A moral fault.
vïse, *n.* An instrument for holding things, closed by a screw.

LESSON 198.

DENOTING SIZE.

" It is not growing like a tree
  In bulk, doth make man better be;
  Nor standing long, to fall at last, dry, bald and sere ;
  In small proportions we most beauty see,
  And in short measures life may perfect be."

bŭlk'-i-ness, *n.* Greatness in size.
ço-lŏs'-sal, *a.* Gigantic.
çôr'-pu-lent, *a.* An excessive quantity of flesh.

çŭm'-broŭs, *a.* Burdensome.
e-nôr'-moŭs, *a.* Great beyond the common measure.
ex-tĕn'-sïve-ly, *adv.* To a great extent; widely.

ġi-ġän'-tĭe, *a.* Very large.

hĕr-eū'-le-an, *a.* Having great strength or size.

hūġe'-ness, *n.* Enormous bulk or largeness.

ĭm-mĕaṣ'-ur-a-ble, *a.* That cannot be measured.

ĭm-mĕn'-sĭ-ty, *n.* Vast in extent or bulk.

lĭll-ĭ-pū'-tian, *a.* Diminutive; very small size.

măġ'-nĭ-fȳ, *v. t.* To enlarge.

măġ'-nĭ-tūde, *n.* Bulk; size.

mŭl'-tĭ-tūde, *n.* A crowd; a great number of persons.

mŭs'-en-lar, *a.* Having well-developed muscles; brawny.

spā'-ciŏŭs, *a.* Vast in extent.

stu-pĕn'-doŭs, *a.* Astonishing magnitude or elevation.

tī'-ny, *a.* Very small.

tre-mĕn'-doŭs, *a.* That which astonishes by its magnitude, force or violence.

LESSON 199.

PRECIOUS STONES.

Full many a gem of purest ray serene,
The dark, unfathomed caves of ocean bear;
Full many a flower is born to blush unseen,
And waste its sweetness on the desert air.—*Grey.*

ăm'-e-thȳst, *n.* A precious stone of a bluish violet color.

bĕr'-yl, *n.* A bluish green mineral of great hardness, and when clear, of great beauty.

eăr'-bŭn-ele, *n.* A beautiful gem of a deep red color.

eăr-nēl'-ian (-yan), *n.* A variety of chalcedony, of a deep red, flesh red, or reddish white color.

ehăl-çĕd'-o-ny or ehăl'-ee-do-ny, *n.* A kind of quartz, usually of a whitish color, and a luster nearly like wax.

ehrȳs'-o-līte, *n.* A mineral, varying in color from pale green to bottle green.

erȳs'-tal, *a.* Clear; transparent.

dī'-a-mónd, *n.* A gem, remarkable for its hardness and brilliancy.

ĕm'-er-ald, *n.* A precious stone of a rich green color.

ġăr'-net, *n.* A mineral of a deep red color.

jäs'-per, *n.* An impure variety of quartz, of a dull red or yellow color.

ō'-nyx, *n.* Chalcedony, consisting of parallel layers of different shades of colors, and used for making cameos.

ō'-pal, *n.* A precious stone, consisting of silex in what is called a soluble state, and a small quantity of water.

pĕarl, *n.* A bluish white, smooth, lustrous jewel.

rŭ'-by, *n.* A precious stone of a carmine red color.

săp'-phire (săf'-ir), *n.* Pure crystallized alumina, next in hardness to a diamond.

sär'-dĭ-ŭs, *n.* A precious stone, probably a carnelian.

sär'-do-nȳx, *n.* A gem of reddish yellow, or nearly orange color.

tō'-paz, *n.* A gem, generally yellow and pellucid.

tûr-quoiṣ' (-koiz' or -keez'), *n.* A mineral of a bluish green color, brought from Persia.

LESSON 200.

DICTATION EXERCISE.

Thus it is over all the earth ! That which we call the fairest,
And prize for its surpassing worth, is always rarest.
Iron is heaped in mountain piles and gluts the laggard forges;
But gold-flakes gleam in dim defiles and lonely gorges.
The snowy marble flecks the land with heaped and rounded ledges,
But diamonds hide within the sand their starry edges.
Were every hill a precious mine, and golden all the mountains;
Were all the rivers fed with wine by tireless fountains;
Life would be ravished of its zest and shorn of its ambition,
And sink into the dreamless rest of inanition.—*Holland.*

LESSON 201.

DENOTING QUANTITY.

True worth is in being, not seeming—
In doing each day that goes by
Some little good—not in dreaming
Of great things to do by and by.—*Alice Carey.*

a-bŭn'-dançe, *n.*   Great plenty.
ăm'-ple, *a.*   Fully sufficient.
eŏm'-pe-ten-çy, *n.*   Sufficiency.
eŏn-sĭd'-er-a-ble, *a.*   Moderately large.
eō'-pĭ-oŭs, *a.*   Plentiful; abundant.
dēarth, *n.*   Want; famine.
ē-noŭgh' (ē-nŭf'), *n.*   A sufficiency.
ĕx-ū'-ber-ant, *a.*   Over-abundant; superfluous.
făm'-ĭne, *n.*   General scarcity of food.
frụit'-fụl, *a.*   Plenteous; productive.
ĭn-ăd'-e-quate, *a.*   Unequal; insufficient to effect the object.
lŭx-ū'-rĭ-ançe, *n.*   Over-abundant.

mēa'-ger,⎫ *a.*   Scanty.
mēa'-gre,⎭
plĕn'-te-oŭs, *a.*   Abundant.
re-dŭn'-dant, *a.*   Exceeding what is necessary.
seănt'-y, *a.*   Hardly sufficient; not ample.
seâr'-çĭ-ty, *n.*   Smallness of quantity.
sŭf-fĭ'-cient (fĭsh'-ent), *a.*   Equal to wants.
su-pêr'-flu-oŭs, *a.*   More than is wanted; excessive.
sûr'-plus, *n.*   An excess beyond what is wanted.

LESSON 202.

HOMOPHONOUS WORDS.

All are architects of Fate, working in these walls of time ;
Some with massive deeds and great, some with ornaments of rhyme.
Nothing useless is, or low, each thing in its place is best,
And what seems but idle show strengthens and supports the rest.—*Longfellow.*

wăste, *v. t.*   To destroy.
wāïst, *n.*   Small part of the body above the hips.

wāde, *v. i.*   To walk in mud or water.
weighed, *v. t.*   Estimated heaviness.

wāït, *v. i.*   To delay.
weight, *n.*   Pressure downwards.

wāve, *n.*   The advancing swell on the surface of a liquid.
wāïve, *v. t.*   To relinquish.

wâre, *n.* Articles of merchandise.

weâr, *v. t.* To consume by use.

wĕek, *n.* Seven days.

wĕak, *a.* Wanting strength.

wrăp, *v. t.* To enfold.

răp, *n.* A blow; (*v. t.*) to strike.

wrōte, *v. t.* Did write.

rōte, *n.* Mere repetition, without attention to the meaning.

wrĭng, *v. t.* To twist.

rĭng, *n.* A circle; (*v. t.*) to resound.

yōke, *n.* That which connects or binds.

yōlk (yōk), *n.* Part of an egg.

LESSON 203.

WORDS REQUIRING CAREFUL DISCRIMINATION.

" Don't brood o'er care—the trouble that you make
Is always worse to bear, and hard to shake :
Smile at the world ; the sorrow that is sent,
Take it, with patience, as your punishment.
He wins who laughs."

ae-çĕpt', *v. t.* To receive with favor.

ex-çĕpt', *v. t.* To leave out.

ăets, *n. pl.* Deeds.

ăx, *n.* A tool for chopping.

af-fĕet', *v. t.* To operate on.

ef-fĕet', *n.* Result.

ălms, *n.* Gifts of charity.

ärms, *n.* Weapons ; limbs.

är'-rant, *a.* Very bad ; wicked.

ĕr'-rand, *n.* A commission.

ĕr'-rant, *a.* Wandering ; wild.

băl'-lad, *n.* A popular song.

băl'-lot, *n.* The ticket cast.

băl'-let (băl'-lā), *n.* A theatrical dance.

băr'-on, *n.* A title of nobility in England.

băr'-ren, *a.* Unproductive ; sterile.

bâred, *v. t.* Made bare.

bĕard, *n.* Hair on the chin.

bĭle, *n.* Secretions of the liver.

boĭl, *n.* A tumor; (*v. t.*) to seethe.

LESSON 204.

Words Requiring Careful Discrimination.

' Perish policy and cunning ;
Perish all that fears the light ;
Whether losing, whether winning,
Trust in God and do the right."

bŏd'-Içe, *n.* A kind of quilted waistcoat with stays, for women.

bŏd'-ies, *n.* Plural of body.

boy, *n.* A male child.

buoy, *n.* A floating cask.

brän, *n.* Coarse part of grain.

brănd, *n.* A mark made by a hot iron.

bŭrst, *v. t.* To break open by force.

bŭst, *n.* A piece of statuary.

eăm, *n.* A part of a machine.

eälm, *a.* Quiet.

eär'-ol, *n.* A song of joy.

eŏr'-al, *n.* Insects and their shells found in the sea, composed almost purely of carbonate of lime.

eâst'-er, *n.* A small wheel on which furniture is rolled.

eäs'-tor, *n.* A substance of a strong smell and bitter taste.

chänçe, *n.* An event happening without any assigned cause.

ehänts, *v. t.* Singing.

elō̧se, *v. t.* To shut.

elōthȩs, *n.* Garments.

eŏn'-fi-dent, *a.* Bold; positive.

eŏn-fi-dänt', *n.* A confidential or bosom friend.

LESSON 205.

Words Requiring Careful Discrimination.

> Virtuous and vicious every man must be,
> Few in the extreme, but all in the degree;
> The rogue and fool by fits is fair and wise;
> And even the best, by fits, what they despise.—*Pope.*

eätch, *v. t.* To seize; to lay hold of.

kĕtch, *n.* A kind of boat.

dĕf'-er-ençe, *n.* Respect for others.

dif'-fer-ençe, *n.* Disagreement; mark of distinction.

dĕnse, *a.* Close; compact.

dĕnts, *n.* Marks; small hollows.

de-sçĕnt', *n.* A coming down.

dis-sĕnt', *n.* Difference of opinion.

de-s̄ĕrt', *n.* Merit; worth.

dḝs-s̄ĕrt', *n.* The last course at the table; pastry, fruits and sweet meats.

de-vi̧se', *v. t.* To contrive; to bequeath.

de-viçe', *n.* Trick.

di'-veŗs, *a.* Several; various.

di-vẽrse', *adv.* In different directions.

ĕm'-i-nent, *a.* Exalted in rank.

ĭm'-mi-nent, *a.* Threatening evil.

e-rŭp'-tion, *n.* Breaking forth.

ir-rŭp'-tion, *n.* Bursting in.

e-mẽrġe', *v. i.* To rise out of a fluid.

im-mẽrġe', *v. t.* To plunge into a fluid.

LESSON 206.

Words Requiring Careful Discrimination.

" He who never changed any of his opinions never corrected any of his mistakes; and he who was never wise enough to find out any mistakes in himself, will not be charitable enough to excuse what he reckons mistakes in others."

fạlse, *a.* Untrue.

fạults, *n.* Errors.

fä'-ther, *n.* Male parent.

fär'-ther, *adv.* More remotely; beyond.

fär, *a.* Distant.

fûr, *n.* Short, thick hair.

fĕll'-er, *n.* One who fells or knocks down.

fĕl'-lōw, *n.* An individual.

fīrst, *a.* Foremost; earliest.

fũst, *n.* Mustiness.

fĭsh'-er, *n.* One who catches fish.

fĭs'-sure (fĭsh'-ụr), *n.* A cleft; a chasm.

fôrm'-al-ly, *adv.* With ceremony.

fôr'-mer-ly, *adv.* In earlier time.

gänt'-let, *n.* A military punishment.

gäunt'-let, *n.* An iron glove.

hăl'-lōw, *v. t.* To keep sacred.

hŏl'-lōw, *n.* A low place.

hä'-lō, *n.* A circle of light.

hŭl-lōō', *n.* A shout; a call.

LESSON 207.

Words Requiring Careful Discrimination.

"There is no greater obstacle in the way of success in life, than trusting for something to turn up, instead of going to work and turning up something."

hăsh, *n.* Minced meat and vegetables.
hărsh, *a.* Austere; abusive.

hŭff, *n.* A swell of anger or pride.
hŏŏf, *n.* Hard part of an animal's foot.

jĕst, *n.* A joke.
jŭst, *a.* Upright; honest.

lēast, *a.* The smallest.
lĕst, *conj.* For fear that.

lĕav'-en, *n.* Yeast.
e-lĕv'-en, *n.* One more than ten.

lie, *v. i.* To rest on a bed or couch.
lāy, *v. t.* To put down.

light'-nĭng, *n.* A flash in the clouds, of electric light.

light'-en-ĭng, *v. t.* Making lighter.

line, *n.* A slender chord.
loin, *n.* A part of the body.

lĭn'-i-ment, *n.* A soft or liquid ointment.

lĭn'-e-a-ment, *n.* Outline; feature.

lŏŏse, *v. t.* To untie, or unbind.
lŏse, *v. t.* To cause to part with unintentionally.

LESSON 208.

Words Requiring Careful Discrimination.

"The purest treasure mortal times afford,
Is spotless reputation: that away,
Men are but gilded loam, or painted clay."

news, *n.* Tidings.
nŏŏse, *n.* A slip knot.

ŏff, *adv.* Away from.
ŏf (ŏv), *prep.* Proceeding from.

păs'-tor, *n.* Minister of a church.
păst'-ūre, *n.* Land used for grazing.

pā'-tiençe, *n.* Calmness.
pā'-tients (-shents), *n.* Those who are sick.

phāse, *n.* That which is exhibited to the eye.
fāçe, *n.* Cast of features; surface of a thing.

pĭl'-lar, *n.* A column.
pĭl'-lōw, *n.* A cushion for the head.

pint, *n.* Half a quart.
point, *n.* The sharp end of anything.

pŏr'-tion, *n.* A part.
pō'-tion, *n.* A dose.

prĕs'-ençe, *n.* Nearness.
prĕs'-ents, *n.* Gifts.

prinçe, *n.* A king's son.
prints, *n.* Impressions.

LESSON 209.

Words Requiring Careful Discrimination.

Dost thou love life, then do not squander time, for that is the stuff life is made of.—*Benjamin Franklin.*

quay (kē), *n.* A bank formed on the side of a river for loading and unloading vessels.

key, *n.* That which opens or shuts a lock.

rinse, *v. t.* To cleanse with water.

rents, *n.* Yearly income; tearings.

sew'-er (sū'-er), *n.* A drain or passage to carry off filth and water under ground.

sew'-er (sō'-er), *n.* One who sews or uses the needle.

stat'-ue, *n.* An image.

stat'-ure, *n.* Height.

stat'-ute, *n.* A law.

spe'-cie (-shỹ), *n.* Hard money.

spe'-cies, *n.* A kind; variety.

spe'-cious (-shŭs), *a.* Apparently right.

stun, *v. t.* To make insensible.

stone, *n.* A piece of rock.

toad, *n.* A reptile.

towed, *v. t.* Dragged through the water by means of a rope.

tow'-er, *n.* A high building.

tour, *n.* A long journey.

worst'-ed (wŭst'-ed), *n.* A well-twisted yarn.

worst'-ed (wûrst'-), *v. t.* Defeated; overthrown.

LESSON 210.

MISCELLANEOUS.

Man lives apart but not alone;
He walks amid his peers unread;
The best of thoughts that he hath known,
For lack of listeners are never said.—*Jean Ingelow.*

trans-par'-en-çy, *n.* Clearness.

treas'-ure, *n.* That which is very much valued.

tre'-mor or **trem'-or**, *n.* An involuntary trembling.

tryst, *n.* An appointed place of meeting.

twink'-le, *v. i.* To flash at intervals.

typ'-ie-al, *a.* Emblematic.

u'-ni-form, *a.* Conforming to one rule or mode.

u-nique' (-nēek'), *a.* Odd; without like or equal.

u'-ni-son, *n.* Harmony; union.

u-ni-vers'-al, *a.* Unlimited.

ur'-gen-çy, *n.* Pressure of necessity.

u'-til-ize, *v. i.* To make useful.

va'-ri-a-ble, *a.* Changeable.

va-ri'-e-ty, *n.* A varied assortment.

ven'-ti-late, *v. t.* To furnish supplies of fresh air.

vent'-ur-ous, *a.* Fearless; daring.

ver'-dan-çy, *n.* Inexperience.

vi-çin'-i-ty, *n.* Nearness.

vo-ea'-tion, *n.* Trade; occupation.

wres'-tle, *n.* A struggle between two, to see which will throw the other down.

LESSON 211.

PERTAINING TO THE CITY.

" List to the city's gaunt, thunderous roar,
Calling and calling for you evermore."

ạl'-der-man, *n.* An officer of a city, next below a mayor in rank.

ăl'-ley, *n.* A narrow walk or passage.

ăl-lŏt'-ment, *n.* That which is allotted.

ăq'-ue-dụet (ăk'-wē-), *n.* An artificial channel for conveying water, especially in large cities.

är-eāde', *n.* A long, arched building, lined on each side with shops.

är'-e-nūe, *n.* A wide street.

eä-fẹ' (kăf-ā'), *n.* A coffee house.

ea-sī'-no, *n.* A building used for social meetings, having rooms for public amusement.

found'-ry, *n.* A building arranged for casting metals.

ġym-nä'-ṣĭ-um, *n.* A place for athletic exercise.

hỹ'-drant, *n.* A pipe where water may be drawn from the mains of an aqueduct.

lo-eäl'-ĭ-tỵ, *n.* Geographical place or situation.

măn-ū-fäe'-to-rỵ, *n.* A house or place where anything is manufactured; a factory.

mãy'-or, *n.* The chief officer of a city.

mu-nĭç'-ĭ-pal, *a.* Pertaining to a corporation or a city.

ôr'-dĭ-nançe, *n.* A rule established by authority.

po-lĭçe', *n.* A body of civil officers who preserve good order and enforce the laws.

rĕṣ-er-vôir' (-vwôr'), *n.* The place where water is collected to supply the city by means of aqueducts.

rĕs-tau-rant' (rĕs-to-räng' or rĕs'-to-rant), *n.* An eating house.

sŭb'-ûrb, *n.* The out part of a town or city.

LESSON 212.

DICTATION EXERCISE.

Here in the city I ponder, through its long pathways I wander.
These are the spires that were gleaming
All through my juvenile dreaming,
When in the old country school house, I conned
Legends of life in the broad world beyond—
Ever I longed for the walls and the streets,
And the rich conflict that energy meets!
So I have come: but the city is great,
Bearing me down like a brute with its weight.
So I have come: but the city is cold,
And I am lonelier now than of old.—*Carleton.*

LESSON 213.

Some of the Cities of U. S. with more than 20,000 Inhabitants.

Life, like some cities, is full of blind alleys, leading nowhere ; the great art is to keep out of them.—*Bovee.*

	Census of 1890.		Census of 1890.
Ăl'-le-ghe-ny, *Pa.*	105,287	€ăm'-bridge, *Mass.*	70,028
Ăl'-too-nä, *Pa.*	30,337	€ăm'-den, *N. J.*	58,313
Au'-bûrn, *N. Y.*	25,858	€ăn-ton, *Ohio*	26,189
Bạl'-ti-môre, *Md.*	434,439	Chăt-ta-nōō'-gä, *Tenn.*	29,100
Băy' Çit-y, *Mich.*	27,839	Chĕl'-sēa, *Mass.*	27,909
Bĭng'-ham-tŏn, *N. Y.*	35 005	Çhĭ-ea'-go (she-kạw'-go), *Ill.*	1,099,850
Brĭdge'-pŏrt, *Conn.*	48,866	Çin-çin-nạt'-ĭ, *Ohio*	296,908
Brŏŏk'-lỹn, *N. Y.*	806,343	€lēve'-land, *Ohio*	261,353
Bŭf'-fa-lo, *N. Y.*	255,664	€ŏv'-ĭng-tŏn, *Ky.*	37,371
Bûr'-lĭng-tŏn, *Iowa*	22,565	€ō'-hōes, *N. Y.*	22,509

LESSON 214.

Some of the Cities of U. S. with more than 20,000 Inhabitants.

There is no solitude more dreadful for a stranger, an isolated man, than a great city. So many thousands of men and not one friend.—*Boiste.*

€oun'-çil Blŭffs, *Iowa*	21,474	Fŏrt Wāyne', *Ind.*	35,393
Dăy'-tŏn, *Ohio*	61,220	Găl'-ves-tŏn, *Texas*	29,084
Dăv'-en-pŏrt, *Iowa*	26,872	Glŏuçes'-ter (glŏs'-ter), *Mass.*	24,651
De-troit', *Mich.*	205,876	Grănd Răp'-ĭds, *Mich.*	60,278
Du-buque' (du-bōōk'), *Iowa*	30,311	Hä'-ver-hĭll (hä'-ver-ĭl), *Mass.*	27,412
È-lĭz' a-beth, *N. J.*	37,764	Hŏ'-bo-ken, *N. J.*	43,648
Ĕl mi'-rä, *N. Y.*	29,708	Hŏl'-yŏke, *Mass.*	35,637
Ē' rĭe, *Pa.*	40,634	Jĕr'-sey Çit-y, *N. J.*	163,003
Ĕv'-ans-ville, *Ind.*	50,756	Kăn'-sas Çit-y, *Mo.*	132,716
Fạll' Rĭv-er, *Mass.*	74,398	Lä €rŏsse', *Wis.*	25,090

LESSON 215.

Some of the Cities of U. S. with more than 20,000 Inhabitants.

Cities have always been the fire-places of civilization, whence light and heat radiated out into the dark, cold world.—*Theodore Parker.*

Lăṇe'-as-ter, *Pa.*	32,011	Lỹnn, *Mass.*	55,727
Lạw'-rençe, *Mass.*	44,654	Mä'-eŏn, *Ga.*	22,746
Lŏs Ăn'-ge-lĕs, *Cal.*	50,395	Măn'-ches-ter, *N. H.*	44,126
Lŏw'-ell, *Mass.*	77,696	Mĕm'-phis, *Tenn.*	64,495
Lọu'-ĭs-ville (lōō'-ĭs-vĭlle), *Ky.*	161,121	Mil-wạu'-kee, *Wis.*	204,468

Mĭn·ne·ăp'·o·lĭs, *Minn.*	164,738	New Hä'·ven, *Conn.*	81,298
Mŏ bīle', *Ala.*	31,076	New Ŏr'·le·anş, *La.*	242,039
New'·ark, *N. J.*	181,830	New Yŏrk', *N. Y.*	1,515,301
New Bĕd'·ford, *Mass.*	40,733	Ōak'·land, *Cal.*	48,682
New'·burgh, *N. Y.*	23,087	Ō'·ma·hạ, *Neb.*	140,452

LESSON 216.

Some of the Cities of U. S. with more than 20,000 Inhabitants.

He who imagines he can do without the world deceives himself much but he who fancies the world cannot do without him is still more mistaken.—*Rochefoucauld.*

Păt'·er·sŏn, *N. J.*	78,347	Seat'·tle, *Wash.*	42,837
Pe·ō'·ri·å, *Ill.*	41,024	Sioux' City, *Iowa*	37,806
Phĭl·a·dĕl'·phi·å, *Pa.*	1,046,964	St. Lou'·is (lōō'·ĭs), *Mo.*	451,770
Pĭtts'·bûrg̃, *Pa.*	238,617	Sў̆r'·a·eūse, *N. Y.*	88,143
Pŏrt'·land, *Me.*	36,425	Tĕr'·re Haute (·hōt), *Ind.*	30,217
Pōugh·keep'·sie (pŏ·kĭp'·) *N. Y.*	22,206	To·lē'·do, *Ohio*	81,434
Rŏch'·es·ter, *N. Y.*	133,896	Wạ'·ter·bur·y (·bĕr·ry), *Conn.*	28,646
Săn Frăn·çĭs'·eō, *Cal.*	298,997	Wilkes'·bär·re (·rĭ), *Pa.*	37,718
Sa·văn'·nåh, *Ga.*	43,189	Wĭl'·mĭng·tòn, *Del.*	61,431
Serăn'·ton, *Pa.*	75,215	Worces'·ter (wŏŏs'·ter), *Mass.*	84,655

LESSON 217.

STATES AND TERRITORIES.

America—the home of the homeless all over the earth!—*Street.*

STATE OR TERRITORY.	SQ. MILES.	CAPITAL.	CENSUS OF 1890.
Ăl·a·bà'·mà, *Ala.*	51,540	Mŏnt·gŏm'·e·ry	21,883
A·lăs'·kà Ter., *Alaska Ter.*	531,409	Sĭt'·kà	1,188
Ar·ĭ·zō'·nà Ter., *Ariz. Ter.*	113,929	Prĕs'·eott	1,759
Är'·kan·sạs (·sạw), *Ark.*	53,845	Lĭt'·tle Rŏck	25,874
€ăl·i·fôr'·nĭ·à, *Cal.*	155,980	Săe·ra·mĕn'·to	26,386
€ŏl·o·rä'·do, *Colo.* or *Col.*	103,845	Dĕn'·ver	106,713
€ŏn·nĕct'·i·eŭt, *Conn.* or *Ct.*	4,845	Härt'·ford	53,230
Dĕl'·a·ware, *Del.*	1,950	Dō'·ver	3,061
Flŏr'·Ĭ·dà, *Fla.* or *Flor.*	59,268	Tăl·la·hăs'·see	2,934
G̃eôr'·g̃ĭ·à, *Ga.*	58,980	Ăt·lăn'·tà	65,533

LESSON 218.

States and Territories.

Teach erring man to spurn the rage of gain;
Teach him, that States, of native strength possessed,
Though very poor, may still be very blessed.—*Goldsmith.*

STATE OR TERRITORY.	SQ. MILES.	CAPITAL.	CENSUS OF 1890.
I'-da-hŏ, *Idaho*	84,290	Boise' Cĭt-ў (bwah-zä')	2,311
Ĭl-li-noiş' (or -noĭ'), *Ill.*	56,000	Sprĭng'-flĕld	24,963
Ĭn-dĭ-ăn'-ȧ, *Ind.*	35,910	Ĭu-di-a-năp'-o-lĭs	105,436
Ĭn'-dian Ter. (ĭnd'-yan), *Ind. Ter.*	65,604	Tah'-le-quah	1,500
Ī'-o-wȧ, *Iowa* or *Ia.*	55,470	Dēs Moĭues'	50,093
Kăn'-sas, *Kan.*	81,700	To-pē'-kȧ	31,007
Kĕn-tŭek'-y, *Ky.*	40,000	Frănk'-fort	7,892
Lọu-ĭ-şĭ-ȧ'-nȧ, *La.*	45,420	Băt'-ȯn Rouge (roozh)	10,478
Māine, *Me.*	33,056	Ạu-gŭs'-tȧ	10,527
Mä'-ry-land, *Md.*	9,860	Ȧn-năp'-o-lĭs	6,000

LESSON 219.

States and Territories.

" What constitutes a State?
Not high raised battlements or labored mound,
Not cities proud with spires and turrets crowned ·
No; men, high-minded men."

STATE OR TERRITORY.	SQ. MILES.	CAPITAL.	CENSUS OF 1890.
Măs-sa-chŭ'-setts, *Mass.*	8,040	Bŏs'-tŏn	448,477
Mĭeh'-ĭ-ğan, *Mich.*	57,430	Lăn'-sĭng	13,102
Mĭn-ne-sŏ'-tȧ, *Minn.*	79,205	St. Pạul'	133,156
Mĭs-sĭs-sĭp'-pĭ, *Miss.*	46,340	Jŭck'-sŏn	5,920
Mĭs-sọu'-rĭ, *Mo.*	68,735	Jĕf'-fer-sȯn €ĭt-y	6,742
Mŏn tä'-nȧ, *Mont.*	145,310	Hĕl'-e-nȧ	13,834
Ne-brăs'-kȧ, *Neb.*	76,185	Lĭṇ'-eȯln	55,154
Ne-vä'-dȧ, *Nev.*	109,740	€ȧr'-sȯn Çĭt-y	3 950
New Hămp'-shīre, *N. H.*	9,005	€ȯn'-eȯrd	17,004
New Jĕr'-şey, *N. J.*	7,455	Trĕn'-tȯn	57,458

LESSON 220.
States and Territories.

"Ill fares the land, to hastening ills a prey,
Where wealth accumulates, and men decay.''

STATE OR TERRITORY.	SQ. MILES.	CAPITAL.	CENSUS OF 1890.
New Mĕx'-ĭ-ₑo Ter., *N. Mex. Ter.*	122,000	Săn-ta Fẹ'	6,185
New Yôrk', *N. Y.*	47,620	Ạl'-ba-ny	94,923
Nôrth Çăr-o-lï'-na, *N. C.*	52 240	Rạl'-eïgh	12,678
North Da-kō'-tä, *N. Dak.*	75,000	Bĭṣ'-märek	2,186
Ō-hī'-o, *O.*	40,760	Ço-lŭm'-bŭs	88,150
Ŏk-la-hō'-mà Ter., *O. Ter.*	4,687	Gŭth'-rie	8,000
Ŏr'-e-ğon, *Or.*	94,560	Sä'-lem	2,600
Pĕnn-sȳl-vä'-nĭ-à, *Pa.*	44,985	Hŭr'-ris-bûrg	39,385
Rhōde Isl'-and, *R. I.*	1,088	{ Prŏv'-ĭ-dençe { New'-pōrt	132,146 19,437
Soath Çăr-o-lï'-nà, *S. C.*	30,170	Ço-lŭm'-bĭ-à	15,353

LESSON 221.
States and Territories.

If you would know and not be known, live in a city.—*Colton.*

STATE OR TERRITORY.	SQ. MILES.	CAPITAL.	CENSUS OF 1890.
South Da-kō'-tà, *S. Dak.*	76,620	Pierre (pē-är')	3,200
Tĕn-nes-sēe', *Tenn.*	41,750	Năsh'-vïlle	76,168
Tĕx'-as, *Tex.*	265,780	Ạus'-tĭn	14,476
Ụ'-tạh, *Utah Ter.*	82,190	Sạlt Lăke Çit'-y	44,843
Vĕr-mŏnt', *Vt.*	9,136	Mŏnt-pē'-lier	3,617
Vïr-ğïn'-ĭ-à, *Va.*	40,125	Rĭch'-mond	81,388
Wạsh'-ïng-tòn, *Wash.*	66,880	Ō-lȳm'-pĭ-à	4,698
Wĕst Vïr-ğïn'-ĭ-à, *W. Va.*	24,645	Chärleṣ'-ton	6,742
Wĭs-çŏn'-sin, *Wis.*	54,450	Măd'-ĭ-son	13,426
Wȳ-ō'-mïng, *Wyo.*	97,575	Çhey-ĕnne' (shĭ-ĕn')	11,690

LESSON 222.
LARGEST CITIES OF THE WORLD.

There is such a difference between the pursuits of men in great cities that one part of the inhabitants live to little other purpose than to wonder at the rest.—*Johnson.*

CITY.	COUNTRY.	POPULATION.
Ăm'-stĕr-dam,	*Hŏl'-land*	328,000
Ănt'-wĕrp,	*Bĕl'-ği-um*	176,000

CITY.	COUNTRY.	POPULATION.
Bŭng-kŏk,'	In'-di-a	600,000
Bär-çē-lō'-nä (or bär-thä-),	Spain	249,000
Bĕl-fàst',	Ire'-länd	208,000
Bĕr'-lin (or bĕr'-lēen),	Prŭs'-si-a (prŭsh'-i-a)	1,122,000
Bĭr'-mĭng-ham,	Eng'-land (ĭng'-)	401,000
Bom-bäy',	In'-di-a	644,000
Bôr-deaux' (-dō'),	Françe	222,000
Brăd'-ford,	Eng'-land (ĭng'-)	183,000
Brĕs'-lạu,	Prŭs'-si-a (prŭsh'-i-a)	279,000
Brŭs'-selş,	Bĕl'-gi-ŭm.	377,000
Bū'-eha-rĕst,	Rou-mä'-ni-a	221,000
Bn'-dù-Pĕsth,	Hun'-ga-ry	365,000
Bue'-nòs Āy'-reş (bō'-),	Ar-gĕn-tine Re-pŭb'-lic, S. A.	178,000
€aï'-ro,	E'-gypt.	327,000
€ŭl-eŭt'-tä,	In'-di-a	683,000
€ärls'-bäd,.	Ger'-ma-ny	20,600
€ăn'-tôn,	Chi'-na	1,500,000
€o-lōgne' (-lōn'),	Ger'ma-ny	130,000

LESSON 223.

Largest Cities of the World.

"Trade's proud empire hastes to swift decay,
As ocean sweeps the labored mole away."

CITY.	COUNTRY.	POPULATION.
€ŏn-stan-tǐ-nō'-ple,	Tûr'-key	600,000
€o-pĕn-hä'-ḡen,	Dĕn'-mark	274,000
Drĕṣ'-den,	Sàx'-o-ny	809,000
Dŭb'-lĭn,	Ire'-länd	249,000
Ĕd'-ĭn-burgh (-bûr-rŭh),	Scŏt'-land	229,000
Fōō-choo',	Chi'-na	600,000
Ḡĕn'-o-à,	It'-a-ly	180,000
Glàs'-ḡōw,	Scŏt'-land	555,000
Hăm'-bûrḡ,	Ger'-ma-ny	290,000
Ha-vän'-à,	Cü'-ba	240,000
Heï'-del-berḡ,	Ger'-ma-ny	27,000
Kī-ō'-to,	Jä-pän'	230,000

CITY.	COUNTRY.	POPULATION.
Lĭṣ'-bŏn,	Pŏrt'-u-gal	246,000
Lĭsle (lēel),	França	178,000
Lĭv'-er-pōŏl,	Eng'-land (ĭng'-)	552,000
Lŏn'-dŏn,	Eng'-land (ĭng'-)	3,832,000
Lŭek'-now,	In'-dĭ-a	285,000
Lȳ'-onṣ,	França	377,000
Măd-rĭd',	Spain	398,000
Măn'-ches-ter,	Eng'-land (ĭng'-)	394,000

LESSON 224.

Largest Cities of the World.

The city is an epitome of the social world. All the belts of civilization intersect along its avenues and it contains the products of every moral zone.—*Chapin*

CITY.	COUNTRY.	POPULATION.
Măr-ṣeilleṣ' (mär-sälz'),	França	360,000
Měl'-boûrne,	Aus-trā'-lĭ-a	352,000
Mĭl'-an or Mĭ-län',	It'-a-ly	322,000
Mŏṣ'-eōw,	Rŭṣ'-si-a (rŭsh'-ĭ-a)	748,000
Mū'-nĭeh,	Ba-vā'-rĭ-a.	230,000
Nä'-pleṣ,	It'-a-ly.	494,000
Nŏt'-ting-ham,	Eng'-land (ĭng'-)	187,000
Ō-děṣ'-sä,	Rŭṣ'-si-a (rŭsh'-ĭ-a)	194,000
Păr'-ĭs,	França	2,269,000
Pē'-king or Pē-kĭn',	Chĭ'-na	500,000
Rĭ'-ō Ja-neī'-rō,	Bra-zil'.	275,000
Shäng'-haī or Shäng'-hi,	Chĭ'-na	278,000
Shěf'-fĭeld,	Eng'-land (ĭng'-)	284,000
Stŏek'-holm,	Swe'-den.	177,000
St. Pē'-terṣ-bûrġ,	Rŭṣ'-si-a (rŭsh'-ĭ-a)	927,000
Sȳd'-neȳ,	Aus-trā'-lĭ-a	187,000
Tō'-kĭ-ō,	Jä-pän'	594,000
Tū'-rĭn or Tū-rĭn',	It'-a-ly	253,000
Vĭ'-ĕn-nä,	Aus-trĭ'-a	1,104,000
Wär'-saw,	Pō'-lànd	384,000

LESSON 225.

MONTHS AND DAYS.

" A life of sober week days, with a solemn Sabbath at their close."

Jăn'-u-a-rỹ, ... Jan.	De-çĕm'-ber, ... Dec.
Fĕb'-rụ-a-rỹ, ... Feb.	Sŭn'-daỹ, ... Sun.
Märch, ... Mar.	Mŏn'-daỹ, ... Mon.
Ā'-prĭl, ... Apr.	Tũeṣ'-daỹ, ... Tues.
Māy, ... May.	Wĕdneṣ'-daỹ (wĕnz'-dỹ), . . . Wed.
Jūne, ... June.	Thûrṣ'-daỹ, ... Thurs.
Ju-lỹ', ... July.	Frī'-daỹ, ... Fri.
Au'-gŭst, ... Aug.	Săt'-ur-daỹ, ... Sat.
Sĕp-tĕm'-ber, ... Sept.	€hro-nŏl'-o-ġỹ, *n.* The science which
Ŏe-tŏ'-ber, ... Oct.	treats of measuring or computing
No-vĕm'-ber, ... Nov.	time by regular divisions or periods.

LESSON 226.

DICTATION EXERCISE.

Remorseless Time!
Fierce spirit of the glass and scythe! What power
Can stay him in his silent course, or melt
His iron heart to pity! On, still on,
He presses, and forever. The proud bird,
The condor of the Andes, that can soar
Through heaven's unfathomable depths, or brave
The fury of the northern hurricane,
And bathe his plumage in the thunder's home,
Furls his broad wing at nightfall, and sinks down
To rest upon his mountain crag ; but Time
Knows not the weight of sleep or weariness, .
And Night's deep darkness has no chain to bind
His rushing pinion.
Time the tomb-builder, holds his fierce career,
Dark, stern, all pitiless, and pauses not
Amid the mighty wrecks that strew his path,
To sit and muse, like other conquerors,
Upon the fearful ruin he hath wrought.—*Geo. D. Prentice.*

These are your school days; given you to obtain a fund of knowledge, and a culture of mind that may unlock for you the exhaustless treasures of Truth.

Neglect these privileges, and the memory of it will never cease to reproach you; but earnestly gather the priceless seed which they afford, and you may look back to these as life's golden hours. In them you will have sown the seed that will ripen into personal harvest of happy usefulness.

And that the paths of Science may lead your reverent feet to the feet of Him whose world she delights to unfold, is the earnest prayer of

LETTER-WRITING:

A MANUAL SHOWING THE

Correct Structure, Capitalization,

PUNCTUATION, FORM AND USES

OF THE VARIOUS KINDS OF

LETTERS, NOTES AND CARDS.

WITH ESPECIAL ATTENTION TO

BUSINESS CORRESPONDENCE.

INTRODUCTION.

A large share of the business done at the present day is by correspondence, and the only writing done by many people is comprised in their letters. A person's business habits and abilities are judged by his letters—and usually correctly. If he writes a well-arranged, neat, business-like letter, we give him credit for possessing like qualities in business. But if his letter is awkwardly worded, slovenly and carelessly written, we conclude he possesses similar traits of character.

It is important, therefore, that early training be given in neatness, correct forms and established customs in writing letters.

This work is designed to be a school text book on business letter-writing, and, as a book of reference, a complete guide in regard to all established rules and usages governing social and official letters, invitations, cards, etc.

The instruction in business letter-writing is, much of it, equally applicable to all classes of letters. The forms given, and the suggestions concerning social letters, invitations, cards, etc., are sufficient to meet the requirements of the majority of people.

THE SCRIPT MODELS will serve as excellent copies in the development of a neat and elegant style of penmanship.

THE FORMS AND EXERCISES given under the different headings, are designed as illustrations of that particular subject, and as examples for practice. Few "model letters" are given, as it is believed the student will be more benefited by writing original letters, after he has had proper instruction, than by copying models. From the large number of exercises in the book, selections for practice may be made, at the option of the teacher.

The teacher may add much to the interest and value of the lessons by himself taking an interest, and giving original illustrations, seeing that the letters and exercises are carefully corrected, occasionally reading meritorious or faulty ones to the class, pointing out the more common errors, etc.

The student is earnestly requested to give to this branch the attention it merits—to make a thorough study of the subject, follow the instructions given, neatly and carefully write his letters and exercises, note corrections and try to avoid the same errors thereafter, and we are sure he will be amply rewarded by the knowledge and proficiency he will gain.

LETTERS.

Letters are prose compositions addressed to some person or persons; they may be divided into *Social, Business, Public* and *Miscellaneous.*

Social letters are letters of sentiment; and embrace domestic or family letters, letters of affection, introduction, congratulation, condolence, advice, and all letters that are prompted by friendship or love.

Business letters are of two classes, personal and official. A *personal* business letter is one on personal or private business. The letters written by persons or firms in connection with their trade, business or profession, belong to this class.

An *official* business letter is one written by or to a person holding a public office, on business connected therewith.

Public letters are addressed to some individual, but published by the press. They are letters in form only.

Miscellaneous letters include those of an unusual character, and that are not elsewhere classified.

The styles and uses of the various kinds of letters are fully explained under appropriate headings, but we shall first examine

The Structure of Letters, which includes Materials, Heading, Introduction, Body, Conclusion, Folding, Envelope, Address, Stamp, etc.

To enable the pupil to readily recognize the component parts of a letter by their names, a skeleton letter is given on the next page.

SKELETON **LETTER.**

HEADING.

ADDRESS.

SALUTATION.

MARGIN.

BODY.

BODY.

COMPLIMENTARY CLOSE.

SIGNATURE.

MATERIALS.

Paper.—The paper used in letter-writing, whether for business or social purposes, should be of good quality; both on account of the better quality of work that can be done with good paper, and because of the impression it makes on one's correspondent; for we judge people largely by the surroundings they choose and the kind of tools they work with.

SIZE.—There are so many styles and sizes of paper used for social purposes that one cannot be governed by any fixed standard.

In business, the sizes most used are note paper, about 6 by 9 inches, and letter paper, about 8 by 10 inches.

COLOR.—White paper is almost universally used in business correspondence, and is in better taste than tinted paper. In social correspondence many different tints are used, and any delicate tint is appropriate. Strong colors should be avoided.

Envelopes.—The envelopes should correspond in color, size and style with the paper.

For social letters, an evelope that will admit the paper in one or two convenient folds should be used.

For business letters, use an envelope that is a little larger than the paper after the letter sheet is folded three times, and the note size twice.

The more common sizes used in business are No. 6, 3⅜ by 6 inches, and No. 6½, 3½ by 6⅜ inches. For official communications, legal documents, etc., use an official envelope—usually about 9 inches long.

Pens.—Good pens should always be used, as no one can do his best writing with a poor pen. Steel pens are now so cheap, and of such good quality, that they are almost universally used for all kinds of business and fine writing.

Ink.—The ink should flow freely and make a fine line. Black ink is now used almost exclusively in all kinds of correspondence, and is in much better taste than colored ink; besides, nearly, if not all colored inks are liable to fade.

HEADING.

THE HEADING of a letter embraces the address of the writer and the date. It may occupy one, two or three lines, according to the length of the address. It should never occupy more than three. The following is the form for an address of one line :

Model 1.

Cleveland, Ohio, Feb'y 12, 1890.

If writing from a large city, and your local address is not well known to your correspondent, your street number should first be given, after which, the proper order is the city, state, day of the month, and year, as in the following :

Model 2.

30 East Boulevard,

Detroit, Mich., Nov. 2, 1889.

If writing from the country, the proper order is the post-office, county, state, and date, as follows :

Model 3.

Vanwert, Queen Co., N. Y.,

February 22, 1890.

In writing from a small place, it is always better to give the name of the *county*, as, when on the envelope, it aids the employes of the post-office department in distributing the mail, and may prevent errors or delay in delivery.

In writing from a well-known school or public institution, it is customary to give its name in the heading of your letter before writing the
address and date, in the following order, which form will occupy three
lines. unless the address is short:

Model 4.

Michigan University,

Ann Arbor, Mich.,

April 4, 1890

If a letter is written from a department of the state or national government, the name of that department is usually given in the heading of
the letter.

When printed letterheads are used, as they are so universally now
by the Departments and leading business houses, only the date needs to
be written in the heading.

When ruled paper is used, the heading should begin on the first
line, about the middle of the page of letter-paper, and to the left of the
middle, if note-paper is used.

If the heading embraces two lines, the second line should begin
nearly an inch to the right of the first, as in model 2.

This heading may, if preferred, be arranged as follows :

Model 5.

202 Broadway, N. Y.,

November 16, 1889.

If the heading occupy three lines, the third should begin as far to
the right of the second, as that is to right of the first, as in Model 4.

On ruled paper, the first line is usually one and one-half to two
inches below the top ; the heading should begin on this line, or, in the
case of a very short letter, on ruled or unruled paper, it should be far

enough from the top to make the spaces above the heading and below the signature about equal.

If two or three lines are used for the heading, care should be taken to arrange the divisions of the heading properly on the lines ; for instance, in writing " 1815 Euclid Ave.," it should all be on one line ; in writing " Jefferson, Ashtabula County," it would not be proper to put " Ashtabula " on one line, and " County " on another.

If the address and date are placed at the close of the letter, as is sometimes the case in social correspondence, they should begin on the next line below the signature, near the left of the page, and if occupying more than one line, the parts should be in the same relative position as when written at the beginning of the letter. The following is an illustration of this form :

Model 6.

Your sincere friend,

Ellen Manning.

20 Newell Ave.,

Argos, Ind., Sept. 3, 1890.

In business letters, the address and date are always written at the top.

Punctuation.—The parts of the heading of the letter should be separated by commas, as in the models. These commas mark the divisions between the different parts of the heading. A period should always follow each abbreviation, and be placed at the end of the heading. It is not now customary to write the abbreviations " th," " st" or " d" after the figures denoting the day of the month, when the year is written. You should write " October 31, 1889," and not " October 31st, 1889."

In the body of the letter, however, or when the year is not written, the letters must be used; as, " Yours of the 31st inst." When the letters are used, they should be written on the line, and not above.

INTRODUCTION.

THE INTRODUCTION of the letter embraces the name and address of the party written to, and the salutation. The salutation is the term " Dear Sir," " Madam," etc. The name of the person addressed should be written on the first line following the heading, and the same distance from the left edge of the paper as the body of the letter.

Name and Title.—It is best to use some title in the address, either before or after the name. The more common titles are *Miss*, *Mrs.*, *Mr.* and *Esq.* If a gentleman has no literary, professional, or military title, his name should be preceded by the abbreviation Mr., or followed by Esq. We do not approve of the custom that is so common of using the title " Esq." indiscriminately in business letter-writing, but consider the title " Mr." more appropriate and in better taste. Mr. and Esq. should never be both used, either in the introduction of the letter or address of the envelope. If you use one omit the other.

Two or more titles of courtesy should not be connected with the same name, except in cases like the following : If a married man has a professional or military title prefixed to his name, Mrs. may be used before it to designate his wife, as *Mrs. Secretary* Blaine, *Mrs. Dr.* Smith, etc. And in writing to a clergyman, whose surname only is known, it is customary to address him as " *Rev. Mr.* Brown." Two or more professional or literary titles may be used with one name, as *Rev.* John Smith, *D. D.*, *LL. D.* When titles are so used, they should be written in the order in which they are supposed to have been conferred.

In addressing a firm of gentlemen, the proper title is " *Messrs.*," (abbreviation for *Messieurs*, French plural of Mr.) ; if young ladies, *Misses ;* married or elderly ladies, *Mesdames* (pronounced *Ma-dahm'*). If the firm is composed of ladies and gentlemen, use no title.

The residence following the name, should embrace the full post-office address of the party written to, and a business letter should contain the full post-office address of the writer as well. It is customary in business letter-writing to write the address in full, and not the name only, at the beginning of a letter. The relative position of the lines in the address should be the same as in the heading, viz : the lines, after the first, each beginning nearly an inch to the right of the beginning of the preceding line.

The salutation is a term of affection, respect, or politeness with which we introduce the letter.

The terms used almost exclusively in business letters are *Sir, Dear Sir, Sirs, Dear Sirs, Gentlemen,* and *Madam.* The salutations employed in addressing one gentleman, are *Sir,* used in writing to public officials, and in the most formal business letters ; *Dear Sir,* the form most used in business; and *My dear Sir,* denoting more familiarity. The proper salutation in addressing a married lady is *Madam,* or *Dear Madam.* In addressing an unmarried lady, the salutation should be omitted, as in Model 8. Write her name and address, then begin the letter. The salutation for a firm of gentlemen, is *Sirs, Dear Sirs,* or *Gentlemen.* Never abbreviate " *Dear* " to " *Dr.,*" or " *Gentlemen* " to " *Gents.*" An almost unlimited number of salutations might be given for social letters, such as *Dear Friend, Dear Mother, My Dear Smith, Friend Brown, Dear Charlie,* etc.

A list of the proper titles and salutations to use in addressing people in various stations in life is given elsewhere in this work.

Position.—In business letters the address is always written at the beginning of the letter, and in military and official letters, the address is sometimes written at the beginning and sometimes at the close. *If the address occupies three lines,* the salutation should begin under the initial letter of the second line, as in Model 5, or under that of the first line, as in Model 6. *If the address occupies two lines,* the salutation may begin as far to the right of the second line as that begins to the right of the first, as in Model 3, or under the initial letter of the first line, as in Model 4. The former is the best arrangement for a wide sheet of paper, and the latter for a narrow one. *If the address occupies but one line,* the salutation should begin about one inch to the right of the marginal line, as in Model 2, or directly under the ending of the name, if it is short, as in Model 1.

Punctuation.—A comma should follow each part of the address, name of the post-office, etc., and a period should be placed at the end of the whole address, as in the models.

If a title follows the name, it should be separated from the latter by a comma, and if two or more titles are used a comma should separate them. Every abbreviation must be followed by a period. The salutation should be followed by a comma, or if the letter begins on the same line, by a comma and a dash. In more formal letters, a colon should follow the salutation instead of a comma.

Capitals.—Every important word of the address should be capitalized, and the first letter of every noun in the salutation should begin with a capital.

MODELS OF INTRODUCTION.

Model 1.

Friend Brown:

I was very glad to receive your kind note, etc.

Model 2.

My dear Irene:

You must not forget your promise to visit us, etc.

Model 3.

Messrs. N. Q. Percy & Co.,

Auburn, N. Y.

Gentlemen:—Inclosed, etc.

When the address occupies two lines, the salutation may begin as in Model 3, or under the beginning of the name, as in Model 4, and the body of the letter on the same or the next line.

Model 4.

V. L. Porter, D. D.,

Quincy, Ill.

Dear Sir:—

Please send us by return, etc.

Model 5.

Messrs. Adams & Newton,

14 Republic St.,

Annandale, Va.

Gentlemen:—Inclosed please, etc.

Model 6.

Mr. N. R. Andrews,

744 Broadway,

New York.

Dear Sir:—In reply to your favor, etc.

Model 7.

Mrs. Annie Perkins,

Dear Madam:

Accept our best wishes, etc.

This form may be used for social letters. In business letters to married ladies, adopt the arrangement in any one of Models 3, 4, 5 or 6, writing "Madam" or "Dear Madam" for a salutation.

Model 8.

Miss Nina Raymond,

Pemberton, Va.

Your order of the 14th, etc.

Use this form in writing a business letter to an unmarried lady, or the name only, " Miss Mary Marshall," may be used.

BODY OF THE LETTER.

THE BODY of a letter is the communication, exclusive of the heading, introduction, and conclusion.

Beginning.—The body of the letter should usually begin under the end of the salutation; but if the address is long, as in models 3, 5, 6, it may begin on the same line, in which case a comma and a dash, or colon and dash, should be placed between the salutation and the first word of the letter, with only enough space for the punctuation mark and the dash.

Margin.—There should always be a blank space on the left-hand side of the page, but none on the right. The width of this margin depends upon the size of the paper. On letter-paper, it should be one-half to three-fourths of an inch, and on note-paper, about one-fourth of an inch.

The margin should be perfectly even.—The habit of writing it so, may be acquired by at first drawing a pencil line where the lines should begin, or using a sheet of paper on which a heavy, black line has been ruled, under the paper on which you are writing. If a pencil line is ruled, it should always be erased after the letter is written, but it is better not to use the pencil line except in practicing.

Paragraphs.—A letter should be paragraphed the same as other compositions. In dismissing one theme, mark the beginning of the next by a broken line that, catching the reader's eye, prepares him for the change. Do not make too many paragraphs. All paragraphs, excepting the first, should begin as far to the right of the *marginal line* as the latter is to the right of the edge of the paper. The arrangement of paragraphs in written letters should be about the same as in printed books, excepting the first paragraph.

Neatness.—Never send a letter in which there are blots, erasures, or interlineations; it is better to copy such communications. Blots and erasures are indications of carelessness and of liability to make mistakes. Our correspondents judge us largely by the appearance of our letters, and we should be careful as far as is in our power to cultivate and retain their good opinion.

Penmanship.—No accomplishment can be of greater worth in business than good penmanship. It is an invaluable first introduction to a business place, and often the cause of promotion. While time is required to make one's accomplishments in other lines known, his good penmanship speaks for itself on sight.

The penmanship should be neat, plain, and as rapid as is consistent with these qualities. Avoid flourishes, and it is better to write without shading than to shade too much. No one can become a good penman without an effort on his own part, and a good hand-writing is almost sure to come to those who are willing, persistent, careful and earnest in their endeavors to acquire it. Careful practice will constantly improve one's hand-writing, while carelessness may spoil a good style already acquired. A carelessly written letter is not only prejudicial to the writer and disrespectful to his correspondent, but consumes time of the latter in deciphering it,—something the writer has no right to ask.

A man with an established reputation can possibly afford to write a poor hand, but any one starting in business life certainly cannot.

Our advice is, to write no more letters than you can write well. Write plainly, neatly, slowly if you must, but write just as well as you can ; you cannot afford to write otherwise.

CONCLUSION.

THE CONCLUSION of a letter embraces what follows the communication itself.

Complimentary Close.—The complimentary close is the phrase of respect, courtesy or endearment written at the end of the letter. The words used vary according to circumstances and taste, as in the salutation. For *social* letters, an almost infinite variety of forms might be given; such as, "Yours truly," "Your friend," "Your father," "Ever yours," "Very sincerely yours," "Faithfully yours," etc.

The words used for the complimentary close are varied according to the relations of the parties; the complimentary close depends somewhat upon the salutation also, and the same words should not be used in both. If a person is addressed as "dear friend" in the salutation, the word "friend" should not be repeated in the complimentary close; and if a person is addressed as "dear friend" in the salutation, "respectfully" would be a very *formal* word to use in the complimentary close. The word "remain," used in the complimentary close, implies previous correspondence.

In *business* letters, the words most used for the complimentary close are "Yours truly" and "Yours respectfully." These may be emphasized by using the word *very* after "Yours" in either form; as, "Yours very truly," or varied by inversion of the words; as, "Truly yours" or "Respectfully yours."

Official letters have a more formal close than any others, such as,

> *I am, Sir,*
> *Your obedient servant,*

> *I have the honor to be (or remain)*
> *Your obedient servant,*

> *I have the honor to be (or remain)*
> *Very respectfully,*

These forms of official etiquette are not strictly adhered to. The term "Your obedient servant," so generally used in official letters, is also a very appropriate term to use in writing to a patron or superior.

Signature.—Every letter should be signed. Some people have the habit of sending letters to friends without signature, or of carelessly sending out important business letters unsigned. If the letter contains a remittance, or anything of importance, the name should be written in full. A letter that is miscarried from insufficient address, or fails for any other cause to reach the party for whom it is intended, is sent to the "Dead-letter Office," whence it is returned to the writer, if known. Thousands of dollars are lost annually (over $40,000 last year) through the failure of writers to sign their full names to letters containing money.

Friendly letters or those not containing matters of business importance may be signed in an informal manner.

Write your name plainly.—Some people seem to have an idea that because they know what their names are every person to whom they write will know also. When they come to the close of their letters, they scrawl their names in such a manner that nobody can read them. In almost any other place we can tell from the context what a word is, even if it is not distinctly written, but most *names* need to be written plainly.. Much valuable time is wasted in trying to decipher illegible signatures.

If the writer is a lady, in writing to a stranger she should sign her name so as not only to indicate her sex, but also whether she is single or married; if a single lady, she may write the title "Miss," in a parenthesis, and if a married lady, she should use the title "Mrs." If she fails in this, her correspondent will not know whether to address her as "Sir," "Miss," or "Madam." A married lady generally uses her husband's name, or initials; as, "Mrs. John Smith," "Mrs. J. W. Smith." She *may* use her own name, and *should* do so if she is a widow.

Official signature.—A person in an official, or a prominent business position, may follow his name with words denoting his position; as, "John Jones, Chairman of Executive Committee;" "L. G. Smith, Assistant Cashier," etc.

If the address is placed at the close of the letter, instead of at the beginning, it should be arranged the same as when used at the head of the letter, written on the next line below the signature and beginning on the marginal line, as previously stated.

Arrangement and Position.—The complimentary close should be written on the next line below the body of the letter, and if long, it may occupy one, two, or three lines. It should begin directly under the initial letter of the first word in the heading, or a little to the left of the middle of the page, if the address is not at the top.

The signature should be written on the next line below the complimentary close, beginning far enough to the left so that the end of the signature will come to the right edge of the paper.

Punctuation.—A comma should be placed after the complimentary close, and if it is long, the parts of the same should be separated by commas, as per models. A period should follow the signature.

The address, when placed at the close of the letter, is punctuated the same as when written at the beginning.

MODELS OF CONCLUSION.

Model 1.

Respectfully,

William R. Brown.

Model 2.

Yours truly,

Evans, Field & Co.

Per B.

Model 3.

Your affectionate sister,

Violet

If the address is written at the close, it may be arranged as in the following:

Model 4.

I am, sir,

Your obedient servant,

Peter Raymond.

Prof. Norman Adams,

Providence, R. I.

Sometimes the date only is written in the heading, and the post-office address should then follow the name, as below:

Model 5.

Very truly yours,

Leroy Howard,

Rochester, Ind.

FOLDING.

Although the folding of a letter is a very simple matter, it is often very awkwardly done. The right way to fold is as easy as a wrong way, and gives your letter a very much better appearance.

Letter-paper.—A sheet of letter-paper may be folded in two ways; *first,* to fit an ordinary business envelope, and *second,* to fit an official envelope, which is a little longer than the paper is wide.

FIRST METHOD.—The correct way to fold for an envelope of the usual size, is to make three folds; first, hold the paper as shown in

1

Figure 1, and fold from the bottom nearly to the upper edge of the paper, as in Figure 2, or far enough to fit the envelope; then turn the paper, as in Figure 3, and fold from the right and left edges about equal distances, as in Figures 4 and 5, so that the sheet, after being folded, is a little smaller than the envelope.

Avoid folding the full width of the envelope from the right, leaving only a very narrow fold from the left. It is much better to make the folds equal from right and left edges of the paper, leaving the width of the envelope in the center.

Care should be taken to bring the corner of the paper, as it is folded, clear to the edge of the sheet, where the fingers of the left hand should hold it firmly, while the fold is creased down with the right. If the fingers are soiled, use an ivory paper knife or other article for creasing down the fold. It should be pressed down smoothly, but not enough to break the paper. The illustrations here given, will make clear the method above described.

2

SECOND METHOD.—To fit an *official* envelope, fold the sheet from the bottom up, nearly as far as the envelope is wide, then from top down to this point, thus giving two folds and three thicknesses of paper. Supposing Figure 3 to show the full size of a sheet of letter-paper, this method of folding is illustrated by Figures 4 and 5.

Note-paper.—There are *three* ways in which note-paper may be folded; FIRST, for the common sizes, which are supposed to be a little narrower

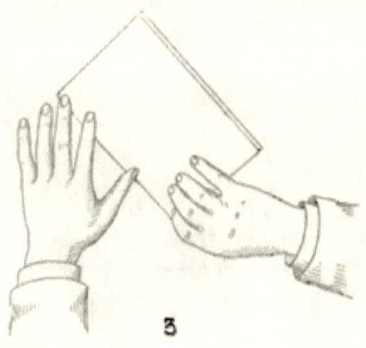

3

than the envelope is long, you should fold the paper twice; first, from the bottom upward a distance a little less than the width of the envelope, and then fold the top down to the same point; the paper will then be a little smaller each way than the envelope. This method is illustrated by Figures 3, 4 and 5, supposing Figure 3 to represent a sheet of note-paper.

4

SECOND, if the envelope is shorter than the width of the paper, the latter should be given two folds; first, from the bottom to the top, and then from right to left until the edges of the paper meet; this method of folding gives four thicknesses of paper. It is very rarely necessary to use this style of folding.

THIRD, for a large, square envelope, such as ladies often use, if the paper is made to match, as it should be, only one fold is necessary, from the bottom to the top, as in Figure 2.

5

Putting letter into envelope.—There is a right way to do even this; take the envelope in the left hand with the opening up, and the back of the envelope towards you, then with the right hand place the letter in the envelope, the part last folded in first; in this way the corners of the paper do not catch in putting it in, and when the letter is taken out, it is right side up as it is opened. See Figure 6.

Unless there is something to enclose later in the letter, it is well to form the habit of sealing the envelope as soon as your letter is placed therein.

The envelope should be addressed before putting the letter in it.

6

THE SUPERSCRIPTION.

THE SUPERSCRIPTION (address upon the envelope), consists of the
name and title of the person written to, and his residence or post-office
address; the latter is usually the same as the inside address. The name
should be plainly written, and care taken to put the letter in the right
envelope. People have been placed in very embarrassing situations, for
lack of care in this direction; a young man has been known to send his
wash-woman a letter intended for his sweetheart, and his lady correspondent a letter begging for more time in the payment of his laundry bill.

Titles.—Politeness requires that some title be used on the envelope;
a professional or official title, if the party has one, and if not, one of

Model 1.

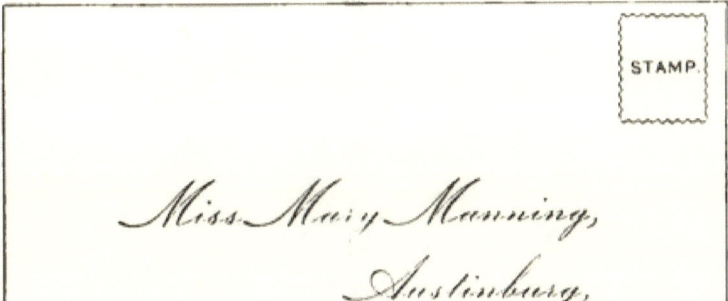

the common titles, *Mr.*, *Esq.*, etc. But as a matter of fact, most business men dispense with this formality at the present day, to save time.

If a business letter is written to a person acting in an official capacity,
his office should be designated in the address; as, "William K. Vander-
bilt, Pres. of N. Y. C. R. R. Co."

A list of the proper titles to use in addressing various persons in
prominent positions, is given elsewhere.

Residence.—By the residence we mean the full post-office address.
If a person lives in a large city, it includes the number and street (or
post-office box), city and state—as in models 2, 3 and 4; if in the country, it means the post-office, county and state—as in model 1. The
state is sometimes omitted in writing to persons in large and well-known

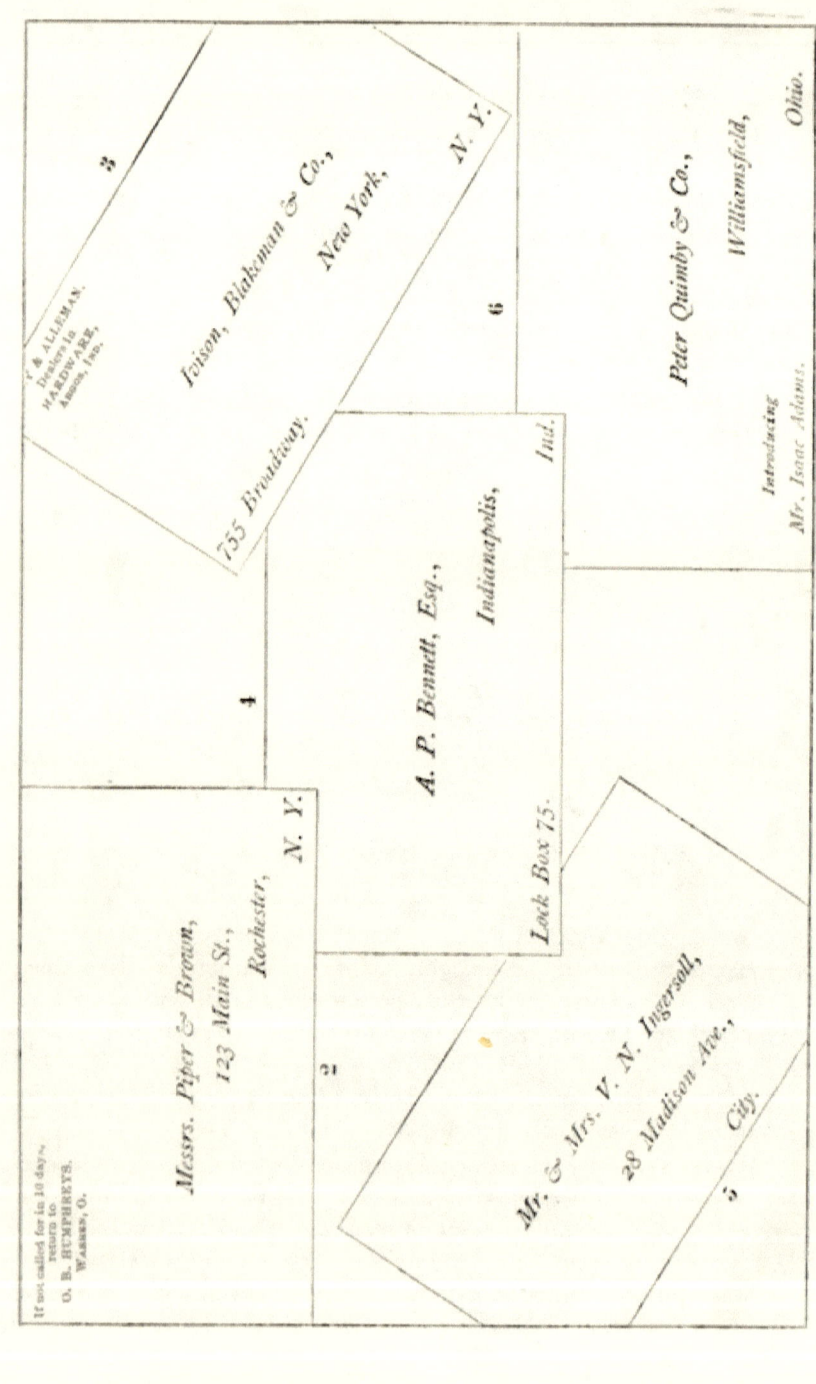

cities, but this is not a good custom, as there are usually several smaller places in the country by the same name, and postal clerks generally look in the right hand lower corner first, for the state. They can handle letters with less delay if the state is given ; and, abbreviating as we do in writing states, it takes but an instant of time.

Arrangement and position.—The writing should be in straight lines, parallel with the upper and lower edges of the envelope. The upper edge is the one that opens, and should be farthest from you, when you address the envelope.

If a person has difficulty in getting lines straight and parallel with the edges, it is a good plan to rule with heavy, black lines, a sheet of paper a little smaller than the envelope, and place it inside of the latter while writing, being careful to remove it before putting in the letter. If the envelope is so thick that you cannot see the lines through, the next best plan is to rule very light pencil lines, and erase them after the writing is dry. Never line with a pin, or any other sharp-pointed instrument, and dispense with all aids as soon as possible.

THE NAME should be written a little below the middle of the envelope, commencing far enough to the left so that the spaces on the right and left of it are about the same; each subsequent line in the address should commence a little farther to the right than the preceding one, and all be arranged so that the state is written near the right hand lower corner.

The proper order for the parts of the address, are :

For a country address,	For a city address,
Name and Title,	Name and Title,
Post-office,	Number and Street,
County,	City,
State.	State.

The county, number and street are, however, more frequently placed in the left hand lower corner on a line with the state, as in models 1, 3 and 4. The latter is a good form to use, as by having one less line to the right, that part of the address is plainer. The number of the post-office box may occupy a line following the name, or be written in left hand lower corner, as in model 4.

If a letter is to be delivered in the same city it is written, it is customary to use the word "City" to take the place of the post-office and state. In such cases the address consists of name, street number and word "City," and should occupy three lines, as in model 5.

If a letter is sent by a friend, his name should be written in the left lower corner.

Some urge that the order of addresses here given be reversed, and the name of the state be written first, because that is the order in which postal employes read the address. We do not see that this is sufficient reason for the change. If the postal clerks know where to look for each portion of the address, they can see as quickly in the form now in use, and this style of address certainly has a better appearance on the envelope; besides, at the office of *delivery* the present form gives the order in which the parts of the address are read.

Legibility.—The address on the envelope should be plainly written, especially the state and post-office. Some of the abbreviations which are used for the names of the states are so similar in form, that it is especially important they should be written plainly; as, *N. J.*, *N. Y.*; *Cal.*, *Col.*; *Mo.*, *Me.*; *Neb.*, *Nev.* 6,464,870 pieces of mail matter were sent to the "Dead-letter Office" last year for various reasons. Of these, 435,416 were *misdirected*, and 18,895 were *not addressed* at all.

Addressed and special request envelopes.—To save your correspondents trouble, and insure accuracy of address, an envelope a size smaller than the one in which your letter is sent, and with your own address printed upon it, may be inclosed.

A special request envelope is one with a card, giving your name and address, printed in the left upper corner, as in model 2. This card may also indicate your business, and serve as an advertisement.

All letters that for any reason are not delivered to the party addressed, are sent to the "Dead-letter Office," unless they have this card printed on the envelope. If you desire your uncalled for letters returned promptly, this card may be preceded by the clause, "If not called for in——days, return to," as in model 2.

The special request may be *written* if you do not use printed envelopes. Envelopes simply giving your name and address, are supposed to be returned in thirty days.

Sealed letters are returned without payment of additional postage, if the envelope bears your name and address.

Packages that appear to the postmaster to have sufficient value to warrant it, are returned to the sender if his address is on the package, and the return postage collected at the original mailing office. Circulars, catalogues, etc., are returned *only* when their wrapper bears the special request, "Please return to——," etc., and then the return postage is collected as on packages.

Inclosing stamp.—In writing to a person on a subject that does not directly interest him, and concerns only yourself, you should always enclose a stamp if you expect a reply. A single stamp enclosed should be fastened to the paper, so it may not drop out and be lost when the letter is opened. This may be done by sticking a very small corner of the stamp, or the gummed border of one from the outside row of a sheet of stamps, to the head of your letter.

Punctuation.—A comma should follow each part of the address, excepting the last, which is followed by a period. If a title follows the name, a comma should be used between the name and the title; if two titles are added, place a comma between them. A period should follow each abbreviation.

Capitals.—All important words, and all abbreviations should begin with capitals. Ordinarily, every word in the superscription is capitalized.

Notice carefully the arrangement, position and punctuation of the sample envelope addresses given in the accompanying models.

STAMP.

No domestic letter, that is a letter addressed to any post-office in our own country, will be forwarded until one two-cent stamp is placed thereon. If the letter is over weight and bears *one* two-cent stamp, the Department will collect the balance of the postage from the person to whom it is addressed. Of course it is always better, however, to see that your letters have sufficient stamps before they are sent out.

Position.—The stamp should be placed on the upper right hand corner of the envelope, about one-eighth of an inch from the end, and half as far from the upper edge; it should be right side up, with the edges parallel with the edges of the envelope. Placing the stamp on the envelope wherever you happen to is an evidence of carelessness, and disrespect for your correspondent. It is just as easy, and takes no more time, to put the stamp in the proper place.

Amount.—The present rate of postage on letters is two cents an ounce, and each fraction thereof; that is, if the letter weighs any more than one ounce, it requires more than one stamp. An abstract of the latest postal laws in regard to rates, is given on another page.

A. R. Lyons, Esq.

Brooklyn.

L.I.

DICTION AND CONSTRUCTION.

The diction of letters is not so formal as that of books. One should use common words, and express himself as he would in conversation.

Small words.—In our letters, as in conversation, we should not use too many large words. Give preference to the common and home words of our language. Our best orators and writers, you will notice, use very few uncommon words. It is usually better to use "*do*" than "*perform;*" "*see*" than "*perceive;*" "*tired*" than "*fatigued;*" "*have*" than "*possess;*" "*Sunday*" than "*Sabbath,*" etc.

Foreign words.—Use few if any foreign words and phrases. In correspondence they are usually indulged in by those who like to display learning, rather than by the best educated.

Slang words and phrases.—It is quite common nowadays to acquire in conversation or on the street a vocabulary of slang words. It is bad enough to use these in conversation, without putting them in writing. Do not use them in letters.

Grammatical accuracy.—A person who has to do business correspondence should understand the ordinary rules of grammar, and though he may not express himself in every instance in the best form, as he would in a studied composition, he should be careful to avoid grammatical errors. Any one will find the reading of good books and papers a great aid to him in the correct use of language.

Clearness.—In business correspondence especially, a person should express himself so that he will not be misunderstood. Make your statements pointed and direct, and so clear that they cannot be misinterpreted.

Sentences.—Short sentences, particularly in business correspondence, are to be preferred to long ones. It is a common fault to run sentences together, uniting them by "and" and "but," when it would be far better to make distinct sentences.

CAPITALS.

Some err in using too many capitals, and others in not using enough. Careful observation of capitals in standard books and papers, is an excellent way of learning their correct use.   A thoughtful study of the following rules will enable any one to avoid errors in his correspondence.

Full instruction has been given on preceding pages as to the capital·ization of the heading, introduction, close and superscription of letters. It is allowable and customary, in writing sums of money, especially in the body of a check, draft or note, to use capitals to begin every noun ; as, "One Thousand Four Hundred and Seventy-five Dollars."   It is also allowable in writing headings or advertisements, to capitalize important words.   In other cases follow these rules :

Capital letters should be used :—

1st.   To begin every sentence.

2d.   To begin every line of poetry.

3d.   To begin every quotation forming a sentence; **as,**
Pope says, " Hope dwells eternal in the human breast."

4th.   To begin all words denoting the Deity; as,
" Trust in Providence."   It is also customary to capitalize all personal pronouns referring to the Deity; as, "Trust in *Him* and *He* will give you strength."

5th.   To begin proper nouns and titles; as,
" Ben Hur was written by Gen'l Lew Wallace, of Crawfordsville, Ind."   In geographical names, composed of proper and common nouns, such as " New York city," " Ohio river," only the first part should be capitalized, unless the name is used in the address, because it may be used alone.   But in case of such names as " Jersey City," " White Mountains," etc., both must begin with capitals, because both are necessary to describe the place.

6th.   To begin the names of city, county, state and national official bodies and departments of the government, and official titles of the officers of the same ; as,
City Council, Infirmary Directors, State Legislature, Post-office Department ; Mayor, Sheriff, Governor, Minister to Russia (but not a sheriff, a constable, a policeman, a justice of the peace, except directly preceding a name).

7th.   To begin the names of all organized bodies, companies and political organizations ; as,
The Odd Fellows, The Burrows Bros. Co., National Guard.   The names of officers of societies and of railroads should not be capitalized unless immediately preceding a name.

8th.   To begin proper adjectives, the names of all religious sects all political parties, and adjectives or verbs derived from them ; as,
The American people; Baptist; Republican; the Congregational church ; the Republican party.

9th.   To begin names of things spoken of as persons, and of especially important things, events or bodies of men ; as,

"Upon this, *Fancy* began to bestir herself;" Declaration of Independence;
the Reformation; National Republican Convention.

10th.   To begin the names of the months, days of the week, names
of streets, and holidays.

Names of the seasons should not begin with capitals, unless they are person-
ified.

11th.   The pronoun I, and interjection O should be capitalized.

12th.   To begin words denoting certain regions; as,

Transatlantic, the North, the South, the East, the West, and their correspond-
ing adjectives, when applied to divisions of a country; as, the North of Africa,
Southern Ohio, Pacific Coast.

13th.   To begin the words State and Territory where referring to
one of the United States, *but not "church and state," and similar uses.*

14th.   To begin words used to indicate the Bible directly ; as,

The Scriptures, Gospel of Luke, etc., but not in "to preach the gospel,"
"scriptural doctrine," etc.

15th.   To begin the names of important buildings and localities; as,

The Public Library ; the High School (but not when spoken of in a general
sense; as, "our high schools"); Central Market ; the Penitentiary ; but not jail,
prison or post-office, because commonly spoken of in a general sense.

PUNCTUATION.

The proper punctuation of the heading, introduction and close of
letters is given in the instruction on those subjects and accompanying
models.

Should not be neglected.—Some business men write so carelessly and hurriedly that they almost entirely neglect the use of punctuation marks.   Business letters, as well as other written documents, should
be carefully punctuated.   By neglecting to do so or punctuating incor-
rectly, the meaning of the sentence is often entirely changed.

Punctuation (from the Latin *Punctum,* a point) is the art of
dividing written composition by means of points to make it correctly express the desired meaning.   Punctuation was not generally known until
about 1600 A. D., after the invention of the art of printing.   Punctua-

tion cannot be made a mere mechanical process; it is hardly possible to give rules that will apply in all cases. The best one is the *rule of common sense.*

Importance.—The importance of the subject makes it worthy of careful study and practice, by any one who would write a good and intelligible letter.

Sometimes serious or ludicrous mistakes occur by the careless misplacing or omission of punctuation points.

John Quincy Adams once gained a law suit involving $50,000, the decision of which turned on the position of a comma.

The Tariff Act passed by the XLIId Congress provided that fruit plants, and certain other commodities, should be admitted free of duty. In engrossing or printing the Act, a comma was inserted between fruit and plants, consequently, "all fruits," and "all plants" were put upon the "free list," and this mistake, (if mistake it was) cost the United States about $2,000,000. A special Act of Congress was necessary to get rid of that comma.

A toast at a public dinner was, "Woman; without her, man would be a savage." The next day it appeared in print, "Woman, without her man, would be a savage."

A report of a Clergyman's temperance sermon read, "A young woman in my neighborhood died suddenly last Sunday, while I was preaching the gospel in a state of beastly intoxication." A comma after the word gospel, would have made the sentence read, "A young woman in my neighborhood died suddenly last Sunday, while I was preaching the gospel, in a state of beastly intoxication."

The following notice was once read in church: "John Brown having gone to sea (see) his wife, desires the prayers of the congregation in his behalf." The comma should have been placed after the word sea.

Punctuate the following lines so as to make them express a fact:

> Every lady in the land
> Has twenty nails upon each hand
> Five and twenty on hands and feet
> This is true without deceit.

AN EPITAPH—PUNCTUATE TO SUIT.

He is an old and experienced man in vice and wickedness he is never found opposing the words of iniquity he takes delight in the downfall of the neighbors he never rejoices in the prosperity of any of his fellow creatures he is always ready to assist in destroying the peace of society he takes no pleasure in serving the Lord he is uncommonly diligent in sowing discord among his friends and acquaintances he takes no pride in laboring to promote the cause of Christianity he has not been negligent in endeavoring to stigmatize all public teachers he makes no exertions to subdue his evil passions he strives hard to build up Satan's kingdom he lends no aid to the support of the Gospel among the heathen he contributes largely to the evil adversary he pays no attention to good advice he gives great heed to the devil he will never go to heaven he must go where he will receive the just recompense of his reward.

PUNCTUATION MARKS.

The principal points used in punctuation are the following:

The Period (.) should follow every declarative and every imperative sentence, and every abbreviation; as,

Your favor received. Dare to do right. Prof. C. O. D.

The Interrogation Point (?) must be placed after every question; as,

Who wrote " Beautiful Snow ?" An interrogation point should also be used after an interrogative phrase in a sentence, and in such cases the next word does not begin with a capital; as, "The question, What do we live for? is a solemn one."

The Exclamation Point (!) is used after words, phrases or sentences denoting strong emotion; as,

Alas! I am undone. " Would that I had perished !" The above note in reference to the Interrogation, also applies to the Exclamation.

A Colon (:) is used before a quotation, enumeration, or observation, that is introduced by "thus," "as follows," "the following," or any equivalent expression; as,

He answered my argument thus : "The man who lives by hope will die by despair."

SECOND. A colon must be placed between the great divisions of sentences, when minor subdivisions are separated by semicolons; as,

"You have called yourself an atom in the universe ; you have said that you were but an insect in the solar blaze : is your present pride consistent with these professions?"

THIRD. A colon is used between the members of a compound sentence, when there is no conjunction between them and the connection is slight; as,

" Never flatter the people : leave that to such as mean to betray them."

FOURTH. When the time of day is denoted by figures, a colon is placed between the hours and minutes; as,

School begins at 8:45 A. M.

A Semicolon (;) is placed between the members of compound sentences, unless the connection is very close; as,

" Lying lips are an abomination to the Lord; but they that deal truly are His delight."

SECOND. A semicolon is placed between parts of sentences which are subdivided by commas; as,

"Mirth should be the embroidery of conversation, not the web; and wit the ornament of the mind, not the furniture."

THIRD. A semicolon must be placed before the conjunction *as*, when it introduces an example; as,

"We, the people of the United States, etc."

FOURTH. When several long clauses occur in succession, all having common dependence on some other clause or word, they must be separated by semicolons. If the clauses are short, they may be separated by commas.

The Comma (,) is used to separate words, phrases, clauses, and short members, closely connected with the rest of the sentence, but requiring separation by some point in consequence of the construction or arrangement.

SECOND. When, to avoid repetition, *and, or, nor*, or a *verb* previously used is omitted, a comma takes its place.

The Dash (—) is used to denote a break in the construction, a suspension of the sense, a sudden interruption, and hesitation in the speaker; also after other points when a greater pause than they denote is required.

Marks of Parenthesis—( )—are used to inclose words which explain, modify, or add to, the leading proposition of a sentence, when introduced in such a way as to break the connection between the dependent parts and interfere with their harmonious flow.

An interrogation point within parentheses is often placed after an assertion to throw doubt on it; as,

"When I get the office (?), I shall spend my leisure time in reading."

An exclamation point similarly enclosed, denotes wonder, irony, or contempt; as,

"This accurate scholar (!), who went to high school and graduated at Yale, has actually made half a dozen grammatical mistakes in one short paragraph."

The Apostrophe (') is used to denote the omission of a letter or letters; as, *'tis, I'll, o'er.* The apostrophe is used to denote the possessive case of nouns; as, *America's wealth.*

Quotation Points (" ") are used to enclose words quoted from

Newport, R.I. June 1, 1887.

My dear Julia:

You must not forget your promise to spend your vacation with us
this season. We have plenty of room,
and your presence will add greatly to
our enjoyment.

Yours sincerely,

Mary Keene.

an author or speaker, or represented in narratives as employed in dialogue; as,

"By doing nothing," says an old writer, "men learn to do evil." "Come' quick! or I perish," shrieked the exhausted hunter.

Single points are used to enclose a quotation within a quotation ; as,

"'Many's the slip,'
Hath the proverb well said, ''twixt the cup and the lip!'"

MISCELLANEOUS HINTS.

Do not write anonymous letters. Avoid writing with pencil, or with ink of any other color than black. Do not fill a letter with apologies and repetitions. Do not use figures in the body of a letter, except in writing dates and sums of money. As a rule, private matters should not be mentioned in business letters.

Upon receipt of a letter containing money, immediately count the sum, and note same on the letter. Do not be afraid to write of common-place things in social correspondence. It is usually the small things of every day life that prove most interesting in such letters.

Style.—The style of the letter should correspond to the subject, and the relation between parties. To friends, familiar; to relations, affectionate ; to children, simple and playful ; to inferiors, courteous ; to superiors, respectful ; on important subjects, impressive ; in condolence, sympathetic ; in congratulation, joyous.

It is impossible to give any rule that will apply to all cases. Perhaps a good rule would be, to write as you talk ; however, we usually have to use fewer words than we would in conversation on the same subject. This is especially true of business letters. *They should be brief and to the point* ordinarily, though not so brief as to make an unpleasant impression on the reader. Sometimes it is advisable or necessary to have a business letter almost the reverse, making the statements or explanations full and complete. In almost every case the person will need to use his own judgment and taste as to the style to adopt in a given case.

Public and descriptive letters admit of the use of more or less flowery language, but in ordinary letters, such figures should be used sparingly, as they would be under like circumstances in conversation. Do not write about nothing, or repeat simply for the purpose of filling space.

Complete letter-writers are books giving model letters, so-called, on all subjects. Some young people fall into the habit of copying these almost word for word, instead of writing original letters. This is a bad practice; it is better to send a poorly constructed letter, of which you are the author, than a "model" one copied.

A case is related of a young man who copied and used such a letter proposing marriage, and received a reply saying, "you will find my answer on the next page." It was a polite refusal.

Emphasis.—In writing, we denote emphasis by underlining words. Some persons are in the habit of filling their letters with underlined words. This is not commendable. Few if any words should be underlined in letters.

Answers.—As a rule every letter should be answered, if it is not insulting. If it is, the letter may be ignored, or returned. The latter is usually the better way.

Letters requiring an answer, should be answered promptly. In fact, prompt people are usually the most successful in business. Of course the answer will ordinarily correspond in style to the letter, being written upon the same subject.

Recapitulation.—It is well in the beginning of a business letter to refer to the subject and date of the letter to which it is an answer. This will call to the mind of your correspondent his letter to you, and perhaps save him time in looking up the subject, besides your letters then, when filed, are something of a history of the transaction.

Care of letters.—Answered and unanswered letters should be kept separate. An answered letter on an important subject should always be filed for reference. There are very many systems of filing now used in business. If you employ no better method, the letters may be simply folded to a uniform size, and on one end of the back the name of the writer, date of its receipt, and date of answer may be written. It is also well to briefly indicate the subject of the communication. This will often save time in opening a letter and reading it.

Copying letters.—It is well to preserve copies of all important letters. The plan most used by business men is to make letter-press copies, which gives a *fac simile*. If the letter is dictated to a stenographer, his short-hand notes may be preserved.

Postscripts.—The writing of postscripts is largely a matter of habit. Try to think of all you want to say before you begin writing and put it in the body of the letter. If a matter of sufficient importance is thought of afterwards, it may be written in a postscript,—with this exception : a message of compliment or affection should never be written as a postscript. Words which, if written in the body of the letter would be decidedly complimentary, may appear insulting if put in a postscript as an after-thought.

Beginning and ending.—Social and private letters should begin in an easy and natural way. Business letters may be a little more formal or abrupt in the beginning. The former should generally close with some expression of affection or compliment, in addition to the complimentary close. Such expressions are often a part of the last sentence.

Care in writing.—As a rule, it is better not to write a letter when excited or angry. More care should be used in this respect in writing than in speaking. Words spoken are soon forgotten, but what is *written* may be kept as a record against us for years. For this reason, it is wise to wait until one can soberly decide just what is best to write.

Truthfulness.—In writing, as in talking, we should always be strictly truthful. Untruthfulness often leads to unfair dealing and possibly to crime, while strict truthfulness and honesty in small as well as large things, gains the confidence of others, and is best as a matter of policy, if for no higher motive. True and lasting success comes only from honor and strict integrity.

Abbreviations.—As a rule, no abbreviations should be used in the body of a letter. Do not write " & " for " and," and spell out all words in full instead of contracting. If any abbreviations are used, employ the terms that are accepted by common usage. Do not abbreviate an abbreviation, as " *Mess.*" for " *Messrs.;*" " *Ad.*" for " *Adv.;*" etc.

Junior and Senior.—The abbreviations for these words are " *Jr.*" or " *Jun.,*" and " *Sr.*" or " *Sen.*" The former is used by the son and the latter by the father, when both have the same name. The son usually discontinues the use of " *Jr.*" upon the death of his father. The abbreviation should immediately follow the name ; it does not take the place of any title, and should begin with a capital.

Nota bene.—This means "mark well," and the abbreviation is N. B. Like the postscript, it follows the signature to the letter.

Paging.—If a letter consists of more than one sheet, the leaves should be paged and arranged in proper order.

Postal cards.—The introduction and complimentary close may be omitted in writing postal cards, and nothing but the address is allowed upon the face of a postal.

If an answer is required, the writer's full address should be given unless it is well known by the person addressed. Postal cards, on which anything is pasted or fastened in any way, are unmailable.

Important or private matters should never be written on postal cards.

Titles and signatures.—People of good taste do not use titles in signing letters. *Rev.*, *Hon.*, *Prof.*, etc., are prefixed to the names of gentlemen by others, but should not thus be used by themselves.

LETTERS OF INTRODUCTION.

A LETTER OF INTRODUCTION is one written for the purpose of introducing a person to a friend or acquaintance, and is commonly used only when it is not convenient to personally introduce the party. There are two kinds of letters of introduction, *social* and *business*. The following general suggestions will apply to both classes :

Be careful whom you introduce.—Do not introduce any one socially, with whom you think your friend would not like to associate. By introducing an improper person to a business acquaintance you may do the latter a great injustice.

Should be short.—Letters of introduction should be short, as they are usually delivered in person, and it is embarrassing to wait for the reading of a long letter.

Praise.—One may use the language of cordial friendship, but extravagant eulogy is out of place in written as well as oral introductions. It is possible to do your friend an injustice by over-praising him, as well as by failing to state his real merits.

Should not be sealed.—A letter of introduction should always be delivered to the one introduced unsealed, that he may see its contents if he desires to do so.

The superscription.—The envelope address of a letter of introduction is the same as if it were sent by mail, except that the words, "introducing ——" are written in the lower left hand corner, as on envelope model 6.

Proper delivery.—The proper way to deliver a letter of introduction is to send it to the person to whom it is addressed, with the name and address of the person introduced. The former should then call on the latter and extend his hospitalities.

In most cases, however, especially if it is a business letter of introduction, the bearer presents the letter in person. Care should be taken to present it at a time when it will cause the least inconvenience to the person addressed.

A Business Letter of Introduction.

Dayton, O., Nov. 3, '89.

Messrs. A. Burt & Co.,
    St. Louis, Mo.

        Gentlemen :—This will introduce to you our friend and former book-keeper, Mr. Chas. D. Ranney, who visits your city to engage in the hardware business. He is a capable, energetic, honorable gentleman, and will, we are confident, be very successful in his new venture.

Any courtesies you may show him will be duly appreciated by

        Yours truly,

        Smith & Brown.

LETTERS OF APPLICATION.

By this heading we mean letters applying for employment. As the success of the applicant often depends entirely upon his letter, careful attention should be given to the following:

Should be carefully written.—His letter of application is often the only evidence of the writer's fitness for a position; great care should therefore be taken in the writing and in the wording of the letter. Numerous advertisements seen in the papers close with the words, "apply in your own hand writing," showing the importance that business men place upon good penmanship. Read your letter over carefully before sending, and if you see any way in which the wording might be improved, or find a single mistake, the letter should by all means be re-written.

Your success in the securing of the place may depend upon this slight extra trouble on your part. If the position is an important one, you will be almost sure to fail in securing it, unless your letter of application is carefully written.

Wording of the letter.—The applicant should usually state what his education has been, what experience he has had in business, if any, state his age, qualifications, etc., and give any general information concerning himself which he thinks would interest the person addressed. It is well to enclose copies of letters of recommendation, if he has such. While the applicant should state his qualifications clearly, it is equally important that he state them modestly as well.

A SPECIMEN LETTER.

Washington, D. C., Jan. 2, '90.

Mr. E. R. Harvey,

   City.

    Dear Sir:—In reply to your advertisement in this morning's Star, I hereby apply for a position in your office. I am eighteen years old and a graduate of our High School, and Business College.

    Can refer you, by permission, to the Principal of either school, also to Mr. C. A. Frost, in whose office I was employed one year. Hoping for a favorable reply, I am,

            Very respectfully,

              Charles Deering.

LETTERS OF CREDIT.

 A LETTER OF CREDIT is one in which the writer loans credit to the bearer; that is, he guarantees the payment of a certain sum in case the person asking credit fails to pay.

 In style, it closely resembles a letter of introduction. The model below is a good specimen of letters of this class.

SPECIMEN LETTER.

Andover, O., Sept. 8, 1889.

Messrs. Root & McBride Bros.,

   Cleveland, O.

    Gentlemen:—Please allow the bearer, Mr. James C. Ranney, a credit for any goods he may wish, to an amount not exceeding $1,500, on four months' time, and I will be responsible to you for the prompt payment of same.

    Should he make any purchases of you on account of this letter, please notify me of the amount, and in case of failure in payment of account when due, let me know it immediately

            Yours truly,

Mr. Ranney's signature.*   Chas. A. Hubbard.

  James C. Ranney.

 *If the bearer is not known to the party of whom credit is asked the letter should contain his signature.

LETTERS OF RECOMMENDATION.

A RECOMMENDATION is sometimes given in a letter of introduction, but is generally a separate letter. Great care should be exercised in giving letters of recommendation. Do not recommend any one too highly and never recommend an unworthy person; innocent persons may suffer by placing confidence in the letter which over-praises. Recommendations may be special or general. Special letters are addressed like ordinary letters, to some person, while the other class should be addressed in a general way " To whom it may concern," or "To the public," etc.

The following are examples of the two classes :

123 E. 14th St., New York,
January 14, 1890.

Mr. E. A. Hammond,,
Chicago, Ill.

Dear Sir:

The bearer of this letter, Miss Millie Humphreys, visits your city to find employment as an amanuensis. She has been with us during the past three years, has given excellent satisfaction, and only leaves our employ because she has friends in Chicago and prefers a residence in that city.

Miss Humphreys writes short-hand rapidly, and makes an excellent transcript on either the Remington type-writer or caligraph.

If you can aid her in securing employment, it will be a special favor to her as also to ourselves.

Very truly yours,
J. C. Williams & Co.

New Orleans, La., July 1, 1889.

To whom it may concern :

This is to certify that Mr. Charles A. Scott has been in our employ during the past three years. He is a faithful, hard working and reliable young man, and we take pleasure in recommending him to any one in need of such services as he can render.

Respectfully,
John C. Brown & Co.

LETTERS ACKNOWLEDGING RECEIPT OF MONEY.

A RECEIPT should always be sent, for money received in a letter. This receipt may be embodied in the form of a letter, or may be a separate receipt; in either case, the amount received should be stated and also the account or thing for which it was received. The receipt, of course, should be sent promptly, that the sender may know his remittance has reached you.

Specimen Letters.

Cleveland, O., Jan. 1, 1890.

Messrs. Samuel Morgan & Co.,

San Francisco, Cal.

Gentlemen :—Your favor of the 25th ult., enclosing New York draft for $26.30 in payment of your account, came duly to hand.

Thanking you for promptness in remitting, and hoping to receive further orders, we are,

Very respectfully yours,

S. C. Brown & Co..

Some firms use a printed form similar to the following for such purposes, in which case it is only necessary to fill the blank spaces :

OFFICE OF

J. H. HAMMOND & CO.,

85 Main Street.

Buffalo, N. Y., ... *188* ....

Dear Sirs :

Your favor enclosing ....

.... *duly received,*

for which please accept thanks.

Yours very truly,

Cincinnati, Ohio, Dec. 20. 1881

Ivison, Blakeman, Taylor & Co.

753 & 755 Broadway, New York.

Gentlemen:— Please send us by Express
500 Gross Spencerian No. 1 Pens, and draw at
sight for amt. of invoice.

Yours respectfully, Chas. Adams & Co.

LETTERS ORDERING GOODS.

A LETTER ORDERING GOODS should contain very few words, except the order, unless there are some special instructions to be given. The order may be embraced in the body of the letter, or may be written on a separate sheet. If the list of goods is written in the letter, it is well to make a separate line for each item, beginning these lines directly under each other and to the right of the marginal line of the letter, as in the following model :

Detroit, Mich., Oct. 1, 1889.

Messrs. Ivison, Blakeman & Co.,

    753 and 755 Broadway,

      New York, N. Y.

Gentlemen :—Please send at once by "American Express" the following goods:

    25 sets Spencerian new standard copy slips.

    50 gross Spencerian pens No. 1.

    4 gross oblique pen holders.

    2 doz. Webster's Handy Dictionary.

Yours truly,

John Jones.

In ordering any kind of goods, state distinctly just what is wanted, so there may be no error in filling your order. Unless the party knows from your previous orders the conveyance by which you wish the goods shipped, it is well to state your preference.

Goods sent C. O. D.—Packages are often sent by express, C. O. D. (collect on delivery). When this is the case, the bill is payable to the Express Co. on receipt of goods. Packages on which a small amount is to be collected, or those to strangers, are often shipped in this way. Ordinarily the person receiving the package by this method pays the express charges on the goods, and also pays for returning the money. The Express Co. collects the return charges of the *shipper*, however, unless he has written on his invoice, or envelope containing same, the words "collect return charges."

LETTERS ENCLOSING A REMITTANCE.

It is not considered safe to enclose currency or silver in a letter. The more common ways of remitting are by draft, check, money order, express order, registered letter, and postal note.

Checks.—Most business houses, at the present day, pay nearly all their local bills by bank checks. As a rule these should not be sent to out of town correspondents, as the receiver would then usually have to pay for their collection. Some firms, whose dealings are almost entirely with persons doing a regular banking business, remit their checks in payment of bills, marking them " New York Exchange." In such cases the receiver deposits them the same as drafts, without having to pay for their collection.

Drafts.—Bank drafts, usually New York Exchange, may be purchased of your local bank. This is perhaps the safest and most convenient way of remitting money. Banks do not like to issue drafts for sums less than $5, and for smaller amounts, money orders or postal notes may be purchased.

To order.—A draft or check should always be made " to order," unless the person to whom it is given makes a special request otherwise ; to save him the trouble of identification, it may then be made to " bearer." If the draft or check is made *to order*, it is necessary for the payee to endorse it before he can collect the same, and it then becomes to the payer a receipt for the amount.

Enclosing a draft or check.—It is better to fold a draft or check with the letter ; this makes the best fold for it, and it is not apt to drop out when the letter is opened.

Endorsement.—A draft or check should always be endorsed across the left-hand end ; then, as the bank clerk turns the paper over with his right hand, the endorsement is right side up and at the top of the check. If endorsed across the right-hand side the clerk will have to turn the check end for end to read the endorsement.

Money orders.—Money orders are issued by the post-office department on all the principal post-offices in the United States, at the following rates :

Orders not exceeding	$ 5 . . 5c.	Over $40 and not exceeding $50 . . 25c.
Over $ 5 and not exceeding 10 . . 8c.	" 50 " " 60 . . 30c.
" 10 " " 15 . . 10c.	" 60 " " 70 . . 35c.
" 15 " " 30 . . 15c.	" 70 " " 80 . . 40c.
" 30 " " 40 . 20c.	" 80 " " 100 . . 45c.

A single money order may include any amount from one cent to one hundred dollars, inclusive.

These are made to "order" and the receiver must be identified before he can collect them. This, therefore, is a very safe way of remitting money.

Express orders.—The principal express companies now issue money orders payable either to "order" or "bearer" at the following rates:

$ 5 00	. . . . 5c.	$30 00 . .	. . . . 12c.
10 00	. . . . 8c.	40 00 . . . . 15c.
20 00 . . . . 10c.	50 00 . . . . 20c.

Over $50 00 proportionately.

This, also, is a very safe way of making remittances.

Registered letters.—The post-office department register either letters or packages to any post-office in the U. S. The fee for registering a letter or package is 10 cents, in addition to the postage. The postage and register fee must be fully prepaid. A receipt is given by the department for such letter or package, and it is receipted for by each employe through whose hands it passes. This is an inexpensive and comparatively safe method of sending small sums.

Postal notes.—Postal notes may be purchased at any money order office for any amount less than $5. Fee, 3 cents each. As they are payable to the bearer, to use them is little more secure than to remit currency. However, for small sums, as fractions of a dollar, a postal note is usually a safe medium.

Money by telegraph.—Telegraph and express companies will telegraph their agents at any important city or village office, to pay money to a person specified. The rates in addition to the cost of telegram, are about as follows:

Sums of $100 or less, one per cent., or 50c to $1.

Over $100 to $200	. . . .	$1 25
" 200 to 300	. . . .	1 50
" 300 to 400	. . . .	1 75
" 400 to 500	. . . .	2 00

Larger sums in proportion.

A letter with a bill.—A letter explaining what a remittance is for should always accompany it, except when the amount is for payment of a bill which is enclosed. In such cases, a letter may be written, but if one is not, it would be understood for what purpose the remittance was made.

Be careful in addressing envelopes containing valuable papers. Last year the 5,467,042 letters and packages opened at the Dead-letter Office were found to contain money, drafts, checks, notes, postal notes, postage stamps, etc., to the amount of $1,384,563.21.

Specimen Letters.

Andover, Ashtabula Co., O.,

Nov. 6, 1889.

The Tribune,

New York city.

Please find enclosed post-office money order for $1.00 to pay for the weekly "Tribune" one year from Nov. 1st, 1889.

Yours truly,

Henry Adams.

The following letter should contain two enclosures, the draft and the bill. A similar form may be used for letters enclosing checks, money orders, express orders, etc. :

Baltimore, Md., July 3, 1890.

Ranney & Raymond,

Boston, Mass.

Gentlemen :—Inclosed please find N. Y. draft for $36.73 in full of our account.

Please receipt and return bill, and oblige,

Yours truly,

John Jones.

LETTERS ENCLOSING INVOICE.

When goods are shipped, a letter or invoice, or both, should always be mailed to the consignee. Unless some special information is to be given, it is customary for business men to simply mail the invoice of goods, and perhaps state thereon the conveyance by which the goods were shipped. Some are accustomed to enclose the invoice in a letter of one or two lines, similar to the following :

244 John St. New York.

August 19, 1885.

Winch & Vernon:

Auburn. N. Y.

Gentlemen:— Inclosed please to find our
invoice of the articles ordered in your favor
of August 15. The goods have been packed
with care, and forwarded by Express.

Yours respectfully,

James W. Lennox

IVISON, BLAKEMAN & CO.,

PUBLISHERS,

753 and 755 Broadway.

New York, Oct. 3, 1889.

Mr. John Jones,

Detroit, Mich.

Dear Sir:—Enclosed please find invoice of goods ordered by you on the 1st inst., and shipped you to-day by "American Express."

Hoping they will reach you in good condition, and prove satisfactory, we are,

Very truly yours,

Ivison, Blakeman & Co.

PUBLIC LETTERS.

PUBLIC LETTERS are communications for publication, written in the form of a letter. They are generally addressed to some individual. This form of writing is adopted because it arouses personal interest in what is said, and admits of a more informal style of composition. Most of the letters published in newspapers are addressed either to the editor, or some public man.

How to write for the Press.—Write plainly, on one side of the paper only. Be careful in the spelling, capitalization, paragraphing, etc. Number the pages. Always give your own name and address; not for publication, necessarily, but as a guarantee of good faith. If you do not wish your name published you may sign the letter with an assumed name, but in addition you must not fail to give your own name and address, otherwise your letter will certainly find its way into the waste basket.

LETTERS OF CONGRATULATION.

A LETTER OF CONGRATULATION is one written to a friend who has had some good fortune. It should, of course, be written in a cheerful, lively style suited to the occasion. Any thing of an unpleasant nature concerning yourself, matters of advice, or other subjects, should not be mentioned in such a letter. The following model is one of this class of letters :

Cleveland, O., Aug. 8, 1889.

Friend Charles:

I am greatly pleased to learn that, notwithstanding the general dullness of business, you have succeeded in obtaining a clerkship. I doubt not your
firm will regard themselves fortunate in securing your services. In the meantime,
accept my congratulations upon your success.

Hoping your stay may be permanent and prosperous, I am,

Truly yours,

Irving Eliott.

C. A. Leonard,
    Washington, D. C.

LETTERS OF CONDOLENCE.

A LETTER OF CONDOLENCE is one written to a friend who has suffered
some loss or bereavement.   Such a letter is one of the most difficult of
all to write.   It requires good taste and sympathetic feeling.   In offering
condolence, carefully avoid recalling to the sufferer the details of the
case, and do not attempt to argue on the subject.   Reasons that should
appeal to the head cannot affect the heart.   Of course, never insinuate
that your friend is in the least directly or indirectly to blame.   What is
most needed at such a time is sympathy.   Endeavor, as much as is possible in words, to show your friend that you are ready and anxious to
share his grief, and your sympathetic feeling will thus lessen the sorrow.

The following letter, written to John Adams on the death of Mrs.
Adams, is one of the finest models of letters of this class:

Monticello, November 13, 1818.

The public papers, my dear friend, announce the fatal event of which your
letter of October the 20th had given me ominous foreboding. Tried myself in the
school of affliction, by the loss of every form of connection which can rive the
human heart, I know well, and feel what you have lost, what you have suffered, are
suffering, and yet have to endure. The same trials have taught me that for ills so
immeasurable, time and silence are the only medicine. I will not, therefore, by
useless condolences, open afresh the sluices of your grief, nor, although mingling
my tears with yours, will I say a word more where words are vain, but that it is
of some comfort to us both that the time is not very far distant at which we are to
deposit in the same cerement our sorrows and suffering bodies, and to ascend in

essence to an ecstatic meeting with the friends we have loved and lost, and whom
we shall still love and never lose again. God bless you and support you under
your heavy affliction.

Th. Jefferson.

TELEGRAMS.

TELEGRAMS are so much used now in business, that to be able to
write out a good message is one of the qualifications desirable for a business man. Some people do not seem to be able to express their meaning
in few words. Such should write what they wish to say, and then cut
out all unnecessary words.

Telegraph companies usually charge a certain rate for ten words, and
so much per word for each one more than that number. The sender,
therefore, if he pays for the message, saves money by expressing himself
in few words. It is better to put in one or two words more, however,
and be sure that your meaning will not be misunderstood, than to con-
dense so much that there is liability of doubt in a matter of importance.

Night messages.—Telegraph companies send messages at night,
when their business is light, at greatly reduced rates. Such messages are
not delivered until the following morning.

ADVERTISING.

The writing of circulars and newspaper advertisements has come to
be an art at the present day. In our larger cities, men who make this their
profession give their entire time to writing advertisements for whom-
ever may apply, and is willing to pay them for such services. With the
competition we have now, in almost all kinds of business, there is no
doubt that the success of many firms is due largely to their style of advertising. The subject, therefore, is worth special and careful attention.
To know just what to say, and how to say it, in a way that will attract
the attention and win the patronage of the reader, is an art well worth
acquiring. With the ceaseless and sharp competition that most business
houses have to meet, it seems necessary to do more or less advertising,
in one way or another. We should, therefore, study to make our advertisements attractive and to the point. As a general rule, the business
man can, on account of his better knowledge of his business, write

his own advertisements better than any one he can employ. To be able to do this, however, requires study and practice on his part. Some of the largest advertisers have many other things to give their attention to, and employ a man who spends his whole time in looking after their advertising. In firms, one member of the firm usually has sole charge of the advertising department. The man who would be successful should not under-estimate the value of advertising.

NOTES AND CARDS.

Most of us have more or less to do with visiting, business and professional cards, and the various social forms, such as invitations, acceptances, regrets, cards of thanks, etc.

A few general hints are here given in reference to them without devoting much space to this part of the work.

Special features.—The following are the ways in which notes differ from letters; they are more formal; they are written wholly in the third person; the date is usually at the bottom, and the signature is generally omitted.

Care should be taken not to change from the third person to second or first.

The following is an example of such error :

" Miss Jones is much obliged to Mr. Smith for his handsome Christmas present. I would have written you sooner if I had not been out of the city."

Materials.—The paper and envelopes used should be plain and of rich quality. For weddings only pure white should be used, but delicate tints are allowable for other occasions. White is always in good taste.

Size.—The styles as to size and shape vary so much and change so often that no definite information can be given on this subject.

Envelopes.—Invitations to parties, weddings, etc., are generally enclosed in two envelopes; the inside envelope of the same quality as the paper, the outside one not so fine. The full post office address is written on the outer envelope, and the name of the person or persons invited, on the inner one. Answers to invitations do not require two envelopes, nor do personal or private notes.

FRENCH PHRASES.—The following French phrases and words, or their initials, are sometimes used on notes and cards:

R. S. V. P.—*Repondez s'il vous plait*,—answer, if you please.

P. P. C.—*Pour prendre conge*,—to take leave.

Costume de rigueur,—full dress, in character.

Bal masque,—masquerade ball.

Soiree dansante,—dancing party.

These phrases are, however, passing out of use.

WEDDING INVITATIONS.

INVITATIONS TO WEDDINGS should be issued ten days or more before the ceremony, by the parents or nearest friend of the bride.

They may be engraved, written, or printed from type, on cards or note paper. The note form is preferable for an invitation of this kind.

One form of invitation is here given. If the favor of an answer is requested, the letters " R. S. V. P.," or the phrase, are placed at the bottom.

Mr. & Mrs. E. P. Collins

request your presence

at the marriage of their daughter

Edith

to

Mr. Harry K. Holloway,

Tuesday, March twenty-sixth,

Eighteen hundred and eighty-nine,

at five P. M.

Grace Church,

Kansas City, Missouri.

Announcement.—Sometimes an announcement card or note is issued after the wedding, announcing the marriage, and enclosing a reception card to the friends whom the parties desire to receive.

The following is one of the numerous forms that may be used:

Mr. Charles S. Cadwallader,

Miss Caroline A. Young,

Married,

Wednesday, April twenty-first, 1886.

At Home,

Thursday, May 27th and June 3d,

96 Prospect Ave.,

Buffalo, N. Y.

Anniversary Weddings.—People sometimes celebrate anniversaries of their marriage, and this is a commendable custom, if the occasion is made one of congratulation and reminiscence, not of formality and ostentation.

The *first* anniversary is called the Paper Wedding; *fifth*, Wooden Wedding; *tenth*, Tin Wedding; *fifteenth*, Crystal (glass) Wedding; *twentieth*, China Wedding; *twenty-fifth*, Silver Wedding; *thirtieth*, Pearl Wedding; *fortieth*, Coral Wedding; *forty-fifth*, Bronze Wedding; *fiftieth*, Golden Wedding; and the *seventy-fifth*, Diamond Wedding.

DINNERS.

A well appointed dinner is one of the pleasantest occasions of social life. The company being more select than at ordinary parties, greater care is observed in regard to all arrangements. To avoid mistakes, one should be careful in the invitation as to the day and hour, and each one should be addressed to the person for whom it is intended.

The invitations may be either written or printed.

Mr. and Mrs. C. J. Stradley

request your presence

at the marriage of their daughter

Lida,

&

Henry T. Loomis

Tuesday Evening, December 26th

at eight o'clock,

Rochester, Indiana.

1882.

PARTIES.

Simple forms **are in** best taste **for** invitations to parties. **The follow-**ing is commended **as a** model :

Senator and Mrs. *Sherman request the pleasure of your* company, *on Wednesday Evening, January fourth, from* eight *to* twelve *o'clock.*

209 Indiana *Avenue.* R. S. V. P.

Familiar Notes.—If the parties are on intimate terms, the formal style of invitation may be omitted, and that of a familiar letter used instead, or for a child's party a style like the following :

1884.   1889.

> Come and see me, little friend,
> Some afternoon at three ;
> Bring your Dolly, if you can,
> And stay till after tea.

Harriette Ellen O'Donald,

At Home,

Friday afternoon, May third,

Three o'clock.

215 E. Tenth St., Topeka.

ACCEPTANCES AND REGRETS.

Answers to invitations are of two kinds: acceptances and regrets.

When Necessary.—Invitations to receptions, weddings, parties, and all other social entertainments, except dinners, do not require an

acceptance, unless they contain the letters R. S. V. P., or their equivalent.   A failure to answer, is understood as an acceptance.   If a person
is unable to attend, a regret should always be sent.

Dinners.—An invitation to a dinner or gathering of any kind
where it is understood a certain number are invited, should always be
accepted or declined.   If after accepting, a person finds it absolutely
necessary to absent himself, he should immediately send a regret, stating
reasons why he cannot attend.

The time to send.—An invitation to a dinner should be answered
immediately.   Other invitations requiring an answer should be answered within three days after receiving.   If a person finds at the last
moment it is impossible to attend, a regret should be sent the day after
the party.

Whom to address.—An answer, in general, should be addressed
to the person giving the invitation, but to a joint invitation from husband
and wife, ("Mr. and Mrs. John Smith") it should contain a recognition
of both, and the envelope be addressed to the wife alone ("Mrs. John
Smith.")

Style.—An answer should correspond in style to the invitation,
and be correspondingly formal or familiar.

Reason of non-acceptance.—If a regret is sent, it is more friendly
and courteous to give reasons for non-attendance, than to simply decline,
without giving cause.

Delivery.—Notes addressed to a person living in another city, or
out of town, are of course sent by mail, and are sent in this way to persons living in a distant part of the city.   In other cases they are usually
delivered by private messengers.

CARDS.

CARDS may be divided into the following classes: Visiting, ceremonial, professional and official, and business.

Visiting cards.—The proper uses of a visiting card are, first;

To announce the visitor's name.—On calling, a card is handed to the
person who opens the door, and the caller inquires for the person or persons for whom the visit is intended.   If "not at home," the caller leaves

Messrs Ulrich & Vernon,

44 Main St.

Auburn, N.Y.

Mr. and Mrs. Charles Newman request
the pleasure of Dr. and Mrs. Dimon's company at
dinner, on Thursday, February 18th, at six o'clock

a card, turning over one end or side, to denote a call in person; second,

To announce a guest's name at a reception.—When a person attends a party or reception, he should hand his card to the usher at the door, and always leave one in the card receiver. Third,

To announce a departure from home.—A person living in the city may, on going away for a long absence, send to his friends a card with the letters P. P. C. on one of the lower corners. Fourth,

To announce a return.—It is proper to announce a return to the city, by sending cards to visiting friends. Fifth,

To accompany a letter of introduction.—As before stated, a person's card should be sent with a letter introducing him. It should bear his temporary address and be enclosed in an envelope with the letter. Sixth,

To make one's self known to a stranger, a person may use his card for introducing himself. Seventh,

To serve as a credential.—A card, especially a business or professional one, may be presented to a stranger to convince him that you are the person you represent yourself to be.

Inscription.—In addition to the name, the residence may also be given in the lower right-hand or left-hand corner. If a lady has a regular day or days for receiving, she sometimes announces this in the lower left-hand corner, as, "Wednesdays," or "Thursdays and Fridays," etc.

If a daughter accompanies her mother in calling, one card may be used for both names, the daughter's being placed about one-half inch below her mother's. The elder of two or more daughters in the same family usually omits her first name on her card; as, "Miss Smith," while the younger daughter uses the given name; as, "Miss Mary Smith."

Titles.—A title may be used or not, according to the taste of a person. Professional men and persons in high official positions, use their professional title on cards. Persons should not assume the title of Honorable, unless they occupy a public office entitling them to it. A man and his wife sometimes use a joint card; as, "Mr. and Mrs. Smith," "Dr. and Mrs. H. A. Brown," etc.

A married lady, if her husband is living, uses her husband's christian name or initials instead of her own; as, "Mrs. James A. Brown."

Style.—Visiting cards vary in style and size to suit the taste and changing fashions. They should always be plain and neat. The most elegant cards are engraved or written; printed ones are not now used by the more fashionable people.

Ceremonial cards.—Cards may be used to convey invitations to parties, receptions and weddings, but notes are preferable in most cases.

Betrothal cards.—It is customary among some to announce a betrothal, and for this purpose either cards or notes may be used.

The following wording is a good form: " Mr. Solomon Weiss, Miss Rebecca Wolf, betrothed, December 6, 1889."

Presentation Cards.—Cards are very convenient as substitutes for notes, to accompany a book or any other gift.

Memorial cards.—It is customary in England, and to some extent in this country, to send memorial cards to friends of a deceased person. Such cards have a black border, narrow for the young, wide for the aged. Memorial cards should be sent out about one week after the funeral.

Professional and official cards.—Cards are used by professional men and public officers for professional and official purposes; the same card may be used, however, for social and business purposes. Such cards contain, besides the person's name, his professional or official title.

Business cards.—Most business men use cards to show the business in which they are engaged, and to give their address. These are generally used more as a matter of convenience than for advertising purposes; however, they may be made to answer the latter purpose.

Some are handsomely engraved, but they are usually printed from ordinary type. They should be plain, neat and tasteful.

TITLES.

There are no rules for the use of titles, except those established by usage. We give elsewhere a list of the principal titles and their correct use and abbreviations, as recognized in the best social, business and official circles.

Titles may be divided into three general classes, *social, scholastic, and official.*

Social titles.—Titles of courtesy and respect have universal application and should always be used, unless some official or professional title supersedes them.

The ordinary titles are *Mister, Messrs., Master* (applied to boys), *Mistress* (pronounced misses), and *Miss,* all of which are prefixed to the name; also, *Sir, Gentlemen* (plural only), *Madam,* and *Ladies* (plural only), which are always used without the name, as in the salutation of a letter. *Sir, Esquire, Master,* and *Miss,* are used both in the singular and plural. *Mrs.* and *Madam* in the singular only. *Messrs.* is the French plural of **Mr.,** there being no English plural to this word. Messrs. should never be, as it sometimes is, used without the names of the persons. It is no more proper to use *Messrs.* as the salutation of a letter than to use its singular, *Mr.* The plural of the salutation Madam is *Ladies.* There being no plural in our language for Mrs., the French plural of Madam, *Mesdames* (abbreviation *Mmes.*) is sometimes used. This is the only title available in addressing a firm of ladies; otherwise, they would have to be addressed individually; as, " Mrs. Jones & Mrs. Smith."

Mrs. and Lady.—It is not in good taste to use "Lady" instead of "Wife" or "Mrs.," although this custom was formerly in good usage in England. You should write "Mr. Smith and Wife," or "Mr. & Mrs. Smith," instead of "Mr. Smith and Lady." "Mrs." or "Miss" should never be used without the name any more than "Mr."

Mr. and Esquire.—These terms, as generally used, are interchangeable, but the former has a wider application than the latter.

"Mr." may be applied to men of all classes, but "Esquire" is properly applied only to persons of some prominence in society Members of the Legal profession are almost always addressed in writing as Esquire.

Special uses of Mr., Mrs. and Miss.—Though not directly pertaining to correspondence, there are some uses of these titles which are worthy our notice.

To DENOTE PROMINENCE.—As men rise to distinction, all their titles are often dropped, and the plain "Mr." used, which receives lustre from their own character and work, and becomes to them a sign of true nobility. Hence we say, Mr. Sumner, Mr. Chase, Mr. Lincoln, Mr. Gladstone, and other titles, such as senator, excellency, or honorable, would not be so expressive of the high esteem and respect with which such men are regarded by the people.

"*Mrs.*" and "*Miss*" are used in the same way to denote distinction; as, Mrs. Stowe, Miss Dickinson. In speaking of persons of the very highest distinction, all titles may be rejected ; as, for example, Shakespeare, Milton, Martin Luther and Daniel Webster, are most honored in their own illustrious names alone.

It is presumptuous and disrespectful to mutilate and contract the names of prominent and elderly persons; as, "Andy Johnson," "Ben Wade," "Joe Johnston," etc.

THREE SPECIAL USES OF MR.—1. If a person is the only one of the name in a certain place, or his name is an unusual one, the title "Mr." may be prefixed to the family name alone; as, "Mr. Jones," "Mr. Thackeray."

2. "Mr." is used among gentlemen meeting in a social, literary or scientific way, in addressing all their companions, whether they have a professional title or not; as, Mr. Everett, Mr. Bryant. This dropping of all other titles is due to the fact that on the floor of such assemblies all members are on an equality.

3. "Mr." is often used before a professional or official title of prominent persons; as, "Mr. Senator," "Mr. President," etc. "Reverend" is also similarly used, or with "the" prefixed; as, "the Rev. Dr. Smith," "the Rev. Father Brown." The title "Rev." should never be used immediately before the surname. Mrs. may be used in the same manner in speaking of, or addressing married women; as, "Mrs. General Sheridan," "Mrs. Chief Justice Fuller."

Scholastic titles.—These are degrees and honors conferred by scientific schools, colleges, universities, and other institutions of learning, or acquired in the practice of the learned professions. Regular degrees are conferred upon those completing a prescribed course and passing a certain examination; *honorable* degrees on persons who have become distinguished in public life or in literary and scientific studies.

Reverend.—The title "Rev." is not regularly conferred, but always given by consent to those who have passed a required examination and been regularly ordained.

President, Chancellor, Rector, Dean, Professor and *Master*, as titles, belong to the office rather than the officer, and when the duties of these offices are discontinued, the titles are usually dropped. After long and distinguished service, however, the title may be retained.

Professor.—The title of professor may be possessed by courtesy or *right*. It belongs of *right* to any one elected by the proper authorities to a regular chair or professorship in an educational institution, organized with full departments and faculty, and conferring degrees under legal charter.

Professor is now applied, however, to a salaried graduate actually employed in teaching, or whose duty it is to teach.   The title is given, by courtesy, to scholars and scientists who have become noted as specialists in any department of knowledge, and to persons who have distinguished themselves as educators.

Abuse of the title.—It is very common at the present day, for dancing masters, horse tamers, barbers, corn doctors, white washers, and . pretenders of all kinds, to assume the title of *professor*, with the view to appear, in the eyes of the ignorant, of more importance than their calling or their attainments warrant.

This tendency to bring an honorable title into contempt should be discouraged by all intelligent people.   *Professor*, as well as other titles, should be used sparingly and with discrimination.

Master.—Master is used in England and in some parts of this country instead of Principal or Teacher, but the word is very rarely used now in the United States.

Doctor of Medicine (M. D.)—This title is used by *right* only by regular graduates of a medical college in good standing, and may be obtained by a person of either sex.   A lady who is entitled to this degree may be addressed as "Carrie Smith, M. D.," or "Dr. Carrie Smith."

Abuse of this title also, is no uncommon thing.   In society, and especially in our larger cities, there are many persons who usurp this professional title and inflict upon the public unprofessional practice, for the sake of filling their pockets with money obtained by false pretense, from ignorant or trusting patients.   Do not recognize or patronize such quacks. It is better always, in all professions, to go to men of good standing and in regular practice.

Official titles.—These include the titles applicable to officers in the Naval, Military, and Civil service of the U. S., and of the several states.   The officer, on retiring from public service, again becomes a private citizen, but it is customary, as a compliment, to continue the official title during life, unless superseded by one more honorable.

Honorable, and abuse of same.—The title "Honorable" is applicable to judges, mayors, senators, representatives in Congress, the heads of government departments and others of similar rank.

(For full list, see "Classification of Titles.")

The abuse of the title "Honorable" has brought it into such disrepute that it has less value than it should have.

Only those whose character, ability, and services have caused their election or appointment to the most important and responsible positions of the nation, state, or city, should be given the title of "Honorable." The title once acquired is retained through life.

Military and Naval titles.—Military and Naval, like professional titles, are properly retained after long or distinguished service. A title really belonging to an officer is that named in his commission.

GENERAL POSTAL INFORMATION.

First class matter.—Postage two cents for each ounce or fraction thereof. Embraces all matter wholly or partly written, or which is so done up as to prevent examination without destroying the wrapper, and must be prepaid at least one rate, two cents. Drawings, written cards, plans and designs are first class.

Second class matter.—Pertains to publishers and news dealers. Embraces newspapers and periodicals, but they may be mailed by others than publishers, at the rate of *one cent* for each *four ounces* or fraction thereof, when they are enclosed in one wrapper, and must be fully prepaid by stamps affixed.

Third class matter.—Postage *one cent* for each *two ounces* or fraction thereof. Embraces books (printed), and all printed matter in unsealed wrappers, and the limit in weight is *four pounds*, except in the case of a single book, which weight is unlimited and must be fully prepaid. Photographs are now third class.

Fourth class matter.—Postage *one cent* for each *ounce* or fraction thereof. Embraces all mailable matter not specified above, and must be so done up as to admit of examination and fully prepaid. Labels, patterns, playing cards, visiting cards, address tags, wrapping paper, blotting pads, bill heads, letter heads, envelopes with printed address thereon, and all other matter of the same general character. Merchandise and samples are fourth class.

Unmailable matter.—Liquids, (except when packed as provided by regulation), poisons, explosive or inflammable articles, or any article which is liable to injure the mails or persons handling the same. Sharp pointed instruments, except when properly done up, are unmailable, also any matter not addressed to a post-office.

Drop letters.—The rate on letters to be delivered at the same office as mailed, is *one cent* if it is not a free delivery office. At offices where the mail is delivered by carriers the rate is *two cents*.

Special delivery stamps.—A "special delivery stamp" placed on a letter or package, in addition to the regular postage, will insure its immediate delivery, within certain limits, at any post-office in the United States. Such mail is delivered to persons living within the carrier districts in large cities or within one mile of the post-office at offices not having carrier service. "Special delivery stamps" cost ten cents, and can only be used for the special purpose they were designed for and not for the payment of regular postage.

Postal cards are unmailable when anything is pasted or attached thereto, or when anything not necessary to complete the address is written or printed on the address side.

Confectioneries are unmailable except when done up in tin boxes, which box must again be placed in a pasteboard box.

Fruits, except dried, are unmailable. Any matter exhaling bad odors is unmailable.

To Canada and Mexico.—The rates of postage are the same as in the United States, except that sealed packages other than letters in their ordinary shape and form are absolutely excluded.

Registered letters.—Letters may be registered to all offices of the United States, and to most foreign countries. Registry fee, ten cents in addition to the regular postage.

Postal notes.—Payable at any money order office, are issued for any amount from one cent to $4.99; fee, three cents.

Money orders on all principal offices of the United States may be purchased, payable "to order." For rates, see page 158.

TYPE-WRITING

The type-writer has come into quite general use and all business men are fast recognizing the fact that it is a great aid in facilitating correspondence; therefore, we think it is quite proper that some special instruction should be given in reference to type-written letters. Nearly all that has been said under other headings applies equally to type-written letters, and in addition we offer the following suggestions:

A thorough acquaintance with the machine and the manipulation thereof is of first importance. To do good work good tools must be used, and these tools must be kept in first-class condition. All good mechanics observe this rule, and the use of the type-writer is no exception.

Care of the machine.—The machine must be kept clean, and all wearing parts—guide rails in particular—should be well lubricated with the best sewing-machine oil, and then wiped perfectly clean. *This should be attended to daily.*

Any and everybody cannot use your machine without changing it more or less, no two operators having exactly the same style. When others do use it, see that they do not abuse or impair its mechanism.

Touch.—An even touch must be cultivated, and all jerky movements avoided, as such are detrimental to speed, and cause many mistakes to be made.

Correct fingering should be given careful attention. An explanation of the best methods can be found in the leading type-writer instructors, of which there are several good works published. The exercises should be practiced carefully and understandingly, and more attention given at first to a smooth, even style, than to speed.

Spacing.—Spacing must be uniform to produce a good effect, otherwise the work will present an uneven appearance. A space must be made after punctuation marks, except where they separate figures; as, $9,000,837.00, and three spaces must be made after a period when it ends a sentence, also the same number after exclamation and interrogation points.

In taking hurried copies, the appearance of the work is not so important as getting it out in the shortest time possible, and spacing is omitted after punctuation marks.

Form.—Special attention must be paid to paragraphing, so that the work may present a well-balanced appearance. Each change of subject matter should begin with a new paragraph. The arrangement of the introduction and close of a letter must be well fixed in mind with regard to the points of the scale where each part commences. It is well to have a fixed rule for the beginning of each. The numbers in the following form indicate the figures on the type-writer scale where it is best to begin each part:

Cleveland, O., July 4, 1889.
30

Mr. John Adams,
1

St. Clairsville, O.
5

Dear Sir:
1

I have your favor of the 27th ul-
5
timo, and in reply, etc.,

Very truly yours,
30

Andrew N. Merchant,

Supt.
50

In the above the salutation might begin at 10, and the body of the letter following it on the same line, with a dash between, or the salutation at 10 and the body of the letter on the next line at 11.

Spelling, capitalization and punctuation.—Do not pass any word of which you may have a doubt regarding its spelling without consulting your dictionary at once. Bad spelling is really more to be avoided than any other error. Many, who are otherwise proficient, fail in securing positions on account of their incorrect spelling.

The rules for capitalizing and punctuating, given elsewhere, should be carefully observed.

The period is the only point of separation used by stenographers in taking notes, the commas, colons, semi-colons, etc., being inserted in the transcript as the context suggests.

Common sense is a faculty that may be used to great advantage in short-hand and type-writing work. If the amanuensis writes from his notes "We will expect you *hear* on the 14th inst.," etc., his *common sense* should have taught him to spell the word *h-e-r-e*. Before handing in his copy for approval the operator should carefully read it himself, looking for errors in spelling, punctuation, capitalization, and such mistakes in the words as are referred to above. A model type-written letter is given on the next page.

O. & C. St. Mary's Falls Canal.

UNITED STATES ENGINEER OFFICE,

34 West Congress Street,

Detroit, Mich., May 4, 1889.

Messrs. Lamont, Fuller & Smith,
    242 Superior St.,
        Cleveland, Ohio.

Gentlemen:--In response to your request of the 3d inst., I send you here-
with copy of History of ''Sault Ste.
Marie Canal,'' in which is printed a
tabular Statement of the Commerce
through St. Mary's Falls Canal from its
opening in 1885, to the close of 1887.
Also a copy of my report for the year
1888. Also a copy of Ex. Doc. No. 52,
House of Representatives, 50th Congress, 2d Session, which brings the sta-
tistics of the Canal down to the close
of 1888.

        Very respectfully,

            O. M. Poe

            Colonel of Engineers,
        Bvt. Brig. Gen. U. S. A.

3 Inclosures.

CLASSIFICATION OF TITLES

AND THEIR

ABBREVIATIONS.

Scholastic **Degrees are** always abbreviated. In addressing an officer of high rank, abbreviations **are not** allowable ; as, President, Governor. Many **abbreviations** of titles **may be used** in catalogues, on the title-pages **of books, and other places,** that are not allowable in addressing letters. In the **address, no degree is used** lower **than** Master or Doctor. We may write " James Brown, **M. D. or A. M.,"** but not " James Brown, A. B. or B. S." A person that has **no title higher than a** bachelor's **degree, should be** addressed simply *Mr.* or *Esq.*

TITLES OF RESPECT AND COURTESY

Mister . . . . **Mr.**	Mistress **(pronounced** Missis) . . . **Mrs.**
Messieurs **(Fr. pl. of Mr.)** . . . **Messrs.**	Mesdames **(Fr. pl.)** . . . . . . Mmes.
Gentlemen . . . .——	Madam . . . . Mad.
Sir, **Sirs** . . . .——	Madame **(Fr.)** . . . . Mme.
Esquire, **Esquires** . . . . Esq., **Esqs.**	Ladies . . . . ——
Master **(a boy)** . . . .——	Miss, **Misses** . . . . ——

SCHOLASTIC TITLES.

All of **the** following **degrees** and many **others are authorized, but these are** the **more** common ones : **B. C. L., D. C. L., and a few** others **are** conferred only by foreign universities. **Harvard** College **confers only the** following degrees ; *Regular—* **A. B., A. M., Ph. D., B. D., LL. B., S. B., S. D., C. E., M. D., D. M. D. ;** *Honorary—*LL. **D., D. D.** Yale confers **nearly the** same, **with the addition of** Ph. B., D. E., and Mus. D.

The Latin terms are given only when they are necessary **to explain the** abbreviation.

DIVINITY.

Bachelor of Divinity . . . . . . **B. D.**
Doctor of Divinity . . . . **D. D.**
Doctor of Divinity, *Sanctæ Theologiæ Doctor* . . . . **S. T. D.**
Doctor of Divinity, *Doctor Theologiæ* . . . . **D. T.**
Professor of Divinity, *Sanctæ Theologiæ Professor* . . . . **S. T. P.**

LAW.

Bachelor of Laws . . . . . . **LL. B.**
Master of Laws . . . . **M. L.**

Doctor of **Laws** . . . . **LL. D.**
Dr. of **Laws,** *Jurum Doctor* . . . **J. D.**
Doctor of Civil Law, *Juris Civilis Doctor* . . . . **J. C. D.**
Bachelor of Civil Law . . . . **B. C. L.**
Doctor of Civil Law . . . . . **D. C. L.**
Dr. of **both Laws,** Canon and Civil, *Juris utriusque Doctor* . . . . **J. U. D.**

MEDICINE.

Doctor . . . . **Dr.**
Bachelor of Medicine . . . . . **M. B.**
Doctor of Medicine . . . . . **M. D.**

Master in Surgery, *Chirurgiæ Magister*,
. . . . **C. M.**
Graduate in Pharmacy . . . **Phar. G.**
Master in Pharmacy . . . . **Phar. M.**
Doctor in Pharmacy . . . . **Phar. D.**
Doctor of Dental Surgery . **D. D. S.**
Doctor of Dental Medicine . **D. M. D.**

PHILOSOPHY AND SCIENCE.

Bachelor of Philosophy . . . . **Ph. B.**
Doctor of Philosophy . . . . . **Ph. D.**
Bachelor of Science . . . . . . **B. S.**
Master of Science . . . . **M. S.**
Doctor of Science . . . . **S. D.**

ARTS AND LETTERS.

Bachelor of Arts. . . . **B. A. or A. B.**
Master of Arts . . . . **M. A. or A. M.**
Bachelor of Letters, *Baccalaureus Liter-
arum* . . . . **B. Lit.**
Doctor of Letters, *Literarum Doctor*,
. . . . **Lit. D.**
Doctor of Polite Literature, *Literarum
Humaniorum Doctor* . . . . **L. H. D.**
Poet Laureate (Eng.) . . . . . **P. L.**

MUSIC.

Bachelor of Music . **M. B. or B. Mus.**
Doctor of Music . . **D. M. or Mus. D.**

DIDACTICS.

Bachelor of the Elements . . . **B. E.**
Master of the Elements . . . . **M. E.**
Bachelor of Science . . . . . **B. S.**
Master of Science . . . . . . **M. S.**
Bachelor of the Classics . . . **B. C.**
Master of the Classics . . . . **M. C.**

TECHNICS.

Civil Engineer . . . . **C. E.**
Topographic Engineer . . . . . **T. E.**
Dynamic Engineer . . . . **D. E.**
Military or Mechanical Engineer . **M. E.** .

The degrees of Bachelor and Master in each of the departments of engineering, and in chemistry and architecture are authorized, but are rarely conferred.

FELLOWSHIPS, ETC.

American.

Fellow of the Am. Academy, *Academiæ Americanæ Socius* . . . . . **A. A. S.**
Member of Am. Antiquarian Society, *Americanæ Antiquarianæ Societatis Socius* . . . . **A. A. S. S.**
Member of the Am. Oriental Society, *Americanæ Orientalis Societatis Socius* . . . . **A. O. S. S.**
Member of Am. Phil. Society, *Societatis Philosophicæ Americanæ Socius* . . . . **S. P. A. S.**
Fellow of the Mass. Medical Society, *Massachusettensis Medicinæ Societatis Socius* . . . . **M. M. S. S.**
Fellow of the Historical Society, *Societatis Historiæ Socius* . . . . **S. H. S.**
Fellow of Connecticut Academy, *Conn. Academiæ Socius* . . . . . . **C. A. S.**

These are the only American societies that confer memberships or fellowships that are recognized as titles.

TITLES OF SERVICE EX–OFFICIO.

THE CLERICAL SERVICE.

A Bishop (Epis., Cath., *et al.*) :— Right Reverend . . . . **Rt. Rev.**
A Bishop (Methodist):—Reverend, **Rev.**
A Presiding Elder (Methodist):—Reverend . . . . **Rev.**
A Rector, Minister, Priest, Rabbi, or Reader . . . . **Rev.**

THE CIVIL SERVICE.

National Government.

The Chief Executive :—

1. Civil: The President . . . **Pres.**
2. Military : Commander-in-Chief of the Army and Navy.

The Vice-President, Ex-Officio President of the Senate:—
Honorable. . . . . Hon.

Chief Justice of the Supreme Court:—
The Chief Justice . . . . C. J.
His Honor . . . . ——

Associate Justices:—
Justice . . . . Jus.
His Honor . . . . ——

Foreign Ministers:—
His Excellency . . . . . . H. Exc.
Honorable. . . . . Hon.

Members of the Cabinet and Members of Congress . . . . Hon.

Heads of Bureaus, Asst. Secretaries, Comptrollers, and Auditors of the Treasury, Clerks of the Senate and House of Representatives . . . Esq.
By Courtesy . . . . Hon.

All other U. S. Officers . . Esq. or Mr.

STATE GOVERNMENTS.

The Governor . . . . Gov.
Civil: His Excellency . . . H. Exc.
Military : Commander-in-Chief.

Sen. Judge of Supreme Court :—
Chief Justice . . . . C. J.
His Honor . . . . ——

Associate Justices:—
Justice . . . . Jus.
Judge . . . . ——
His Honor . . . . ——

Lieutenant Governor, Heads of Departments, State Senators‡, Law Judges
. . . . Hon.

Mayors of Cities:—
Honorable . . . . Hon.
His Honor . . . . ——

Members of the House of Representatives‡ . . . . Esq.
By Courtesy . . . . . . Hon.

Aldermen, Magistrates, and all officers not specified . . . . Esq.

PROFESSIONAL SERVICES.

Officers of Universities and Colleges:—
Chancellor. . . . . Chanc.
Vice-Chancellor . . . . . V. Chanc.
President . . . . Pres.
Vice-President . . . . . . V. Pres.
Provost . . . . Prov.
Dean . . . . ——
Rector . . . . Rect.
Registrar . . . . Reg.
Librarian . . . . Lib.

Faculty and Instructors:—
Professor . . . . Prof.
Lecturer . . . . ——
Tutor . . . . ——

‡ There is a difference of opinion as to whether the title of "Honorable" should be applied to members of the two houses of the Legislature. It is the custom of the State Department at Washington to apply the title of "Esquire" to members of both.

The customs of the states vary. Perhaps the greater weight of opinion is in favor of the application of "Honorable" to members of the State Senate, and "Esquire" to those of the House of Representatives. In some states, the title "Honorable" is applied to the Speaker of the lower house, but not the other members.

THE MILITARY AND NAVAL SERVICE.

The command pertaining to the rank of general and line officers is printed under the title in finer print. Commands, however, are subject to change by assignment, and the laws governing the army organization have left it in an anomalous state, and the rank of commands in an unsettled condition. The titles of the general and line officers, placed opposite in the two columns, indicate relative rank in the two departments of service.

Military Service (U. S. A.)	Naval Service (U. S. N.)
GENERAL AND LINE OFFICERS.	**LINE OFFICERS.**

General . . . . **Gen.**	Admiral . . . . **Adm. or Adml.**
The armies of the U. S.	The fleets of the U. S.
Lieutenant General . . . . . **Lt. Gen.**	Vice-Admiral . . . . **V. Adml.**
An Army Corps, and Territorial Division.	A Fleet or Fleets.
Major General . . . . . . **Maj. Gen.**	Rear Admiral . . . . **R. Adml.**
A Division, and Territorial Division.	A Fleet or Squadron.
Brigadier General . . . . . **Brig. Gen.**	Commodore. . . . . **Commo.**
A Brigadier, and Territorial Department.	Squadron, Ships of first class.
Colonel. . . . . **Col.**	Captain. . . . . **Capt.**
A Regiment.	Vessels of second class.
Lieutenant Colonel . . . . . **Lt. Col.**	Commander . . . . **Com.**
A Battalion, second in command, Regiment.	Vessels of third class.
Major . . . . **Maj.**	Lieutenant Com. . . . . . . **Lt. Com.**
A Battalion, third in command, Regiment.	Vessels of fourth class.
Captain . . . . **Capt.**	Lieutenant . . . . **Lieut.**
A Company.	Executive Officer of fourth class.
First Lieutenant . . . . 1st **Lieut.**	Master . . . . **Mas.**
A Platoon, third in command, Company.	Assistant Navigator.
Second Lieutenant . . . . . 2d **Lieut.**	Ensign . . . . **Ens.**
A Platoon, third in command, Company.	
Cadet . . . . —	Midshipman . . . . **Mid.**
Student at West Point Military Academy	Student of Annapolis Naval Academy.

STAFF OFFICERS.	**STAFF OFFICERS.**
Adjutant General . . . . . **Adj. Gen.**	Surgeon General . . . . . **Surg. Gen.**
Rank of Brigadier General.	Rank of Commodore.
Assistant Adj. Gen. . . . . . **A. A. G.**	Medical Director . . . . . . **Med. Dir.**
Rank of Colonel to Major.	Rank of Captain.
Inspector General . . . . . **Insp. Gen.**	Medical Inspector . . . . **Med. Insp.**
Rank of Colonel.	Rank of Commander.
Assistant Insp. Gen. . . . . **A. I. G.**	Surgeon. . . . . **Surg.**
Rank of Colonel.	Rank of Lieutenant Commander.
Quartermaster General . . . **Q. M. G.**	Past Asst. Surg. . . . . . . **P. A. Surg.**
Rank of Brigadier General.	Rank of Lieutenant.
Asst. Q. M. Gen. . . . . . **A. Q. M. G.**	Assistant Surgeon . . . **Asst. Surg.**
Rank of Colonel.	Rank of Master to Ensign.

Deputy Q. M. G . . . . . Dep. Q. M. G.
Rank of Lt. Colonel.

Quartermaster . . . . Q. M.
Rank of Major.

Asst. Quartermaster . . . . . A. Q. M.
Rank of Captain.

Commissary Gen. of Subsistence, C. G. S.
Rank of Brig. Gen.

Asst. C. G. S . . . . A, C. G. S.
Rank of Colonel to Lt. Colonel.

Commissary of Subsistence . . . C. S.
Rank of Major to Captain.

Surgeon General . . . . . Surg. Gen.
Rank of Brigadier General.

Chief Medical Purveyor, Chf. Med. Pur.
Rank of Colonel.

Surgeon . . . . Surg.
Rank of Major.

Asst. Surgeon . . . . . . Asst. Surg.
Rank of Captain to 1st Lieutenant.

Paymaster Gen . . . . P. M. G.
Rank of Colonel.

Assistant P. M. G . . . Asst. P. M. G.
Rank of Colonel.

Paymaster . . . . Pay M.
Rank of Major.

Chief of Engineers . . . . . . Chf. E.
Rank of Brigadier General.

Chief of Ordnance . . . . . Chf. Ord.
Rank of Brigadier General.

Judge Adv. Gen . . . . J. A. G.
Rank of Brigadier General.

Judge Advocate . . . . J. A.
Rank of Major.

Chief Signal Officer . . . . . C. S. O.
Rank of Colonel.

Paymaster General . . . . . P. M. G.
Rank of Commodore.

Pay Director . . . . Pay Dir.
Rank of Captain.

Pay Inspector . . . . . . Pay Insp.
Rank of Commander.

Paymaster . . . . P. M.
Rank of Lieutenant Commander.

Past Asst. P. M . . . . . P. A. P. M.
Rank of Lieutenant.

Assistant Paymaster . . . . . A. P. M.
Rank of Master.

Engineer-in-Chief . . . . Eng.-in-Chf.
Rank of Commodore.

Chief Engineer . . . . Chf. E.
Rank of Captain to Lieutenant.

Past Asst. Eng . . . . . . P. A. Eng.
Rank of Lieutenant to Master.

Assistant Engineer . . . . . . A. Eng.
Rank of Master to Ensign.

Cadet Engineer . . . . . Cadet Eng.
Graduates of Naval Academy.

Chaplain . . . . Chap.
Rank of Captain to Lt. Com.

Chief of Construction . . . . Chf. Con.
Rank of Commodore.

Naval Constructor . . . . . Nav. Con.
Rank of Captain to Lieutenant.

Commandant . . . . Comdt.
Navy Yards and Stations.

Navigator . . . . Nav.
Master of a Vessel.

Captain (by courtesy) . . . . . Capt.
Master of a Merchant Vessel.

THE DIPLOMATIC AND CONSULAR SERVICE.

Envoy Extraordinary and Minister Plenipotentiary . . . . . E. E. and M. P.
Minister Plenipotentiary . . Min. Plen.

Minister Resident . . . . . Min. Res.
Minister Resident and Consul-General
. . . . M. R. and C. G.

Secretary of Legation . . . **Sec. Leg.**	Deputy Consul . . . . **D. C.**
Interpreter . . . . **Int.**	Consular Agent . . . . . . **Con. Agt.**
Consul-General . . . . **C. G.**	Commercial Agent . . . . **C. A.**
Vice-Consul-General . . . . . **V. C. G.**	Agent . . . . **Agt.**
Consul. . . . . **C.**	Marshal . . . . **Mar.**
Vice-Consul . . . . **V. C.**	Consular Clerk . . . . **C. C.**

FORMS OF ADDRESS AND SALUTATION.

The form of address is printed in plain Roman type, the *salutation in italic.*

PERSONS IN THE LEARNED PROFESSIONS.

THE CLERGY.

A Bishop (other than a Methodist).

To the Right Reverend ——, D. D., Bishop of Ohio. *Right Reverend Sir :—,* or *Right Rev. and dear Sir :—.*

Address a Methodist Bishop as *Rev.* simply.

A Rector, Minister, Priest, Rabbi, or Reader.

To the Rev. ——.   To the Rev. Dr. A—— B——.   The Rev. H. M. Ladd, D. D., Pastor (or Rector, as the case may be) of —— Church, Cleveland. *Sir:—. Reverend Sir:—. Rev. and dear Sir :—.*

THE BENCH AND THE BAR.

The Chief Justice of the Supreme Court of the United States.

To the Hon. ——, Chief Justice of ——, etc. To the Chief Justice of the Supreme Court, etc. *Sir:—. Mr. Chief Justice:—. Your Honor:—. May it Please your Honor:—. May it Please the Honorable Court:—.*

"Your Honor," "May it Please," etc., are terms used in court, not in private letters.

An Associate Justice.

To the Honorable ——, Justice, etc. Or, Honorable Justice ——. *Sir:—. Your Honor:—, etc.*

Other Judges.

The Hon. ——, Judge of the Court of Quarter Sessions (or as the case may be). Or simply, The Honorable A—— B——. *Sir:—. Dear Sir:—. Your Honor:—, etc.*

Lawyers, Justices of the Peace, etc.

James A. Brown, Esq. *Sir:—. Dear Sir:—.*

THE MEDICAL PROFESSION.

A Physician or Surgeon.

Dr. C. A. Scott. Or, C. A. Scott, Esq., M. D. *Sir:—. Dear Sir:—.*

A Dentist.

Dr. John Allen. Or, John Allen, Esq., D. D. S. (or D. M. D.) *Sir:—. Dear Sir:—.*

New Haven.

Nov. 17. 1878

Friend Lyons,

I regret that I did not see you during your recent visit to our city.

When you are again here please to give me a call; as I would like to speak to you of something that interests us both.

As ever, Yours,

M. J. Curtis.

LITERARY AND SCIENTIFIC MEN.

The President of a College.

The Rev. J. H. Fairchild, D. D., LL. D., President of Oberlin College. Or, The Rev. Dr. **Fairchild** (with or without the designation). *Sir :—. Dear Sir :—. Rev. and dear Sir :—,*

A Professor.

Henry Lewis, D. D., LL. D., Professor of Greek in —— College. Or, Prof. Henry Lewis, D. D., LL. D. Or, Dr. Henry Lewis, Prof. of ——, etc. *Sir :—. Dear Sir :—.*

OFFICERS IN THE CIVIL SERVICE.

The President of the United States.

To the President, Executive Mansion, Washington, D. C. *Sir :—,* or *Mr. President :—.*

The Vice-President.

To the Honorable **Levi P. Morton, Vice-President of the U. S.** Or (unofficial), **Hon.** Levi P. Morton. *Sir :—.*

Cabinet Ministers

To the Honorable Redfield Proctor, Secretary of War. Or, To the Honorable the Secretary of War. Or, Hon. Redfield Proctor. *Sir :—.*

All others not specified who are entitled to "Honorable," are **addressed in a** similar manner

Foreign Ministers.

To his Excellency **Robert T. Lincoln,** Envoy Ex., etc., at the Court of St. James. *Your Excellency :—. Sir :—.*

Assistant Secretaries, **Heads of Bureaus, etc.**

To ——, Esq., Assistant Secretary of State. *Sir :—.* (Sometimes, by courtesy, addressed as *Hon.*)

The Governor of a State.

To His Excellency J. B. Foraker, Governor of the State of Ohio. Or, His Excellency Governor J. B. **Foraker. Or, To His Excellency the Governor.** *Sir :—, Your Excellency :—.*

Heads of State Departments, **Members of the State Senate, etc.**

Hon. ——, Attorney-General of N. Y. *Sir :—.*

OFFICERS IN THE MILITARY OR NAVAL SERVICE.

ARMY OFFICERS.

The **General of the Army.**

To General **W. T. Sherman, Commanding the** Armies of the United States. Or, General **W. T. Sherman, Commanding U. S. A.** Or, To the General of the

Army. (It is a rule of the War Department at Washington, to address all officers
by their office, not by name.)   *General:*—, or *Sir:*—.

The general practice in the army is to use the military title (*General, Col., Captain,* etc.) in
the salutation, in addressing all officers above the grade of Lieutenant.   A Lieut. has the salutation of *Sir.* In the superscription, his rank is generally mentioned. In army correspondence
the address is generally, not always, written at the top of the letter.

A Colonel.
Col. ——, commanding 1st Cavalry.   Or, Col. ——, U. S. A.   *Colonel:*—.

The Quarter Master General.
The same as a business man; and other officers of the Army are addressed in
a similar manner.

NAVY OFFICERS.

The Admiral of the Navy.
To Admiral D. G. Farragut, Commanding the Fleets of the U. S.   Or, Admiral
D. G. Farragut, Commanding U. S. N. Or, To the Admiral of the Navy.   *Sir:*—.

In the Navy, *Sir* is invariably used as the salutation; and the address, consisting of the
name, title, and command, is written at the bottom.   The following is an extract from the Navy
Regulations:—
"Line officers in the Navy, down to and including Commander, will be addressed by their
proper title; below the rank of Commander, either by the title of their grade, or *Mr.* Officers of
the Marine Corps above the rank of 1st Lieut. will be addressed by their military title, brevet or
lineal; of and below that rank, by their title of *Mr.* Officers not of the line will be addressed by
their titles, or as *Mr.* or *Dr.*, as the case may be."

A Commodore.
Commodore A—— B——, commanding South Atlantic Squadron (or as the case
may be).   Or, Commodore A—— B——, U. S. N.   *Sir:*—.
Other officers of the Navy are addressed in a similar manner.

LEGISLATIVE AND OTHER ORGANIZED BODIES.

Communications to an organized body are usually addressed to the President
of that body as its chief representative. The communications may, however, be
addressed to the body itself.   In such cases it goes to the President, and is by him
formally presented.
Communications, especially petitions, are often addressed "To the president
and members of ——," etc.

The Senate of the U. S.
To the Honorable the Senate of the U. S. in Congress Assembled.   *Honorable
Sirs:*—. Or, *May it please your Honorable Body* (or *the Honorable Senate*) :—.

The President of the Senate.
To the Honorable the President of the Senate of the U. S. Or, To the Honorable Levi P. Morton, President of the Senate of the U. S.   *Sir:*—. Or, *Honorable Sir:*—.

The House of Representatives.
Address and salutation similar to those of the Senate.

The Speaker of the House.

To the Honorable the Speaker of the House of Representatives. *Sir :—*, or *Mr. Speaker :—*.

State Legislatures.

They are addressed in the same form as the House of Congress, except, of course, the name, and the formula "in Congress assembled."

The title "Honorable" is generally applied to Legislative bodies if addressed collectively, even though the individual members are not entitled to it. For example, in most states in addressing the House of Representatives of the State, we would use the title "Honorable," but in addressing an individual member, as stated elsewhere, we would use the title *Esq.*, with the salutation *Sir.* The same applies to city governments. In some states, the Speaker of the House is addressed as "Honorable."

A Court.

To the Honorable Judges of the —— Court. *Your Honors:—.* Or, *May it please your Honors:—.*

A Board of Education.

To the President and Members of the Board of Education (or whatever the corporate name may be). *Sirs :—.* Or (if in the city), *May it please your Honorable Body : —.*

As stated above, communications (except petitions) are generally addressed to the President of such bodies, as follows :—

The President of a Board of Education, Directors, or Commissioners.

To ——, Esq., President of the Board of School Commissioners of Baltimore City. *Sir :—.*

To a Company.

To ——, Esq., President of the L. S. & M. S. R. R. Co. Or, To ——, Esq., President of the —— Insurance Co., New York. *Sir :—.*

A PETITION.

To a Legislature.

To the Honorable the Senate and House of Representatives of the Commonwealth of Pennsylvania. *The undersigned respectfully represent,* etc. Or, *The petition of A. B.* (or the undersigned) *humbly showeth,* etc.

Close, when there are several signers :—*And your petitioners, as in duty bound, will ever pray,* etc.

(Signatures.)   (Signatures.)

In a petition to Congress, or to either House, add the words "in Congress assembled." A petition to a Court or other body is in the same general form.

CLASSIFIED LIST OF ABBREVIATIONS

(Exclusive of those Denoting Titles.)

CHRONOLOGICAL.

TIME OF DAY.

Hour, h.; minute, min.; second, sec.
Forenoon (*ante meridiem*) . . . . A. M.
Afternoon (*post meridiem*) . . . . P. M.
Noon (*meridiem*) . . . . M.

MONTHS.

Month, months . . . . . . mo., mos.
Last month (ultimo) . . . . ult.

This month (instant) . . . . . . inst.
Next month (proximo) . . . . . prox.

YEARS AND ERAS.

Year, years . . . . yr., yrs.
By the year (per annum) . . . per an.
Before Christ . . . . B. C.
In the Christian Era (*anno Domini*) A. D.
Week . . . . wk.

RELATING TO BUSINESS.

Account . . . . acct., a/c.
Agent . . . . Agt.
Amount . . . . Amt.
At or to (mercantile) . . . . . @, a.
Average . . . . av.
Balance . . . . bal.
Bank . . . . bk.
Barrel, barrels . . . . bl., bbl. or bls.
Bill Book . . . . B. B.
Bills Payable . . . . B. Pay.
Bills Receivable . . . . . . B. Rec.
Bought . . . . bo't.
Brother, Brothers . . . . Bro., Bros.
Brought . . . . brot.
Bushel . . . . bu., bush.
By the . . . . P., p. or ℔.
Cashier . . . . Cash.
Cash Book . . . . C. B.
Cleared . . . . cld.
Charged . . . . chgd.
Company . . . . Co.
Care of . . . . c/o.
Collector . . . . Coll.
Commission . . . . Com.
Commerce . . . . Com.
Credit, creditor . . . . Cr.
Cent, cents . . . . ct., cts.
Clerk . . . . clk.

Cash on delivery . . . . . C. O. D.
Debtor . . . . Dr.
Ditto (the same) . . . . do.
Discount . . . . dis. or disc.
Dividend . . . . div.
Dollar, dollars . . . . . dol., dols.
Dozen . . . . doz.
Draft . . . . Dft.
Each . . . . Ea.
Errors excepted . . . . E. E.
Errors and omissions excepted . . .
. . . . E. & O. E.
Et cetera (and the rest) . . . etc., &c.
Foot or feet . . . . ft.
Forward . . . . For'd.
Freight . . . . Fr't.
Folio Cash Book . . . . . F. C. B.
Gross . . . . gro.
Gallon . . . . gal.
Half . . . . Hlf.
Handkerchiefs . . . . hdkfs.
Head . . . . Hd.
Hogshead . . . . hhd.
Hundred . . . . hund.
Hundred weight . . . . cwt.
Interest . . . . int.
Invoice Book . . . . I. B.
Inches . . . . in.

Insurance	Ins.	Per cent (by the hundred)	per cent.
Invoice	Inv.	Pennyweight	pwt.
Inventory	Inv't.	Pound, pounds	lb., lbs.
Journal	jour.	Quart, quarts	qt., qts.
Journal Folio	J. F.	Quarter, quarters	qr., qrs.
Ledger	Ledg.	Returned	ret'd.
Ledger Folio	L. F.	Received	rec'd.
Measure	meas.	Receipt	rec't.
Merchandise	mdse.	Schooner	schr.
Memorandum	mem.	Sales Book	S. B.
Number, numbers	No., Nos.	Sailed	sld.
Outward Invoice Book	O. I. B.	Shipment	shipt.
Ounce	oz.	Square	sq.
Package	pkge.	Storage	stor.
Pages	pp.	Steamer	Str.
Pair	pr.	Sundries	sunds.
Peck, pecks	pk., pks.	Thousand	M.
Petty Cash Book	P. C. B.	Tonnage	ton.
Paid	pd.	Volume	vol.
Payment	payt.	Weight	wt.
Pint, pints	pt., pts.	Without deduction	net.
Premium	prem.	Yard, yards	yd., yds.
Per annum (by the year)	per an.		

' RELATING TO LAW AND GOVERNMENT.

Abbreviations of official titles not here given may be found in the Classified List of Titles.

Administrator	Admr.	Congress	Cong.
Administratrix	Admx.	Defendant	Deft.
Attorney	Atty.	Justice of the Peace	J. P.
Against (*versus*)	v. or vs.	Member of Congress	M. C.
Assistant	Asst.	Plaintiff	Pltf.
And others (*et alii*)	et al.	Post-office	P. O.
Clerk	clk.	Post-master	P. M.
Committee	Com.	Right Honorable	Rt. Hon.
Common Pleas	C. P.	Superintendent	Supt.

ECCLESIASTICAL.

Congregational	Cong.	Methodist Episcopal	M. E.
Deacon	Dea.	Protestant Episcopal	P. E.
God willing (*Deo volente*)	D. V.	Presbyterian	Presb.
Jesus the Savior of Men	I. H. S.	Roman Catholic	Rom. Cath.

MISCELLANEOUS.

Ad libitum (at pleasure) . . . . ad lib.	Incognito (unknown) . . . . . Incog.
Alley . . . . Al.	Island . . . . Isl.
American . . . . Am. or Amer.	Lake . . . . L.
Anno Domini (in the year of our Lord)	Manuscript . . . . . . MS. (pl. MSS.)
. . . . A. D.	Mountain or Mount . . Mt. (pl. Mts.)
Anonymous . . . . Anon.	Postscript . . . . P. S.
Answer . . . . Ans.	Pro tempore (for the time) . . pro tem.
Arithmetic . . . . Arith.	Railroad . . . . R. R.
Avenue . . . . Av. or Ave.	Recording Secretary . . . . Rec. Sec.
Borough . . . . Bor. or bor.	River . . . . R.
Christmas . . . . Xmas.	Secretary . . . . Sec.
Corresponding Secretary . . Cor. Sec.	Senior . . . . Sr. or sen.
Corner . . . . Cor.	Street or Saint . . . . . St. (pl. Sts.)
County . . . . Co. or co.	Take Notice . . . . N B.
Court House . . . . C. H.	Township . . . . tp.
District . . . . Dist.	Videlicet (namely) . . . . viz.
East, E.; West, W.; North, N.; South, S.	Village . . . . Vil. or vil.
Executive Committee . . . Ex. Com.	Young Men's Christian Association . .
Id est (that is) . . . . i. e.	. . . . Y. M. C. A.

MISCELLANEOUS EXERCISES.

(Selections may be made by number from this list, at the option of the teacher.)

The short exercises, including the parts of letters, may be written on foolscap paper, using only as many blue lines as are necessary for each, and ruling lines between the forms to separate them.

For each letter written, address an envelope, fold the paper, and place it in the envelope.

HEADINGS AND INTRODUCTIONS.

Arrange, punctuate and capitalize correctly.

1. Write a heading for a letter to be sent from this place to-day.
2. Use these words in a heading: Iowa, 1889, June 20, 753 Elm St., Davenport.
3. Write a heading and introduction for a letter to be sent to Charles Warner & Co., Erie, Pa., from Chicago, Ill., present date.
4. Write a heading for a letter sent from some hotel in New York City.
5. Write a heading for a letter sent from some educational institution, to-day.
6. Write an introduction to a letter to the President of the U. S.
7. Write an introduction to a letter to the Governor of your state.

8. Write a heading and salutation to a business letter to Miss Cynthia Brown, Springfield, Illinois.

9. Write an introduction to a letter to the firm of John Brownlee & Co., publishers of the Christian Gazette, 667 Ash street, Boston, Mass.

10. Write an appropriate salutation to (1) a business firm, (2) a child, (3) an intimate friend, (4) an aged gentleman, (5) a married lady friend, (6) your teacher.

Write correctly the following **headings and introductions .**

11. jan 24th detroit my Dear alfred your letter etc.

12. mr martin My dear sir if it is convenient etc.

13. chicago ill 2d of June 1888 hon J t Brown gov of ohio dear sir can you etc.

14. prof isaac Dodge goshen Indiana my Very dear Sir will you Please etc.

15. ky covington my dear brown February 4th 1880 it is with etc.

THE CONCLUSION.

Write the following, arranging, punctuating and capitalizing correctly:

16. Yours Truly howard Kirtland.

17. Very Respectfully Yours John Hammond.

18. Your sincere Friend Marion.

19. Your Loving Son Harry.

20. We remain As ever very Truly yours Brown Smith & co.

21. Write the conclusion of a business letter from yourself to A. T. Stewart & Co., New York.

22. Write the conclusion of a letter to your most intimate friend.

23. Write the conclusion of a letter to the Post Master General of the United States.

ENVELOPES.

(For these exercises paper may be used instead of envelopes, marking around an envelope with a lead pencil, to give the size and shape of same. Arrange the address properly in this space.)

24. Address an envelope to Jones, Hart & Simpson, 801 Broadway, New York City.

25. Address an envelope to E. E. Northway, 128 Hawthorne Ave., City.

26. Address an envelope to Prof. J. Tuckerman, South New Lyme, Ashtabula Co., Ohio.

27. Address an envelope to Messrs. Smith, Brown & Co., Chicago, Ill., for a letter introducing Mr. Charles Brown.

28. Address an envelope to Prof. J. H. Bryant, Lock Box 73, Jacksonville, Ill.

29. Address an envelope to Miss Mary Miller, Minneapolis, Minn., care Mr. Martin Mercer.

30. Address an envelope to Mr. F. A. Timby, Care Reed & Riley, 14 Fifth Ave., Denver, Col.

INTRODUCTIONS.

31. Write a letter introducing a friend of yours to an acquaintance in Buffalo, asking him to aid him if possible in securing employment in a dry goods house.

32. Your uncle is a Congressman in Washington; write him a letter asking him to show some attention to your friend, the bearer, during his visit at the capital.

33. Write to your sister, introducing an intimate friend who is passing through the city, and calls upon her at your earnest solicitation.

LETTERS OF CREDIT.

34. Write a letter of credit to a firm in New York, asking that Thomas Mayhew be trusted for three months to an amount not exceeding five hundred dollars, for millinery goods.

35. Write a letter addressed to yourself, from the firm in New York, stating that Thomas Mayhew failed to pay for the goods in due time, and asking immediate settlement for the amount.

APPLICATIONS.

36. Write a letter applying for a situation as book-keeper in a grocery, stating qualifications, experience and salary expected; also name some one as reference.

37. Write a letter to the School Board, Jackson, Mich., applying for a position as teacher in the public schools, stating qualifications, experience, grade desired, and salary you will accept; also some special preparation you have made for the work.

38. Write an advertisement for the New York World, stating your desire to secure a situation as amanuensis for some literary or professional gentleman.

39. Write a letter soliciting advertising for the Daily Tribune, published in Boston. State circulation.

40. Write to a friend in Lincoln, Neb., asking what the opportunities of success are there for a young man of your abilities.

Answer the following advertisements:

41.

BOOK-KEEPER AND CORRESPONDent—Wanted, a book-keeper, competent to keep the accounts and assist in conducting the correspondence of an establishment. Address, stating experience and giving references, "Business" - je10-tf

42.

WANTED—Young man stenographer and type-writer, with machine. Address, stating terms, lock box 216, Fostoria, Ohio.

43.

WANTED—Shipping clerk by a large manufacturing concern. Must write a good hand and be thoroughly acquainted with the shipping to all parts of the United States; single man preferred; none but those competent need apply. Address with references at once, P. O. Box No. 408. 4j52-7

44.

WANTED—A lady stenographer who has had some experience on the type-writer. Address, in own hand writing, stating salary wanted, NURSERYMAN, Herald office. 342

45.

WANTED—A young lady for mercantile office; must be a good writer. One with previous business experience preferred. Address in own hand writing, naming references, COMMERCIAL, Sun office. 19

46.

WANTED—Book-keeper (double entry) and correspondent; must be rapid and accurate, good penman, and able to take notes of instructions in short-hand; give age and experience. Address box 179, Leader office. 231

RECOMMENDATIONS.

47. Write a **letter of** recommendation for **John Durand** who has been in your employ five years, stating his ability **as a** book-keeper.

48. Write a **letter of** recommendation for a faithful **teacher.**

49. Write to your pastor asking for a **letter of** recommendation to the church in this city.

50. Write **a letter** to Dr. Joseph **Barnes,** with whom you studied, asking for a testimonial of your qualifications **as a dentist.**

ORDERING MERCHANDISE.

51. Write a letter ordering twelve **kinds of groceries and state the method of** shipment and payment.

52. Write a letter ordering six different **kinds of books, state the amount you can pay in cash** and **the time** wanted on the balance.

53. Write a **letter ordering** millinery goods to **be sent C. O. D.**

54. Write a **letter ordering six** pieces **of dress goods and six articles in the** notion line, **to be sent by express.** State that you **wish to discount your bill.**

INCLOSING INVOICE.

55. Write a letter enclosing an invoice of **groceries.**

56. Write a letter **enclosing shipping** receipt and **invoice of 100** Arithmetics, shipped by fast freight.

57. Write a letter enclosing an invoice **of drugs; also write the invoice, ten** articles.

RECEIPTS AND PAYMENTS.

58. Write a letter acknowledging the receipt of money for an account in full.

59. Write a receipt for money paid you on account.

60. **Write a receipt for money paid you by one person for another, in full of** the latter's **account.**

61. **Write a receipt for three months' rent** paid you for store, 536 Walnut **street.**

62. **Write a letter** enclosing a money order **in payment of the** balance due **on an old account.**

63. Write **a letter to Frank Holmes enclosing an** order drawn in his favor upon Hiram Johnson.

64. Write a letter to R. A. Martin & Co., of your own city, enclosing a check in payment of bills for the month, to date.

65. Write a letter to John Taylor & Co., New York, agents for the Star Line ocean steamers, engaging two passages to Liverpool, Eng., enclosing draft to pay for the same.

66. You have just received a monthly statement of your account from your tailor. Write him a letter enclosing ten dollars to apply on account, and asking for time on the balance.

LETTERS ASKING FOR SETTLEMENT.

67. One of your customers has failed to meet his payments promptly ; send him his account, and ask him to call and settle immediately or make satisfactory explanation of the delay.

68. Write to Dr. Joseph Hill, Pittsburg, asking for settlement of an invoice of drugs shipped a year ago, that were to have been paid for in thirty days.

69. The Howard Publishing Co., Trenton, N. J., owe you two hundred and fifty dollars. Write them a brief note, stating that you will draw on them for the amount on the 1st proximo.

70. Write to your lawyer who has been collecting your accounts and failed to report the same, asking him to call and settle without further delay.

71. Write a courteous letter to Wm. Hays, who is behind with his payments, asking for immediate settlement.

TELEGRAMS.

72. Write a telegram not exceeding ten words, ordering a small invoice of dry goods sent by express.

73. There has been a railroad accident. Send a telegram of ten words to your mother announcing your escape without injury, and that you will be home at 10:30 P. M.

74. Write a telegram of not to exceed ten words, to Spencer & Packard, Chicago, stating goods ordered ten days ago have not arrived and ask why.

75. Telegraph to Hunt & Fisher, Boston, Mass., regarding a clerk you contemplate employing. He was in their employ five years. Use not more than ten words.

CONGRATULATIONS.

76. Write a letter of congratulation to an intimate friend, who is to deliver the valedictory address of his class.

77. Write a letter of congratulation to a friend elected to Congress, after a very exciting and close election.

78. Write a congratulatory note to an author, who is a very near friend, upon the success of his latest work.

79. Write a letter of congratulation to a friend just married.

MISCELLANEOUS.

80. Write a letter to your parents telling of your safe arrival at school and give some incidents of the journey.

81. Write your teacher a note explaining your absence from school during the past week.

82. Write to the President of Cornell University asking for catalogue and circulars.

83. Write to the publishers of the " North American Review," asking them to send you a copy for one year, and state with what number you desire to begin.

84. Write the names of (1) five railways, (2) three express companies, (3) and two telegraph companies.

The following example will illustrate a method of marking errors in students' letters. Use **red ink or** colored pencil to make corrections. **Underline misspelled words**; as, **"improv-."** Draw a line through errors; as, "that," "L," etc. **Insert punctuation marks** where omitted. Indicate changes of location with lines; as, in "|———ment" and "Henry———l." In grading, 100 per cent. may be given for letters perfect in arrangement, **neatness**, capitalization, **punctuation, etc., and five or more per cent.** (as the teacher may elect) deducted for each error.

Dear Father—

Bessie and I are very desirous of attending the ——————— Business College during the Summer, either for the regular course or special branches.

We can take the morning session from 8 to 12 o'clock and have the afternoon for outdoor enjoyment.

Hoping that you will favor this opportunity for our improv|———ment. I am,

Your Loving Son,

Henry.———|

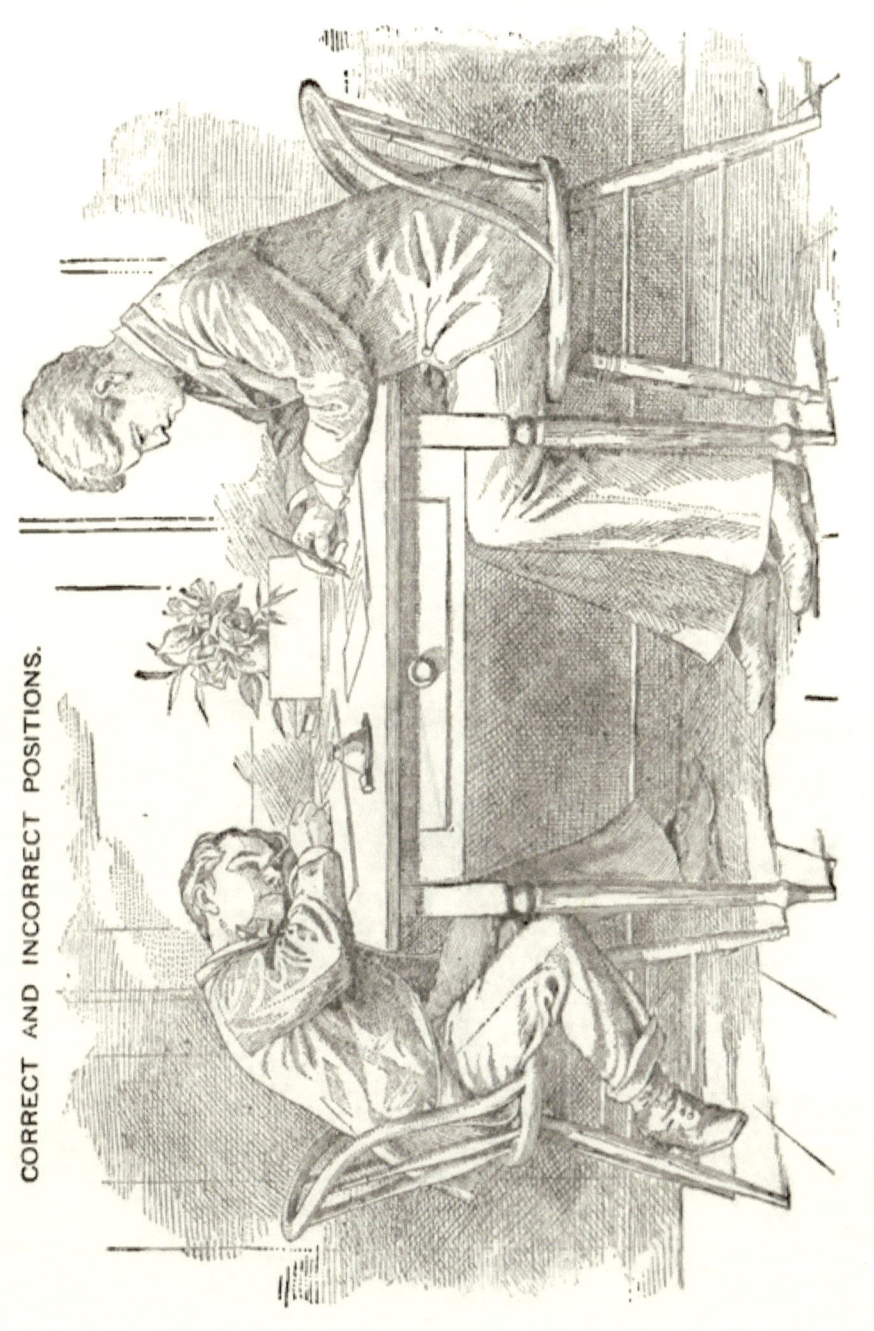

CORRECT AND INCORRECT POSITIONS.